DISTRIBUTED URBANISM

What do Dubai, Detroit, and Tokyo have in common? How are rural and urban conditions merging under the radar of official planning guidelines in Beijing? What type of architecture results from the prevalence of airborne contaminants? What kind of urbanism does Google Earth produce?

As everything from automobile production to energy collection, citizenship to higher education, news media to professional sports relinquish a model of singularity for one of multiplicity, the tools of interaction and design have changed. Exploring these decentralized systems through which cities are increasingly organized and produced, this volume compares emerging design practices in the contemporary production of urbanity.

Distributed Urbanism presents a series of case studies highlighting the architectural implications of remote design agencies on twenty-first-century cities. Edited by Gretchen Wilkins, this collection of essays and projects, both imagined and real, compiles work by leading architects and theorists from a global perspective, including projects in Rotterdam, Tokyo, Barcelona, Detroit, Hong Kong, Dubai, Beijing, and Mumbai.

Gretchen Wilkins is Senior Lecturer in Architecture at RMIT University in Melbourne, teaching in the Urban Architecture Laboratory and is a co-coordinator of the World Architecture Workshop. Previously she was Assistant Professor at the University of Michigan and Research Fellow at the Japan Foundation. She is the editor of *Entropia: Incremental Gestures Towards a Possible Urbanism* (Champ Libre, 2008) and *On-The-Spot: Atelier Hitoshi Abe* (University of Michigan, 2008).

DISTRIBUTED URBANISM

Cities after Google Earth

EDITED BY GRETCHEN WILKINS

LONDON AND NEW YORK

First published 2010
by Routledge
2 Park Square, Milton Park, Abingdon, Oxon OX14 4RN

Simultaneously published in the USA and Canada
by Routledge
270 Madison Avenue, New York, NY 10016

Routledge is an imprint of the Taylor & Francis Group, an informa business

© 2010 Gretchen Wilkins selection and editorial material; individual chapters, the
contributors

Typeset in Sabon by Wearset Ltd, Boldon, Tyne and Wear
Printed and bound in India by Replika Press Pvt. Ltd., Sonepat, Haryana

British Library Cataloguing in Publication Data
A catalogue record for this book is available from the British Library

Library of Congress Cataloging-in-Publication Data
Wilkins, Gretchen.
Distributed urbanism: cities after Google earth/Gretchen Wilkins.
p. cm.
Includes bibliographical references and index.
1. Urbanization. 2. Cities and towns. 3. Google Earth. I. Title.
HT151.W58 2010
307.76–dc22
2009039546

ISBN10: 0-415-56231-7 (hbk)
ISBN10: 0-415-56232-5 (pbk)

ISBN13: 978-0-415-56231-7 (hbk)
ISBN13: 978-0-415-56232-4 (pbk)

CONTENTS

CONTRIBUTORS

Hitoshi Abe is Chair of the Department of Architecture and Urban Design, UCLA, and is a principal of Atelier Hitoshi Abe in Sendai, Japan founded in 1993 and branched in Los Angeles in 2007. His work has been published in several monographs such as *Hitoshi Abe Flicker* (TOTO, 2005), which accompanied an exhibition of his work at the Gallery MA in Tokyo, *On-the-Spot* (Michigan Architecture Papers, 2007), and *HITOSHI ABE* (Phaidon Press, 2009).

Simon Drysdale is an architect currently practicing in Melbourne, delivering high density residential and commercial projects. He has worked and traveled extensively in the Middle East, with a particular emphasis on Gulf Cooperation and Persian Gulf regions.

Jerry Herron is Professor of English and American Studies and Dean of the Irvin D. Reid Honors College at Wayne State University. His publications include *Universities and the Myth of Cultural Decline* and *After-Culture: Detroit and the Humiliation of History*; his work has also appeared in *South Atlantic Quarterly*, *Raritan*, *Social Text*, *Representations*, *Georgia Review*, and *Playboy*.

Robert Mangurian and **Mary-Ann Ray** are principals of Studio Works Architects in Los Angeles, teach at SCI-Arc (Southern California Institute of Architecture) and the University of Michigan, and are co-founders of BASEbeijing. Mangurian and Ray were awarded the Chrysler Design Award in 2001 and in 2008, they received the Stirling Prize for the Memorial Lecture on the City by the Canadian Centre for Architecture and the London School of Economics.

Anuradha Mathur and **Dilip da Cunha**. Mathur is an architect and landscape architect. She is Associate Professor at the School of Design, University of Pennsylvania, Philadelphia. **Da Cunha** is an architect and city planner. He is visiting faculty at the School of Design, University of Pennsylvania, and at the Parsons School of Design in New York. Mathur and da Cunha are authors of *Mississippi Floods: Designing a Shifting Landscape* (Yale University Press, 2001), and *Deccan Traverses: the Making of Bangalore's Terrain* (Rupa & Co., 2006). Their most recent work, an exhibition (and book) titled *Soak: Mumbai in an Estuary* (see www.soak.in) opened at the National Gallery of Modern Art in Mumbai in June 2009.

Masashige Motoe is Associate Professor at IT Communication Design Lab at Tohoku University in Sendai, Japan. His research and projects focus on the field of spatial design in relation to information technology.

Ignasi Pérez Arnal is a professor and architect by Escola Tècnica Superior d'Arquitectura de Barcelona, UPC (1992) and in the MSC of The Big Scale: Projects in the new environments (ETSAB). He is Senior Visiting Professor at Facoltà di Architettura di Alghero, and Director of Erasmus Mundus Master in Sustainable Emergency Architecture (UIC) and of Master Degree of Design and Architecture (ELISAVA).

Dan Pitera is a political and social activist masquerading as an architect. He is the Director of the Detroit Collaborative Design Center at University of Detroit Mercy School of Architecture and was a 2004–2005 Loeb Fellow at Harvard University Graduate School of Design. He likes "fallout shelter" yellow.

Ilka Ruby and **Andreas Ruby** trained as architects and architecture historians respectively and are the founding partners of "textbild," an office for architectural communication operating in the fields of publishing, curating, teaching and consulting (www.textbild.com). Among their many publications are titles such as *Images. A Picture Book of Architecture* (Prestel 2004), *Groundscapes* (Gustavo Gili, 2005), *Urban Transformation* (2008) as well as the forthcoming titles *Of Houses and People* (HDA Publishers, 2009) and *EM2N: Both-And* (GTA Publishers, 2009). In 2008 they founded their own publishing house Ruby Press (see www.ruby-press.com).

Felicity D. Scott is Director of the program in Critical, Curatorial, and Conceptual Practices at the Graduate School of Architecture, Planning and Preservation, Columbia University, and a founding co-editor of *Grey Room*, a quarterly journal of architecture, art, media, and politics published by MIT Press since Fall 2000. She is author of *Architecture or Techno-Utopia: Politics After Modernism* (MIT Press, 2007) and *Living Archive 7: Ant Farm* (ACTAR Editorial, 2008).

Li Shiqiao is Associate Professor at the School of Architecture, Chinese University of Hong Kong. He studied architecture at Tsinghua University and obtained his PhD from AA School of Architecture and Birkbeck College, University of London. He is author of *Power and Virtue* (London and New York, 2007), and *Architecture and Modernization* (Beijing, 2009); his writings also appeared in prestigious journals in architecture and cultural theory.

Michael Speaks is Dean of the College of Design and Professor of Architecture at the University of Kentucky. Former Director of the Graduate Program at the Southern California Institute of Architecture in Los Angeles, Speaks has also taught in the graphic design department at the Yale School of Art, and in the architecture schools at Harvard University, Columbia University, The University of Michigan, UCLA, Art Center College of Design, and the Berlage Institute and TU Delft, in the Netherlands. Speaks is a founding editor of the cultural journal *Polygraph*, and is former Senior Editor at *Any* in New York, where he also edited the book series "Writing Architecture," published by MIT Press. In addition, Speaks served for many years on the editorial advisory board of a+u and is currently a contributing editor for *Architectural Record*.

Johan van Schaik is a co-director of Minifie van Schaik Architects whose work includes residential, educational, public and urban projects. He is a lecturer at RMIT University's School of Architecture & Design and has travelled and worked in Abu Dhabi, Al Ain and Dubai.

Gretchen Wilkins is Senior Lecturer in Architecture at RMIT University in Melbourne, teaching in the Urban Architecture Laboratory and is a co-coordinator of the World Architecture Workshop. Previously she was Assistant Professor at the University of Michigan and Research Fellow at the Japan Foundation. She is the editor of *Entropia: Incremental Gestures Towards a Possible Urbanism* (Champ Libre, 2008) and *On-The-Spot: Atelier Hitoshi Abe* (University of Michigan, 2007).

Jason Young is Associate Professor of Architecture at the University of Michigan and contributing co-editor for *Stalking Detroit* (Barcelona: ACTAR, 2001), an anthology of essays, projects, and photographs offering a thick, analytical description of the city of Detroit during the 1990s.

FOREWORD
"Making data speak"

FELICITY D. SCOTT

What are we looking at when we launch Google Earth, whether on a personal computer or an iPhone, and are presented with digital images of the planet? On the one hand the answer is, of course, very simple: we are looking at a virtual globe comprising multiple layers of satellite imagery, aerial photography, and 3D GIS data mediated through a search program that, as Google tells us, "lets you fly anywhere on Earth." On the other hand, however, this interface and the geospatial data which comprise the apparently integrated simulation of Earth's terrain speak in complex ways to a quite radical transformation in the global environment it simultaneously depicts, a transformation taking place over the last five decades or more, and in which the social, economic, environmental, and geopolitical vectors and fault-lines at work are not unrelated to the forces driving the information technology which subtends those images and their means of dissemination. Our ability to view Earth in this format was enabled, that is, at least initially, by Cold War-motivated research in communications and surveillance technologies and cybernetic control mechanisms, as well as their network-based global infrastructure. That Google Earth marks, in turn, an increasing militarization of our milieu is perhaps most symptomatically revealed in the option to view your simulated flight "anywhere on Earth" as if through the bubble canopy of an F-16 Fighting Falcon. The contributions to *Distributed Urbanism: Cities after Google Earth* do not all mention Google Earth. But, in different ways, and through the lens of architectural and urban responses, they speak in an important manner to contemporary problematics emerging from the technological and geopolitical forces underpinning such an application.

Initially called Earth Viewer (2001), and re-released as Google Earth in 2005, this simulation of Earth might initially remind us of its famous photographic predecessors of the planet as first seen from outer space – from "Earthrise" of 1968, taken during the Apollo 8 mission, to the "blue marble" of 1972, during Apollo 17. Products of the United States' space program, these widely disseminated images had a profound impact on the popular (and architectural) imagination at that moment, providing a visual complement to Marshall McLuhan's notion of a Global Village and for many rendering comprehensible for the first time the systems-based ecological and environmental arguments that we are all, indeed, interconnected, that our actions might have consequences elsewhere. (We could also cite a non-photographic predecessor from the 1950s, R. Buckminster Fuller's electronically controlled

Mini Earth project to demonstrate "the integrating patterns, both expected and unexpected, occurring around the fact of man's constantly shrinking 'one town world,'" and its late 1960s successor, the computerized World Game.[1]) NASA's images seamlessly lent themselves at once to an emerging and counter-cultural environmental consciousness – manifest in Stewart Brand's entrepreneurial use of them on the cover of his *Whole Earth Catalog* – and to advancing the institutions and mechanisms of global governance of a rapidly industrializing Third World or Global South, and in turn the economic and political hierarchies, population displacements, and "distributed urbanisms" of contemporary global capitalism. Here in this volume – from Jason Young's characterization of Detroit's "post-city urbanism" and Jerry Herron and Dan Pitera's reading of this former industrial center as a form of vanishing urbanism or shrinking city, to Ignasi Pérez Arnal's responsive "disaster urbanism" and the unstable territories of Mumbai discussed by Anuradha Mathur and Dilip da Cunha – we find traces of the urban and environmental legacy of those forces of globalization that were always and already foreshadowed in NASA's ability to launch such images.

With Google Earth, however, there is a significant shift at once in the capacities inscribed within the information technology and in the planetary imaginary it sponsors. We are faced here, of course, not simply with images of Earth but with an interactive datascape, a vastly extended, often high-resolution, multi-layered, searchable, manipulable, and digitally transmittable information database or archive, much of which was once available only to military or government agencies. Hence the anxiety it caused regarding rogue, or terrorist appropriations, most potently symptomatized in former Vice President Dick Cheney's demand that his residence at Observatory Circle be obscured through pixelation. The targeting and zooming-in/zooming-out functions of Google Earth (which, as acknowledged by one of its founders, was inspired by Charles and Ray Eames's 1968 film, *Powers of Ten*) both position us very differently and give us access to multiple distinct registers of information. As architect Laura Kurgan demonstrates elsewhere, in her important work on the declassification of satellite data, these images allow us to be "close up at a distance," and in the shifting of scales we can see or read things that might not otherwise be legible. As she recognizes, moreover, the pixels that make up those images are not simply fragments of a "snapshot from outer space" but are pieces of data linked within digital networks to data in other information systems. As data they are not transparent but, as she argues, "need to be interpreted."[2] The functioning of such images, that is, cannot be reduced to technological parameters but has potentially political ramifications. Simon Drysdale and Johan van Schaik point to this potential in "Rubble in the Sand." In the course of their conversation about rapidly developing cities in the United Arab Emirates (UAE), they note that this datascape not only allows architects and their clients to situate their projects – both conceptually and geographically – within this simulated milieu, but also harbors evidence of the environmental injustices and structural inequity to which those with urban expertise might become a kind of witness. That is to say, unlike viewing the heroic and beautiful, if still haunting NASA photographs of a fragile Earth floating distantly in outer space, zooming in to their digital counterparts reveals, among many other things (should one care to search), the archipelago conditions and violent junctures emerging in the wake of contemporary forms of global distribution, whether of bodies, of buildings, of infrastructure, of resources, of finance, of borders, etc. Behind architects' newfound ability when using Google Earth to produce what Drysdale provocatively calls "supersaturated postmodernism," and van Schaik in response, "urban scale sampling," is, to recall, a rigid, authoritative system of codes and protocols that belies any appearance of unhierarchical access to the visible information.

This volume contributes to such problematics as they encounter the domain of architectural and urban research on many fronts. It importantly reminds us of the many strange ways in which architecture resists being fully assimilated into, or is not fully reconcilable with, certain logics of the digital realm; that, in a literal sense, even when engaging information technology the discipline (as with that technology) remains inscribed within a radically material, social, and historical matrix which cannot be entirely subsumed by new medias' mode of operation. And it does so, rightfully, without nostalgia for something like a pure materiality. To point to this disjunctive encounter is not to suggest a limitation to architecture's ability to operate at the forefront of techno-cultural transformation but rather to recognize its capacity to operate as a potent vehicle for critical understandings of the complex, hybrid, often non-linear contours of the contemporary urban condition and what it both gives rise to and systematically occludes. The research on Detroit, for instance, not only points to the way in which the fate of industrial cities are historically intertwined with the emergence of their informatic counterparts (think Silicon Valley) and, in turn, redistributions of labor and industry. As with Hitoshi Abe and Masashige Motoe's *MegaHouse*, it also speaks of the degree to which the industrial, as with architecture itself, lingers in the most material manner in (even haunts) the information age. The phenomenal wealth of the UAE and other oil-rich nations, such as Iraq, also reminds us all too forcefully of the economic value of petroleum-driven industrial technology. Li Shiqiao's remarkable analysis of Hong Kong's environment of off-white shine, among other contributions, in turn reminds us of the historical, social, political, and even climatic specificities and contingencies inscribed within urban environments. Even if formally visible in Google Earth, these details would not be legible or readable in the simulation. Many of the architectural strategies and formulations offered in this volume, that is, implicitly speak to a certain architectural excess or remainder, and hence to the lack of smoothness implied in Google Earth's simulation of the globe.

Architects have long been in the business of imagining future worlds (or Earths). The question raised here is how new technologies and new modes of simulation might function not simply as contemporary tools of analysis and representation but as platforms to forge new conceptual and design strategies that might speak to, or speak back to, the discipline's long-standing commitment to making those worlds more just. All this is to suggest that *Distributed Urbanism: Cities after Google Earth* reminds us that architects can continue to deploy new technologies to critical and creative ends, that in their manner of operating in the interstices of an increasingly complex urban condition, in their productive encounter with social, economic, material, and geopolitical forces, architects can continue to generate strategies and concepts that are not (or not entirely) reducible to corporate management operations and the market. Architects, to reiterate, can make that data speak to other ends.

NOTES

1 R. Buckminster Fuller, "Proposal to the International Union of Architects," in *Your Private Sky: R. Buckminster Fuller: Discourse*, ed. Joachim Krausse and Claude Lichtenstein (Baden: Lars Müller Publishers, 2001), 250.
2 www.l00k.org/?s=closeupatadistance.

ACKNOWLEDGMENTS

This book has emerged from a four-year-long series of collaborations, beginning with a symposium entitled "Borderlands" in Detroit, Michigan. The symposium concluded an international workshop hosted by the Taubman College of Architecture at the University of Michigan in Ann Arbor. I am grateful to Tom Buresh and Doug Kelbaugh for supporting this workshop and to all of the staff and students who participated, especially to Tohru Horiguchi and Masashige Motoe and Yasuaki Onoda from Tohoku University, Senhiko Nakata from Miyagi University, Osamu Tsukihashi from Tohoku Institute of Technology, Elodie Nourigat, Jacques Brion, Romain Jamot, Valerie Horeau from the Ecole Nationale Supérieure d'Architecture de Montpellier (ENSAM) in France, Johan van Schaik and Paul Minifie from RMIT in Australia, and Ignasi Pérez Arnal from the Universtitat Internacional de Cataluña, Barcelona, Spain. The symposium was also supported by the Community Foundation of Southeast Michigan and the James L. Knight Foundation, and hosted by the Museum of Contemporary Art Detroit (MOCAD). Thanks to Gregory Tom and Edward Jackson for their help organizing the events.

Support for this extended body of work was generously provided by the Design Research Institute at RMIT University. Also at RMIT I would like to personally thank Leon van Schaik, Nigel Bertram, Pia Ednie-Brown, and Sue Anne Ware for lending their comments and support at different stages of the project. And to the many other people who helped shape and edit this work, especially Rebecca Roke, Akiko Takenaka, Anna Tweeddale, Justin Szwaja, and Emily Murray. I am especially grateful to Johan van Schaik for his invaluable perspective and insight throughout.

At Routledge I'd like to thank Francesca Ford, Alex Hollingsworth, Catherine Lynn, Louise Fox, and Pamela McLaughlin for their generous assistance throughout the publication process of bringing the manuscript to fruition. Thanks also to those who contributed their graphic work, including Ai Weiwei and FAKE, Corine Vermeulen, Esther Lorenz, Zhan Whang, Pekin Fine Arts, and Andy Sargent of Southsouthwest.

Thanks finally, and especially, to all of the contributors, who generously gave their time, knowledge, and vision to the work, without which this never would have materialized. They are Hitoshi Abe, Dilip Da Cunha, Simon Drysdale, Jerry Herron, Robert Mangurian, Anuradha Mathur, Masashige Motoe, Dan Pitera, Mary-Ann Ray, Andreas Ruby, Ilka Ruby, Ignasi Pérez-Arnal, Felicity Scott, Li Shiqiao, Johan van Schaik, Michael Speaks, Jason Young, and translation by Oscar Yanez del Mazo.

INTRODUCTION

GRETCHEN WILKINS

In April 2009 Mark Zuckerberg announced that Facebook, the social networking website he launched in 2004, had amassed 200 million users.[1] To demonstrate the significance of this figure he contextualized it within global demographic data, for example, how long it took the world to amass 200 million people (20,000 years), how it would rank in size as a country (fifth, bigger than Japan, Brazil, or Russia), and the distribution of users geographically (the highest concentration of 90 users per square mile in parts of Canada and Europe is greater than the average population density of the United States). Ultimately Facebook is simply an interface through which to exchange digital information across the web, like any other of its kind. Yet, positioning the site in a demographic context makes more explicit the ways in which this network connects to others outside the digital realm, where it is then used as a tool to "make a difference" locally through political advocacy,[2] emergency response,[3] or public health.[4]

The distributed nature of social networking follows a general trend toward distribution in everything, everywhere, from automobile production to energy collection, social services to citizenship, news media to professional sports, all of which having to some degree relinquished a model of singularity and centralization for one of multiplicity and interactivity. The connectedness of places and data has increased exponentially over the past decade or more, eventually enabling an environment in which the web is the primary operating system for all things material and digital, actual and imagined, an environment of networked objects of all sorts, tweetjects, blogjects, and the next. These increasingly complex relationships between distributed networks and local conditions have shifted social, economic, and environmental practices, and the practices of architecture and urbanism are similarly affected.

The distributed mechanisms shaping cities tend not to be discipline-specific, nor are the tools we use, or more often adapt, to design, perceive, and inhabit them. This is why it is not far-fetched to speculate on how networks like Google, corporations like General Motors, or sites like Facebook affect contemporary urbanism. Google Earth, as Felicity Scott describes in the Foreword of this book, emerged from a lineage of military defense and surveillance, as so many technological innovations do. But when Google acquired the software license in 2004 and branded Earth in its name, it marked a turning point in the design of cities in the same way Facebook has redesigned friendship. The ability to view, manipulate, travel through, and generally interact with this digital representation of three-dimensional space proved broadly relevant and triggered a series of adaptations and alternative uses. The implications for architecture and urbanism are many, and although Google Earth is certainly not the central hinge from which design practices have changed, it marks a shift in the way we might consider the distributed mechanisms through which cities are organized and produced, and the architectural practices that are emerging in response. *Distributed Urbanism: Cities after Google Earth* is a collection of these responses, a series of case studies both imagined and real, that track the decentralized agencies of design, control, and participation in the contemporary production of urbanity.

A key aspect of Google Earth is its accessibility and interactivity. If it were merely a tool for viewing images its relevance would be reduced to novelty. Rather, it is one of many emerging tools through which we can interact with the physical world remotely and participate in design collectively. Once easily categorized as top-down or bottom-up models, the interactive, mechanisms shaping contemporary urban experiences are somewhere in between. For example, if centrally controlled, localized models prove irrelevant in globalized society, and yet fully market-driven, open-source systems tend to implode if unchecked, the hybrid "market communism" proposed by Michael Speaks in his chapter in this volume about the branding strategies of Rotterdam, or the "New Socialism" Kevin Kelly discusses elsewhere, is another way forward. As Kelly describes,

> The new [operating system] is neither the classic communism of centralized planning without property nor the undiluted chaos of a free market. Instead it is an emerging design space in which decentralized public coordination can solve problems and create things that neither pure communism nor pure capitalism can.[5]

Kelly is referring specifically to digital socialism, but this sentiment is mirrored in the networks that govern urban economics and urban space. Robert Mangurian and Mary-Ann Ray's Rural Urbanism project documents this economic and urban middle-ground in Beijing, where they have located nearly 500 "urban villages" throughout the city. These informal, even illegal, settlements fall outside of the central economic and urban development model, but are nonetheless acknowledged as critical economic components to the overall urban system, and are thus receiving economic and infrastructural support centrally. Neither planned nor erased, neither central nor peripheral, they are part of Kelly's "emerging design space," a space that resists being absorbed completely into the rapidly developing metropolis of Beijing.

Hitoshi Abe's MegaHouse project reveals a similar middle ground in Tokyo, a "design space" that emerged not in the wake of rapid urbanization, but rather during its retreat. Positioned in the context of national depopulation and increasing vacancy, the project proposes a digital interface to activate unoccupied spaces dispersed throughout the city. It is both a new way to occupy the city as well as a new economic model, releasing urban space from the bureaucratic vice grip of long-term leases or individual ownership, models that are increasingly ineffectual in urban real estate.

The rapid acceleration or deceleration of urban production is inherently linked to the fluidity of capital and value, sometimes real and often speculative. Detroit, Dubai, and Tokyo are all products of this boom-and-bust cycle, a course which uses architecture as the primary tool through which to fully realize the limits of the game. Because the velocity of extreme economic cycles is often out of sync with the comparatively sluggish pace of even fast-tracked architectural production, design practices in this context are continually pressured to innovate, at first just to keep up, and later just to survive. At the time of this publication Dubai sits at that precarious inflection point in the bubble curve, the moment the rollercoaster slows just before the peak, with jittery uncertainty lying ahead.

Dubai's post-bubble future is yet to be written, and while some like to suggest it will return to desert or decline in the manner Detroit did, there are too many variables that differentiate Dubai from its predecessors, not the least of which is its relationship to oil-rich Abu Dhabi. Dubai is also unlike other bubble cities in that it combined superlative ambitions with an unlikely tabula rasa condition, the combination of which perfectly suited the kind of fly-in, fly-out expatriate urban design practices enabled by the explosion of easy access to aerial photography. Johan van Schaik's interview with Simon Drysdale discusses the effects of aerial tools like Google Earth on the rapidly developing cities in the United Arab Emirates, evaluating the distortions they create and the limits they impose on the perception of constructed and natural landscapes in this region.

Their discussion highlights the primary issue, and for some the primary concern, of aerial tools and similar mechanisms in contemporary architectural and urban practices, namely the gap between the perception and the experience of cities. The ability to view Melbourne, Las Vegas, or Cambridge, England[6] on a monitor from six inches above or from outer space, on the ground in "Street View" or airborne in the "Flight Simulator" suggests a complete experience but nevertheless leaves blind spots, examples of which are uncovered by Ilka and Andreas Ruby in their chapter, "The City You Can't See on Google Earth." Their chapter, along with Jason Young and Jerry Herron's analyses of Detroit – reporting "on the ground" and from the "borderama" respectively – begins to suggest that this perceptual gap is an agent of design in its own right. That is to say, the blind spots, failures, errors, and omissions of representational tools generally, from virtual globes to "new city photography" to public news media, are in fact the most valuable asset these tools provide. It's not about what they tell you, but what they don't.

As much as these images misrepresent reality, they also misrepresent fantasy. Before visiting a place it's possible to have an entirely erroneous perception of what, and even where, it is. Virtual globes "right" those "wrongs," as Thornton McCamish describes in his essay "The Greatest Earth on Show": "In my experience this is one of the things that virtual globes like Google Earth do best; they show you, with breathtaking clarity, that the world is never quite as you imagined or remembered it."[7] The virtual globes like

Google Earth are not live, nor photographically accurate, since they are quilted together from a series of layers of photographs from different times, but in the manner in which users add tags, stories, histories, itineraries, activism, links to webcams or YouTube videos, this representational fantasy produces a collectively authored reality – a distributed urbanism engendering new spatial practices and types of interface, all with very real economic, environmental, and social implications.

In some cases the gap which is in some cases problematic can in other cases be extraordinarily useful, such as when design intervention is required but physical access simply isn't possible, or isn't the most relevant option. The floods of New Orleans, Mumbai, or Indonesia, the bushfires outside Melbourne, the Swine flu starting in Mexico, the SARS epidemic in Asia and Canada or the pathological blight consuming Detroit are all urbanisms characterized by crisis, where conventional approaches to a site simply don't work. In this context design is a direct response to extreme economic, environmental, or political pressure, understanding the mechanisms inflicting these pressures as a way to reveal alternative techniques for use in the aftermath. Ranging across a wide spectrum of locations and conditions, this final group of projects highlight the very contemporary, even if not strictly new, issue of crisis in architectural practice. Urbanism in this context confronts the residual effects of "massive change,"[8] pressures that are much larger than a single location and which require tools that can interface with both these broad systems, as well as architectural spaces.

Ignasi Pérez Arnal's projects in Peru and Sri Lanka, for example, use a combination of remote networks and global software to "digitally grow" settlements in post-disaster areas where the site is physically (or technologically) inaccessible but where intervention is required immediately. In an argument that recalls the earlier discussion of the Internet of Things, Pérez Arnal posits

> If cities were once planned by and for industrial production via paper-based design with strict regulations on its streets, public spaces, and utilities, they should now be planned via the Internet, as the dynamic of cognitive capitalism bases its projections on the variables of time, mobility, and the displacement of people, goods, and overall information. If the Internet functions as a supporting mechanism to this economy, shouldn't it do the same for developing cities?

Anuradha Mathur and Dilip da Cunha's work confronts similar territory in the context of Mumbai, when the 2005 monsoon transformed this estuary city into a perilous flood ground. Rather than perpetuate the "war against the monsoon" enacted by the city administration, they developed meticulous techniques of representation, observation, and projection in order to locate the elusive balance between control and fluidity, between water and land. Their exhibition SOAK presents Mumbai as a city which refuses to conform to the objectives of those who are perpetually constructing it.

As these last few projects in the book suggest, many of the rules and techniques deployed in the aftermath of urban crisis emerge outside of the discipline of architecture or landscape. They may come from geospatial sciences, information technologies, social demography, or even, as in the case of Hong Kong, bacteriology. In analyzing the origins of contemporary materiality in Hong Kong, Li Shiqiao suggests that Florence Nightingale's *Notes on Hospitals* (1863) might be a more relevant treatise for architectural design in Hong Kong than, for example, Le Corbusier's *Towards a New Architecture*, when the SARS outbreak was manifest architecturally through a series of off-white, glossy surfaces throughout the city. It was as if the hospital was turned inside out and distributed throughout the city, a practice that emerged not from the theories of modernism but from the theories of antisepsis.

If Hong Kong looked to medical practices in confronting their social crisis, Detroit is increasingly looking to social practices to confront their economic crisis. Do-it-yourself urbanism is alive and well-documented, including self-organized services (trash removal, security patrol), infrastructure (street lighting), provisions (urban agriculture), building construction, and increasingly, through the work of the Detroit Collaborative Design Center (DCDC), building demolition. As the thousands of abandoned buildings in Detroit become too expensive for the city to demolish (especially if they cannot provide the basic services described above), Dan Pitera's work in the DCDC employs community activism to elicit government action by visualizing the urban blight, through architectural techniques and volunteerism. The city is pressured to respond to these sites, often producing a new type of public space referred to by Pitera as "productive residue." This type of practice is as much a form of activism as it is a form of architecture, enacted for change and against permanence (of the status quo).

The chapters and projects collected here are presented as a series of case studies, takes on the implications of distributed agencies on the twenty-first-century city. Each piece endeavors to identify a key external pressure and specific architectural response, sampling from a series of locations in a format that is itself distributed geographically. The primary themes of economics, technology, and climate loosely organize the work, but it is quickly apparent that these subjects are inherently interlinked, mutual partners in urban transformation, and thus do not form the primary structure of the book but an undercurrent throughout. Ultimately the ambition of the book is to identify the agents of change in contemporary cities and to speculate on the role these agents have on architectural practice.

Distributed Urbanism marks a moment when tools like Google Earth signify a much broader transformation in integrative design, when environments are shaped from the outside in and the inside out. The integration of peripheral bits of information produced by others, and digital residues that proliferate exponentially, suggest a resilient form of practice that takes place locally and remotely, collaboratively and concurrently. In this context the boundaries of the discipline expand to include digital, physical, and social networks well beyond those specific to design. As the tools producing the "New [digital] Socialism" are extended to architecture, and architecture to them (i.e., Google SketchUp[9]), does architecture become an open-source discipline, collectively designed and fabricated? The effects of digital fabrication technologies and robotics are not addressed in this volume but are clearly part of this discussion at the scale of materials and construction – allowing remote control of architecture in a manner the medical sciences employ at the scale of the body. In short, as the tools of architectural production are increasingly integrated with those of cultural production the discipline of architecture is poised to reassert its relevance across a much broader territory of design and making.

NOTES

1 http://blog.facebook.com/blog.php?post=72353897130.
2 www.facebook.com/facebookforgood.
3 www.nyc.gov/html/oem/html/pr/09_06_16_facebook.shtml.
4 www.facebook.com/album.php?aid=106392&id=20531316728.
5 Kelly, Kevin, "The New Socialism," *WIRED Magazine*, vol. 17.06, p. 120.
6 Three cities currently available at this degree of high resolution.
7 McCamish, Thornton, "The Greatest Earth on Show," *The Age*, September 7, 2008.
8 Refers to the book *Massive Change*, by Bruce Mau, Jennifer Leonard, and the Institute without Boundaries (Phaidon Press, October 2004).
9 SketchUp was a digital modeling software launched in 2000 and acquired by Google in 2006.

1 THE CITY YOU CAN'T SEE ON GOOGLE EARTH

ILKA AND ANDREAS RUBY

The twentieth century has been earmarked by a rapidly accelerated urbanization of the world population. If only 13 percent of the population worldwide lived in cities in the year 1900, the percentage rose to 29 percent in 1950, and, in the meantime, the United Nations predicts a further rise to 60 percent. This means that the city-dweller population worldwide will have risen from 220 million in 1900 to 4.9 billion in 2030.[1]

For years we have been confronted with statistics such as these with only a vague fantasy of what this unimaginable magnitude represents: a mass without measure. In the "Sweet Porridge" fairytale from the Brothers Grimm, the city is buried under a mudslide of porridge which has swelled and ballooned over the top of the pot, until a little girl utters the magic word: Stop. "And whoever wishes to re-enter the city, must eat their way through."

We hear and read a lot about this endlessly expanding city, but we have yet to *see*, as a rule, anything. That we can picture it, in the meanwhile, is thanks in part to a series of photographers who, since the mid-1990s, have grappled with the theme against the backdrop of explosive growth of megalopolises in Asia, Africa, and Latin America. These photographers have "eaten through" every new global city and, as a result, pried opened our eyes (with a giant spoon). In the beginning, it was primarily photographers such as Thomas Ruff, Andreas Gursky, and Thomas Struth – i.e., students of the Düsseldorf Becher school – who transferred their professor's typological-analytical p.o.v. of the kaput industrial architecture of the Ruhr wasteland over to the city as a whole.[2] Later, photographers from other countries such as Frank von der Salm, Valérie Portefaix, and Laurent Gutierrez, and many others created a body of work that makes an appeal for a new genre which we would like to call "new city-photography." That is, the city has become one of the preferred themes of photography since its invention, and yet this "new city-photography" is characterized by a very particular p.o.v. It is a perspective that endeavors to encompass the entirety from an extract of the exploding city of the new millennium; both a wide-angle perspective and a bird's-eye perspective from far above – from the sky-lobby of a hotel, or the observation deck of a highrise or an airport. A large part of the aesthetic workings of the new city-photography arises from the visual opulence of this panoramic perspective: a sense of control through an "over-view" which persuades and originates in the perspective of the field marshal on a battlefield. The inherent repression of this perspective is one that we are no longer conscious of today as it has infiltrated and conditioned our "civil" way of seeing. One only need remember how the function of satellite photos of the earth – originally taken by NASA within a military framework – did an about-face when they turned up as the eye-candy of the chill-out party scene and were set to a groovy electric soundtrack after midnight on *Space Night* (a program from the mid-1990s on German television which was broadcast globally via satellite). Yann-Arthus Bertrand's popular aerial-view photography plays a role here too, as do Alex MacLean's conceptually challenging aerial-view studies. The ultimate democratization of the über-p.o.v. territory – once (with)held by the rich and powerful – was followed up in 2004 with the introduction of Google Earth software: a virtual globe of projected geo-data, aerial, and satellite photography to be used by one and all for free on the Internet. With the computer one could float and fly carefree over landscapes that seemed from above to present a picturesque kaleidoscope of orders and figures. The bewitching thing about these photos was that *everything* looks beautiful, be it a vacation hub in the Bahamas, a slum in São Paulo or a refugee camp in Central Africa. The guaranteed aesthetic effect is without a doubt a reason why the view from above has fallen from virtue within the world of contemporary photography.

THE URBAN TRANSCENDENT

At the same time, the "zenith" view stands within a long cultural tradition of perception. In the end, the view from the sky-lobby visually repeats the classical view from the Belvedere: a pleasure palace with a beautiful view onto the Arcadian countryside. The wildly growing contemporary city, hence, has usurped the role of the landscape for the romantics of the eighteenth century – an embodiment of the transcendent: half-impressive, half-reverence. So wild as the romantic poets, philosophers, and painters let nature seem in her untameness, rawness, and hostility, so too today we quake and quiver with the view onto the out-of-control landscape of the twenty-first century. On one hand, the informal shanty-towns of the megalopolises of Latin America and Africa seem to flow endlessly into the landscape, unremittingly creating new territories of lawlessness and poverty where it could hardly be less difficult to live than in the wilderness. The conditions of life of hundreds of thousands housed in cardboard and plastic-bag shacks both disturb and shock, and yet, secretly, we are fascinated by the bizarre beauty of these settlements covering the natural structure of the skin of the Earth. But on the other hand, there have been metropolises which skyrocketed out of the ground at an amazing speed, meeting the demand of the Asian market to offer millions of people an instant home. Even there, the heart and brain cannot beat to the same drummer: with the history of stagnation of the (essentially built) European city, we are impressed by the energy with which China plans and builds hundreds of new cities, while we cannot even begin to imagine the nightmarish consequences of her planning mistakes. Once the proud cultural testimony to civilization, the twenty-first century city has become a game of Vabanque in an increasingly incalculable global society.

Figure 1.1a Seoul, Korea, public viewing of soccer game on City Hall Plaza, 2006.

Figure 1.1b Kaneohe, Hawaii. Hawaiian Memorial Park Cemetery, 2005.

A MORPHOLOGICAL SWAMP

Without a doubt, in the photographic *vedute* of our wild urban nature, we experience much of the morphology of the contemporary city, the meaning of urban infrastructure, and the relation of the built to the natural landscape. And yet somehow the picturesque city remains strangely out of reach. We cannot understand her because we float above her, unable to confront her eye to eye. In a certain way, this master-p.o.v. echoes the dilemma of modern city planning and her preferred instrument, the Master Plan, i.e., an order placed over the city from above whose hardware components can be arranged like figures on a chessboard, but without making a statement or even a remote connection to the life of the city.

This mechanistic understanding of city-building and city-planning was significantly forged in the twentieth century through the CIAM (Congrès Internationaux d'Architecture Moderne). In 1933, at the Fourth CIAM Congress in Athens, Le Corbusier heralded the doctrine of the modern city in what would become known as the "Charter of Athens" – and would become the most influential model for future new cities in the post-war era. That is, until a group of young architects around Peter and Alison Smithson (who later formed the group TEAM X) protested. In 1956, at the Tenth CIAM Congress in Dubrovnik, they reproached their modern forefathers for having lost touch with the functional optimization of the living and experiencable city space. Le Corbusier's modern city was based essentially on a series of building-volumes that were scattered in arrangements over the tabula rasa of the virgin Earth. The figure of the building advanced to become *the* essential urban element of the city – in the case of Le Corbusier's "Unité d'Habitation," it even takes up an entire shopping street while all the urban space around the building is left to its own devices, only serving park and circulation functions. A consequence of this operation, TEAM X complained, was quite literally the amputation of the street, i.e., the organ which gave the city its life. As an incubator of city social life, the street bundled together public activities and was essentially the place in which collective and social experiences were made possible.[3] Tellingly, significant evidence of this deficit was seen by the Smithsons in the city-photography of their times, namely, through the photos of Nigel Henderson. Like the Smithsons, Henderson was a member of the Independent Group, a progressive association of artists, architects, and theoreticians in Great Britain in the early 1960s. He photographed what seemed at first to be unremarkable street scenes from Bethnal Green, a working-class and immigrant neighborhood in East London. The pictures show how children virtually take over the streets, occupying them for all sorts of children's games. This spontaneous re-programming of the streets, overlooked by Corbusier's rigid scheme of the functional city, seemed to the Smithsons to be a sign of authetic city life:

> In the suburbs and slums the vital relationship between house and street survives, children run about, people stop and talk, vehicles are parked and tinkered with: in the back gardens are pigeons and pets and the shops are round the corner: you know the milkman, you are outside your house in your street.[4]

Henderson's photos are part of a greater tendency of his time, in contrast to the aforementioned panoptic perspective, mostly shot from the standpoint of the pedestrian – such as in the Parisian street scenes of Robert Doisneau or the graffiti walls made eternal through the photographs of Brassai. Already in the 1950s, Italian directors like Roberto Rossellini and Vittorio de Sica had broken loose from the tradition of the studio, taking to the streets and using

Figure 1.2a Dubai, Camel race, 2007.

Figure 1.2b Mexico City. Universidad Nacional Autónoma de México, Campus Plaza, 2007.

lay-actors for their new neorealist films. In the 1960s, the protagonists of the American "Direct Cinema" such as Robert L. Drew, Richard Leacock, and Donald A. Pennebaker got their start. Direct Cinema used the street as a stage for the sphere of Everyday Life, in which a relationship between body and space exists, and in that way we could experience the street not only visually, but also with our bodies.

To the contrary, the often-monumental dimensions of contemporary photography seem to almost make us forget the distinction between image and observer (spectacle and spectator) and even partially convey the illusion that we are sharing the space of what is pictorially represented, when actually we are rather distanced from this reality. Paradoxically, this is how contemporary photography incites a curiosity about its subject – the city – which it, in turn, cannot satisfy.

CITY HOPPING

Interestingly, new city-photography took off at exactly the same time as flying in Europe became notably cheaper. Ryanair, the first budget airline, was founded in 1985; easyJet followed in 1992; and with the deregulation of European air traffic in 1997, the boom of budget flights crossed over to the European continent. In only a few years, the cultural connotations of flying have completely changed. What used to be a costly and exclusive means of travel for business or tourism has changed in just a few years into an air-based form of international public mass transit and triggered a completely new form of short-term city tourism. In the meanwhile, one flies to other cities to do what one would have done in one's own, or at the most, to cities a short road-trip or train ride away for a day of shopping, to see an exhibition, or to visit friends. The Everyday of traveling and the spatial networking of one's own quotidian life with different places lifts away the feeling of distance and strangeness – the constitutional feature of a classical journey – and displaces the dialectic of the familiarity of home and the foreign-ness elsewhere.

With our new mobility, the Elsewhere is not, per se, more strange than our home turf, which, likewise, is not necessarily more familiar than other places. On the contrary, we sense how certain places in different cities grow on us; certain places begin to make us feel more at home than at "home."

Over time, we connect these places encountered on our everyday trips with a synthetic city – a nomadic home reminiscent of the Situationist city as defined by Guy-Ernest Debord, for whom the city never existed as a whole but only in parts – the parts that we actually use every day. Everyone produces in their own manner and through their own specific use of the city their own subjective "version" of the city. In order to illustrate his theory, Debord pointed to a scientific diagram that marked out the movements over the year of a young Parisian girl, which consisted basically of a triangle between her house, her school, and her violin lessons. Based on these observations, Debord drew up a special map of Paris that plucked out the chosen neighborhoods from the totality of the city-body and dropped them like islands in the sea to form a new map which leaves the in-between bits out. Each of these islands was indicated by specific atmospheric qualities, their so-called *unités d'ambiances*. Taken together, these islands create a "psychogeographic profile" that influences our movements through the city, that let us be attracted to certain places and repelled by others. "Psychogeography" is a Debordian coinage used to describe the affects of certain neighborhoods, regardless of whether they are consciously or unconsciously shaped by the emotional world and behaviors of the individual. In contrast to the homogenized city of the CIAM, which could only be equally attractive everywhere

Figure 1.3a Guadalajara, Mexico, Illegal Market, 2007.

Figure 1.3b Otovalo, Equador, Village Market, 2004.

thanks to its functional optimization, Debord searched for the contradictions of the city, the niches which eluded the dominant fabric, in search of discontinuity in a sea of orderly continuity, much like Monsieur Hulot in Jacques Tati's contemporaneous films *Mon Oncle* and *Playtime*. Debord's entreaty for a definition of the city based on individual forms of experience instead of wiping them out finds its expression in the cultural technique of the *dérive*: the art of the drift. Debord understood the "*dérive*" as a kind of

Happening, lifting away the functional-conditioned experience of the city and letting oneself be led instead by its varied signals and "unités d'ambiances."[5]

Because of the affordability of mobility-made-easy through flying, Debord's *dérive* can take place in this "synthetic city" pieced together through elected parts from several cities. In this "global *dérive*," we experience the psychogeographic difference and we connect the dots of the diverse *unités d'ambiances* to form a new urban hypertext; that is, we continue to knit our own subjective city depending on our own concrete actions and movement between cities.

PICTURE-JOURNEYS/IMAGE-TRIPS

In an information society, the physical locomotion from A to B is only one form of traveling among others. The more we let ourselves drift between places, the more clear it becomes that all of these destinations have traveled to us beforehand – in the pictures that we gathered before the journey even began and, with time, have internalized.[6] This pre-picture of the city is essentially our first encounter with the city. The physical movement to the place itself and the indescribable experience of the sensations that take place after the fact will inevitably be set in relation to this first image of the city that we already have saved on the hard drive of our imaginations. Often, experiencing the city will lead to a correction of the image we had of it beforehand, more rosy or more gray, the image and the reality of the experience of the city are never the same. From the quantity alone, the pictures that have traveled to us are a step ahead of our own experience, as in the fairytale of the Rabbit and the Hedgehog – in the train of everyday touristic propaganda, we are haunted by many more images of places than we could ever succeed in traveling to.

Picture-journeys, however, often present problems of orientation that we wouldn't have had through the physical experience of traveling. In general, if we want to identify the pictured city, it is only when we recognize remarkable buildings, such as Cesar Pelli's Twin Towers in Kuala Lumpur, the Pearl Tower in Shanghai, or "city spaces" such as the night-light grid pattern of Los Angeles that stretches all the way to the horizon. Without these landmarks, we are without a clue – one sees only what one knows. It also becomes clear how the array of the visible within the urban spectrum is limited: only the representation of the city at the visual level can be focused on, which then by nature excludes all of the not-visual sensations which help define the city's identity. From looking at a photograph, we cannot know that a city is loud (Cairo), that the air is polluted (Beijing), or, because of its elevation, that its air is so thin that it initially gives you a headache (Quito). From looking at a photograph, we can never conceive that your body will be covered in a layer of sweat as soon as you walk out of an air-conditioned building (Singapore) or what it means to walk about an Arabian city whose streets are conspicuously lacking women (Dubai). From looking at a photograph, we never get the feeling (nor even a glimmer of the idea) of the introverted heaviness of Vienna that haunts us as soon as we set foot in its historical First District. And the photo cannot evoke the subliminal sense of danger that overcomes us when we walk through a nearly unpopulated downtown Detroit, something

Figure 1.4a Honolulu, Hawaii, Shopping Mall Ala Moana, 2005.

Figure 1.4b Dubai, Camel racetrack, 2007.

no local would do, despite the impressive art deco high-rises, primarily devoid of use excepting the few bullet-proof-glass check-cashing counters at which not-terribly friendly people stand waiting to exchange their weekly paychecks for cold hard cash.

In the photographic version of the city – and here the bird's-eye-view variation in particular – the qualifying parameters fall to the wayside from which we can distinguish one city from another. To the contrary, its morphological likenesses are intensified. When we look at a picture of a high-rise-spotted downtown Manhattan and then a similar picture of Hong Kong, we are tempted to compare them as equals, if only because of their visual kinship. But if one were indeed to visit both cities, their extreme differences would stand out. In that way, one could fathom that Rem Koolhaas's theory of the *Generic City* ("Is the contemporary city like the contemporary airport – 'all the same'?"[7]) is rather a phenomenon resulting from the photographic reproduction of cities which does not necessarily reflect the reality of these cities.

OBJECTS IN THE MIRROR MAY BE CLOSER THAN THEY APPEAR

The new city-photography presents neither the sensational conditions of the city, nor the cultural practices informed by them, nor the forms of usage of space. From a European perspective, it would be easy to interpret a photograph of a shopping mall dominating the center of Kuala Lumpur as if the streets were a part of the public space and the buildings a form of private space. But that would be to project the imagination of European public space onto a scene that neglects a level of experience which would be impossible to ignore with both feet on the ground: the climate. Kuala Lumpur lies near the equator and with a tropical temperature over 30°C and 90 percent humidity, it becomes nearly impossible to enjoy being outside for more than just a short moment. The concept of being a flâneur is unthinkable, if only because of the weather. When someone actually goes for a walk outside in Kuala Lumpur then it is with a minimal expenditure of energy so that one sweats as little as possible. The air-conditioned shopping malls of Kuala Lumpur are a part of the public space de facto (not de jure) because they are the only spaces in which one can hang out for a longer period of time and actually experience a sense of community.

And that is why shopping malls in Kuala Lumpur are called "plazas." This, in turn, causes orientation problems for the European tourist in search of a place like Low Yat Plaza, for example, which according to their guide book is the place where they might find electronic gadgets, but it is unlikely that they will realize the local definition of a "plaza" (= building) before they pass out in the unbearable heat from their outdoor quest for just such a place. In the European sense, these shopping malls take on the feeling of being quasi-public not only because of the air-conditioning but also because they are composed of more individual buildings. Indeed, they take on spatial dimensions that we tend to associate more with urban spaces than purely architectural spaces. The transitions from one building to the next are often so inconspicuous, so seamless, that one realizes the change only upon exiting, much like entering a completely new sector of the city in which one must fully reorient oneself. The malls Sungei Wang and Bukit Bintang Plaza in the city center of Kuala Lumpur are connected by a five-story complex of some 180,000 square meters (equivalent to *c.*25 soccer fields). Often having more than one entrance, these malls are part of a network-type structure that spans the city space like a late echo of Alison and Peter Smithson's Berlin Plan or an Asian-built manifestation of Debord's "*dérive.*"

Figure 1.5a Quito, Equador, Centro Commercial Espiral, 2004.

Figure 1.5b Kota Bahru, Malaysia, Car Repair Shop, 2004.

Indeed, because of the climate, it is fully comprehensible why the city planners of Kuala Lumpur would want to have a public space consisting of a sequence of air-conditioned rooms so that one could avoid the heat and humidity of the outside; but this leads to a complication of the architectural concept of the entrance, which is just as disorienting for the European visitor as the interiorization of the public space in and of itself. Often, one enters a shopping mall without even noticing that one has entered another building altogether. The lobby of the Petronas Towers, for example, flows into the Suria KLCC Mall, which is actually its own building. The entrance is completely subordinated and similar to the notable entrance of multifunctional mega-buildings like Times Square Plaza (2003). The building has a footprint of some 700,000 square meters, i.e., 100 soccer fields, and contains Malaysia's largest shopping mall within the first ten floors, with some 325,000 square meters of effective surface (an astonishing figure when compared to Germany's largest mall, the CentrO, with 70,000 square meters, which is comparatively low given its location in one one of Germany's densest urban agglomerations, the Ruhr Area, and its catchment area of 60 million people). The entrance to Kuala Lumpur's "Cosmo's World" is on the fifth floor, an "Indoor Theme Park" complete with a rollercoaster such as one only finds outdoors in Europe. Soaring upwards from the fourteenth to the forty-third floors are the two towers of the conference center and the lobby of Berjaya Times Square Hotel. On the ground floor, one would hardly realize that a hotel exists in the building at all. The entrance at the side of the building, entered by taxi, is completely inconspicuous: an empty corridor with six elevators (and when one arrives via the monorail – which is, likewise, connected to the building of the Times Square Plaza station – one lands immediately in the shopping mall). Only when one knows that one should take the elevator up to the fourteenth floor does one succeed in locating the lobby. The hotel entrance, in other words, is the lobby on the fourteenth floor – its own entrance, that is, doesn't exist. By virtue of the breathtaking boggling of functions, the entrance to the building can no longer express its own categorical content. The function of the entrance is, in the end, based on the climate: it marks the point of departure from the climatic trials and tribulations of the natural city space and the arrival into the artificial climatized city space. This "interiorization" of the public space and the displacement or disintegration of the building's entry way are characteristic features of the urbanity of Kuala Lumpur – invisible in photography of any kind.

FROM THE CITY TO ICON BUILDING

As a result, this selective sensorium of photography becomes a dilemma – within the history of the global competition between cities in a battle for the pot-of-gold of tourism – which uses photography as its main medium of communication, followed by television. On the one hand, they can only win this competition when they can produce a non-interchangeable city profile; on the other, its distinctness must be communicated through the eye of the needle of photography, thus inevitably weeding out the details. Given this catch-22 situation, it becomes obvious why practically every city involved in the market of global tourism endeavors to develop a unique city profile that is visually arresting and communicable: icon-building has become the currency of the urban economy, both symbolic and real. It presents the conundrum of a New Deal that could possibly backfire – if only the handful of star-architects with definitive signatures are contracted. And that these architects are engaged in general in more than just one city, the look of the city face tends to be more identical and interchangeable than distinct or individual. It is the brand-name architects who profit in the end and not the city faces they create.

Figure 1.6a Guadalajara, Mexico, Street Life, 2007.

Figure 1.6b Rome, Italy, Facade Renovation, 2006.

As ever, here Dubai is a step ahead of the game. The most important icons the emirate uses in their tourism statistics are not the buildings but the icons which are made up of artificial land. The planned Palm Islands and (the modestly titled) The World are giant territorial signs that are erected with the view from the airplane (or even from outer space) in mind. Significantly, as soon as one sets foot on the ground, they lose their "iconicity" rapidly, when only the outer edge remains to be seen. Between the never-ending expenditures of the production of an imaginary pre-picture of a city, which one can see in the work-in-progress "Palms" fully completed in (computer-generated) satellite photographs, and its actual phenomenological reality from the perspective of a person on foot opens up an abyss of the visible. In this blindspot of perception, contemporary photography opens up a daunting field of research from which the real fabric of a new urbanity is behind the veil of P.R. images that we must first learn to understand.

NOTES

1 United Nations, *World Urbanization Prospects, The 2005 Revision*, New York, 2006.
2 See Michael Mack, ed., *Reconstructing Space: Architecture in Recent German Photography*, London: AA Publications, 1999.
3 Alison Smithson, ed., "Team X Primer 1953–1962," *Architectural Design*, no. 12, December 1962.
4 Alison and Peter Smithson, Grille 1953, section House + x = street, cited in Jesko Fezer, "Die Idee der Strasse ist vergessen worden" [The idea of the street has been forgotten], *Starship Magazine*, no. 5, 2002, pp. 30–34.
5 Guy Debord, "Théorie de la Dérive," *Les lèvres nues*, no. 9, November 1956, pp. 6–13.
6 Alain de Botton, *The Art of Travel*, London: Vintage International, 2004.
7 Rem Koolhaas, "The Generic City," Rem Koolhaas, Bruce Mau, *S,M,L,XL*, New York: Monacelli, 1995, S.1248.

2 RURAL URBANISM

Thriving under the radar –
Beijing's villages in the city

ROBERT MANGURIAN AND
MARY-ANN RAY

In the era of the city after Google Earth, there appear be new and odd forms of human congregation hatching. One of these "city parts" we have been tracking are the urban villages of Beijing – some being dismantled, others thriving. All Chinese cities have urban villages.[1] While not obviously visible, and occurring mostly under the radar, this form of "rural urbanism" turns out to be extremely prevalent and occurs in countless tens of thousands of urban villages – the *cheng zhong cun*, or villages in the city – throughout Chinese cities today.

Urban villages develop in a number of ways. The simplest is that the village was a "natural" rural village,[2] which had existed for a long time – perhaps hundreds of years – and was located outside the city, then was swallowed up by the growing city in the Mao and post-Mao years. These villages existed for farming and small-scale manufacturing; in Beijing's case, they also serviced Imperial burial sites. Upon being "swallowed up," the now-urban village adapts, changes, and increases in density with concrete and brick structures replacing traditional courtyard houses.

The other prevalent origin for an urban village is that it forms in response to the normal and abnormal parts[3] of the developing city. They supply needed labor, markets, and other amenities for these planned parts of the city. Thus, the airports of Beijing have a number of urban villages surrounding them. Large construction sites, especially for housing, spawn urban villages to supply labor for construction, and subsequently markets for further construction and other needs. The populations of these urban villages are largely the illegal residents known as the "floaters." Capital Steel,[4] an extremely large steel factory established in the Mao era in west Beijing, has spawned numerous urban villages that served to supply excess labor (from the countryside) and shops for all those working and living in the factory compound.

MAPPING RURAL URBANISM IN BEIJING: THE CITY THAT SWALLOWS THE VILLAGE OR THE VILLAGES THAT SWALLOW THE CITY

We first became aware of "villages in the city" after taking a lease on a large studio space in Caochangdi. Caochangdi is one of Beijing's urban villages with the special distinction of having the premiere contemporary Chinese artist Ai Weiwei as one of its residents, as well as being home to many other artists' studios and contemporary art galleries. And yet, like all of the city's urban villages, the daily economy and atmosphere of the place operates more like a rural Chinese community. The art population of Caochangdi forms only a very small part of the overall population of Caochangdi.

In a mapping of the urban villages in Beijing using Google Earth, accomplished by our students from BASEbeijing and the University of Michigan's Taubman College of Architecture, we collected an inventory of nearly 500. Many of these are in the "high-end" Chaoyang District, home to the embassies and the Central Business District, which is by far the highest revenue-producing district in all of China – it grosses 2.5 percent of the entire GDP of China. For instance, there is an urban village around the corner from CCTV, although it is currently being dismantled. This simultaneity of the Central Business and Embassy Districts with urban villages that look like, and operate more like, rural villages produces a set of strange simultaneities of people, architectures, and urbanism. Clearly, these villages are known to Beijing's

Figure 2.1 A mapping of the nearly 500 urban villages within Beijing (Photo Credit: Students of the Taubman College of Architecture, University of Michigan).

officials and planners, but they are allowed to exist "under the radar." They are extremely important to the functioning of the city, or they would not be allowed to exist. But they do not comply with planning guidelines or building standards.[5] The urban villages, at best and with all their vitality and entrepreneurial energy, can be seen to challenge the often lifeless, relentless large-scale housing projects and mega-block office and commercial projects.

OFFICIAL MANDATE FOR THE "NEW SOCIALIST COUNTRYSIDE" AND THE "NEW SOCIALIST VILLAGE"

In a careful analysis of the forces at work, it turns out that the Chinese Central Party is consciously looking the other way while, at the same time, they are scrutinizing the economic and social successes of these villages in the city. The government is not only allowing some of the urban villages to exist

Figure 2.2 Aerial detail of the Embassy District of Beijing showing the simultaneity of urban villages (A), agriculture (B), American Embassy (C), Suburban-style Tract Housing (D), Fourth Ring Road (E), Golf Course (F), Lufthansa Center (G), Five Star Kempinski Hotel (H), and Factories (I) (Photo Credit: Google Earth).

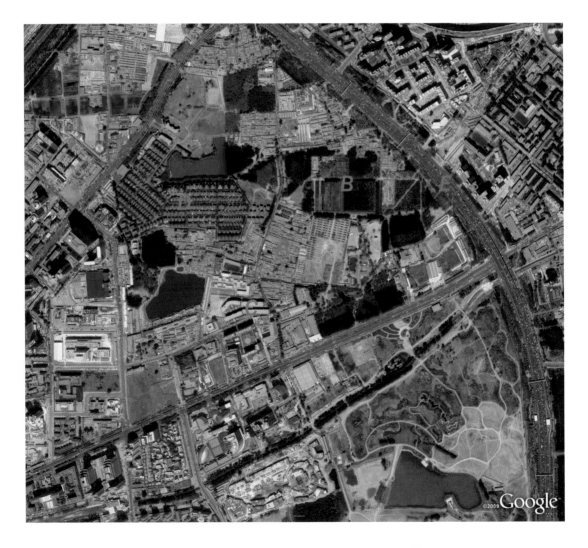

Figure 2.3 A Big Character Slogan Banner hanging in the urban village of Caochangdi translates as: "Participate in the Collective Building of the New Socialist Village."

as is, it is now stealthily supporting the growth occurring from the ground up by entrepreneurial urban villagers. The government is investing in infrastructures and programs under the name of the New Socialist Countryside.[6] The New Socialist Countryside is geared toward improvements of quality of life in rural areas, but it is also being implemented in urban areas where particular villages in the city are officially identified as New Socialist Villages. Hu Jintao, *Time* magazine's Man of the Year in 2007, and the current President of China, with regard to the New Socialist Countryside program says "we will stick to the guideline of giving more, taking less, and being more flexible" (Hu Jintao, 2006). One aspect of the new flexibility is that democracy is in action at the village level in that all village leaders are selected through a local election process.

Thus, there may be a narrow window for another kind of city development that takes into account the improvised nature of the urban villages that produces at times exceptional energy and creativity. In addition, these urban villages seem to fill gaps and account for the ebbs and flows of Beijing's economy.

RURALOPOLITANIS: CONTEMPORARY LACK OF CLEAR DISTINCTIONS BETWEEN RURAL AND URBAN

The New Socialist Countryside section of the most recent Five Year Plan (2006–2010) for China specifically addresses the vast rural population of

24

China – some 700 million people who are mostly farmers. But the line between the rural and urban, and between agriculture and industry, is not so clearly demarked at the end of the twentieth century and beginning of the twenty-first century. For instance:

> Huge gains in agricultural efficiency have emancipated huge numbers of rural laborers from the land, thus laying the basis for the development of farmer-run township enterprises whose competitively priced goods and services sell well across China. They are involved in many sectors, e.g. industry, agricultural products processing, transportation and communications, construction, commerce and catering. By 2004, 22.13 million township enterprises, with 138.66 million employees had generated 4,181.5 billion Yuan in added value, a 13.9 percent increase over 2003. Now the driving force behind the increase in farmers' income and rural economic development, township enterprises have created job opportunities for about 30 percent of rural laborers to date.
>
> (Chen Xiwen, 2006)[7]

HYBRID TOP-DOWN, BOTTOM-UP URBAN EXPERIMENTATION

The New Socialist Village campaign proposes ways to eliminate the burdens imposed by the cities as they have advanced at the expense of, and through the labors of, the rural residents. In order to reverse the massive rural-to-urban migrations (migrants are known as the "floating population" in China), the Central Party has recognized that new hybrid forms of rural and urban

Figure 2.4 High-tension workers who are part of the floating population in Beijing – rural-to-urban migrants who often find housing in the city's urban villages.

(and specifically NOT suburban) may need to be invented. In reality, these urban villages provide the only low-cost housing for the vast migrant labor force in Chinese cities today,[8] and it is happening through a process that might be described as "housing for the people, by the people."

There is a powerful phenomenon taking place today in the wealthier urban villages that illustrates and confirms Robert Neuwirth's statement that "These squatters mix more concrete than any developer. They lay more brick than any government. They have created a huge hidden economy – an unofficial

Figure 2.5 A new multi-story construction being built in Caochangdi during the summer of 2009.

system of squatter landlords and squatter tenants" (Neuwirth, 2006: 10). The only difference in the Chinese cities is that the "squatters" are actually official land lease-holders. Most of these land-holders in the villages in the city are former farmers who have rights to farmland and/or houses in what used to be Agricultural People's Communes but are now urban areas. These former farmers have pooled resources with family members and business partners to collect funds to demolish their existing single-story houses and build illegal – or more accurately, not legal – multi-story buildings. These constructions

Figure 2.6 Mr. Li, a former farmer, is now a landlord who leases housing and retail space in his new illegal multi-storied structure on land leased to him by the central government. Mr. Li supports the demolition and new construction in the village. He says "if the old doesn't leave, the new will never arrive."

Figure 2.7 Funded by the New Socialist Village Countryside program, the urban village of Caochangdi receives new infrastructure in the form of separated sanitary sewers and gas lines.

transform the former farmers – who now have ground-floor retail space and several stories of rentable dwellings to collect on – into "wealthy" landlords.

While these constructions are "not legal," the Party is quietly recognizing that the burgeoning villages in the city are providing a model and new modes of experimentation in this area. There is a kind of stealth support system being provided by the government for some of the most successful villages. For instance, two years ago, under a New Socialist Countryside program, Caochangdi received some major infrastructural improvements including new separated storm and sanitary sewers and gas lines. The phenomenon of the new farmer four-story constructions has been fueled both by the fact that it provides them with revenue-producing rental space, and because it is government policy that if land leases are revoked or given up at some point, the lease-holders are compensated in an amount commensurate to the improvements, additions, and new construction on the land. This top-down support is tenuous and sometimes ambiguous. This summer, land lease-holders in Caochangdi received official notices from the village leadership warning that the village is one of more than a dozen neighborhoods slated for possible demolition and that any construction not completed before certain cut-off dates would not receive financial compensation.

致村民一封信

各位村民：

　　目前，随着全市城乡一体化进程的加快，按照市区政府有关精神，崔各庄乡 15 个村全部列入土地储备范围，已进入城乡一体化拆迁腾退阶段，为避免村民重复建设，造成不必要的经济损失，崔各庄乡党委、政府根据市区精神，经研究决定：

　　自 2009 年 7 月 1 日起，严格禁止二层或二层以上房屋的建设，于 7 月 1 日以后新建的二层或二层以上房屋，在拆迁腾退时不予认定和补偿，由此产生的损失和后果由建房者自负。

　　城乡一体化是历史发展和农村发展的必然，是改善和提高农民生活环境和品质的有效途径。望广大草场地村村民从维护自身利益的角度出发，以积极的态度面对城乡一体化形势，积极配合上级的各项决议。

通 知

崔各庄乡各企事业单位：

　　为深入贯彻市、区关于加快城乡一体化建设的要求，根据市、区有关精神，我乡 14 个村全部被列入土地储备范围，并将在短期内逐步开展拆迁腾退大量工作，为保证拆迁腾退大量工作的顺利开展，特通知如下：

　　一、即日起，严格禁止各企事业单位新建、改建、扩建房屋、厂房。

　　二、2009 年 8 月 4 日后新建、改建、扩建的房屋、厂房，在拆迁腾退时不予补偿，由此产生的损失和后果由建房者自负。

　　三、各企事业单位翻建项目，由各村向乡规划科申报，经审批后方可建设，否则视为违法建设，由执法部门予以强制拆除。

　　特此通知

崔各庄乡人民政府

二〇〇九年八月四日

Figure 2.8 Documents issued by the Caochangdi urban village leadership (June 2009) informing land lease-holders that the village is one of more than a dozen slated for possible demolition, and any construction not completed by the summer of 2009 will not be financially compensated.

AGRI-URBANISM: CONTEMPORARY AND HISTORICAL FORMS OF HYBRID SPACES OF AGRICULTURE AND CITIES

Another phenomenon that demonstrates the lack of clarity between rural and urban is the fact that there are numerous farmers (perhaps as many as one in every ten urban dwellers) living within the cracks of Chinese cities and mostly within the urban villages in the city that were formerly established as agricultural people's communes. In 1969, Jane Jacobs surprised herself and others when she set out to write her book *The Economy of Cities*. In the first chapter, entitled "Cities First – Rural Development Later," she says:

> One of the many surprises I found in the course of this work was especially unsettling because it ran counter to so much I had always taken for granted. Superficially, it seemed to run counter to common sense and yet there it was: work that we usually consider rural has originated not in the countryside, but in cities. Current theory in many fields – economics, history, anthropology – assumes that cities are built upon a rural economic base. If my observations and reasoning are correct, the reverse is true: that is, rural economics, including agricultural work, are directly built upon city economies and city work.

(Jacobs, 1970: 3–4)

29

Whether or not we agree with Jacobs that city economics had to develop in advance of established agriculture, her arguments do make it clear that strong interdependencies between the two are necessary and natural.

The desire for, and perhaps the need for, agriculture in proximity or even in simultaneous coexistence with cities is a growing trend in the developed world, and the press and design journals are always ready to cover news of urban agriculture projects. For China, the need for using any arable land for agriculture, including land in urban areas, is clear since

> China is a country with a large population but less arable land. With only 7 percent of the world's cultivated land, China has to feed one fifth of the world's population. Therefore, China's agriculture is an important issue and draws wide attention from the world. Some foreigners once raised the question, "Who will feed China?" China's leaders and agriculture experts' reply was, "We Chinese will feed ourselves."[9]

CHAIRMAN MAO WAS A (RADICAL) URBAN (ACTUALLY RURALOPOLITAN) PLANNER OF THE ANTI-URBAN ANTI-CONSUMER PRODUCER CITY

The concept of the New Socialist Village emanates from Mao's time, and from his thinking on cities and the countryside. In 1959, Chairman Mao Zedong put forth a radical plan and planning strategy for Beijing. It was a

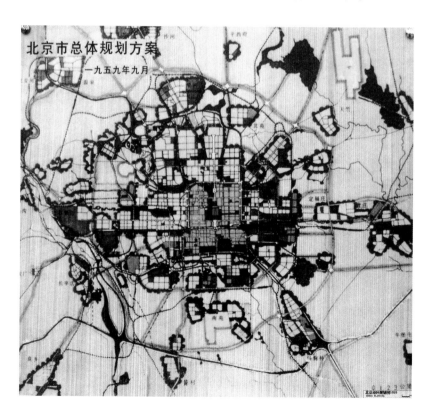

Figure 2.9 1959 planning proposal for the city of Beijing with dispersed units of clumps composed of village, factory, and agriculture with green coverage in between.

proposal for an anti-urban, anti-consumer city, and it anticipated the ruralo-politan developments as seen in the new urban villages, in new green city and urban agriculture movements, and in the officially mandated current program for the development of the New Socialist Countryside.

This little-known plan for Beijing was drafted in 1959 with a team led by Liang Sicheng working with three other Chinese and four Soviet planners.[10] It is said that Mao played a primary role in the thinking behind the plan. The plan put forth a radical idea about a kind of ruralized urbanism by dividing the city into "Dispersal Units" composed of dozens of tripartite settlements of *commune housing*, *factory*, and *agriculture*. This was a proposal for a "pro-ducer city" (*shengchan chengshi*) as opposed to a "consumer city" (*xiaofei chengshi*). In between, the plan called for forests or more agriculture so that the city would reach 40 percent greenery coverage.

BEIJING URBAN VILLAGE CATALOG: THE CLASSIC, THE EXCEPTIONAL, AND THE SURREAL ANOMALY

Within the collection of nearly 500 urban villages of Beijing, there is a range of typologies, atmospheres, and economies. While the above-mentioned urban

Figure 2.10 An urban village with factories, agriculture, and the runway of the airport used by the leaders of China – west Beijing (Photo Credit: Google Earth).

Figure 2.11 An urban village with factories, agriculture, and a freeway interchange – north/ east Beijing – fourth ring road (Photo Credit: Google Earth).

plan for Beijing was never officially adopted, one author mentioned that in practice, it had profoundly shaped the actual formation of the city. And indeed, if one looks between the cracks, or from the vantage point of Google Earth, these hundreds of villages in the city are the "spitting image" of one of the "Dispersal Units" proposed in the 1959 plan with the tripartite components of village, factories, and agriculture. Driving through the normative city, the urban villages go undetected since they are screened from view by large swaths of trees as part of Beijing's urban afforestation program or by high whitewashed screen walls.

Many of these villages are thriving, even if under the radar. Their success is most often due to the fact that the villagers and newly arrived migrants have taken advantage of particular conditions and have established economic advantages from them. For example, Gaobeidian, a very ancient village along a canal in the now highly developed extension to Beijing's Central Business District in the mid-eastern part of the city, has continued a tradition of wood-

working and furniture-making crafts. This industry, along with some associated tourism, has allowed the village to survive and advance even in the face of impending development and soaring real-estate values. Another successful village is Bo Luo Ying. Situated between two wealthy, mostly expat, gated suburban-style housing developments in northeast Beijing, Bo Luo Ying has established itself as a service spot for the foreigners who go there for pharmaceuticals (both legal and illegal), antique shops, massage parlors, pubs, and Internet cafes. It serves as an antidote to the sterile and exclusive private communities that surround it (devoid of shops and street life), and it in fact provides the only highly public and active social space and nightlife for miles around.

Some villages are disappearing or going through a dismantling process, usually by orders given from above and overseen by the Chai Chien, the Demolish and Relocation Bureau. Bei Hu Qu is a village formerly associated with an adjacent liquor factory. It now exists as a recycling center for materials of all sorts that sits within a landscape of encroaching golf courses that cater to the nearby high-density housing district of Wang Jing. The village is seemingly suspended within the demolition and relocation process as about 30 percent of the families there are *ding zi hu*, or nail households. As Sylvia Wallis has written in her *Brief Lexicon of Chinese Urbanism*[11] "Stubborn

Figure 2.12 A whitewashed screen wall that blocks the view of the rubble, recycling yards, and nail households of Bei Hu Qu village from the golf courses and city surrounding it.

Figure 2.13 In Bo Luo Ying village, a box in a recycling pile from a relocating expat who has just moved into the adjacent gated villa compound.

Figure 2.14 Thriving nightlife in the urban villages.

families resist leaving their traditional homes despite the insistence of developers seeking to make enormous profits. *ding zi hu* are as difficult to pullout from their bulldozed neighborhoods as nails from old wood studs." Village life goes on amid mounds of rubble now covered by weeds and exposed tile floors of the former rooms reoccupied as gambling, hangout, market, and laundry-work spaces.

Figure 2.15 The urban village of Bei Hu Qu lives on amid an environment of 70 percent demolition, encroaching golf courses, and the distant high-density housing district of Wang Jing.

CAOCHANGDI: FARMERS, FLOATERS, TAXI DRIVERS, ARTISTS, AND THE CONTEMPORARY ART MOB CHALLENGE AND REMAKE A PIECE OF THE CITY

As mentioned earlier, we came to know about the urban villages of Beijing after finding ourselves with the studio BASEbeijing[12] and a house in Caochangdi. Caochangdi is the subject of our recently published book, *Caochangdi: Beijing Inside Out*.[13] Even though Caochangdi is bounded by, and literally touching, both the Fifth Ring Road and the Airport Expressway – two highly traveled thoroughfares – Caochangdi is virtually invisible to the city surrounding it due to a combination of the height difference between the village and the roadways and the thick swaths of trees between them. Once inside the village, what produces a strange urban conundrum and sets Caochangdi apart from 500 or so other urban villages in Beijing is that since the beginning of the twenty-first century, it has become a locus of art production

Figure 2.16 Aerial view of Caochangdi village (Photo Credit: Google Earth).

and international art galleries.[14] *Vanity Fair* reported that at a recent auction, a fair amount of this art was connected to Caochangdi,[15] the village that *Condé Nast Traveler* recently described as one of the "newest cool places" (along with Harlem, Brighton, and Valencia). The Caochangdi Art Hood-slash-Village is just the beginning of a rather wild mix that forms a heterotopia extraordinaire. The traditional village fabric sits in the midst of a landscape of ring roads, expressways, train tracks, mid-rise housing, suburban villas, factories, high-end international galleries and art studios, taxi-cab

drivers' dormitories, residents, shop and restaurant owners, landlords for migrant workers' housing, and agriculture. And, Martha Stewart has paid a visit to the village.

An alphabetical catalog of buildings in Caochangdi reveals a wild mix of programs that exist simultaneously and have resisted any tendency toward a collapse of difference. These range from a dog-meat restaurant to a Korean Christian Church operating under the cover of an animation training school, a blue-chip art gallery based in Lucerne and Beijing, a Belgian foundation for

Figure 2.17 Martha Stewart visits Ai Weiwei in Caochangdi to speak with him about his design and lifestyle (Photo Credit: Ai Weiwei and FAKE).

Figure 2.18 A design by Ai Weiwei and FAKE design (Photo Credit: Ai Weiwei and FAKE).

Cancer Diagnosis, Therapy, Sterilization and Proton Ionization Solutions for Hygiene, the house and studio of Ai Weiwei and FAKE Design, IOWA – a compound of Quonset huts transformed into an American-style suburban home and Mongolian corn-fed beef restaurant – housing for taxi drivers, an art school, and a driving school boasting simulated freeway on- and off-ramps for new drivers. And the list continues. This difference is seen in the commotion of action taking place on the street and in the architecture and buildings in Caochangdi. A mule cart rolls by a parked Bentley and then through an impromptu market. There is a mix of original village structures, ad hoc shacks, brand new multi-story concrete-frame brick buildings built by entrepreneurial farmers, and the "high architecture" studios and galleries designed by Ai Weiwei and FAKE, and others.

The culture of the copy is alive and well in Caochangdi village and is in fact thriving in its entrepreneurial illegal environment. FAKE's design studio is in the village, and, led by Ai Weiwei, the office has designed and built several projects. The farmers, who now have no land to farm, occupy themselves by adding value to the property leased to them by the government through constructing multi-story buildings on the land where their one-story

Figure 2.19 An imitation of a FAKE design across the street from the original (fake FAKES).

houses once stood. The farmers have definitely taken notice of the language and the look of the FAKE architecture and of the wealthy foreigners who are paying high rents for them. The farmers have started to make fake FAKEs.

THE POST-GOOGLE CITY

In this period of cities in the post-Google era, we hope that some of us remain interested in looking deeply into the real and varied mechanisms affecting human congregation around the world these days. As Robert Neuwirth (2006: xiii) has pointed out, by 2050 more than one-third of the entire population of the world will be living in illegal urban "squatter" settlements.

It might be possible that some funny hybrid effort combining illegal building by citizens with centrally planned infrastructure, and even architecture with a capital A, as seen in Caochangdi, might be one way to wiggle out of that gloomy statistic and into a new vital urbanism.

PROJECT CREDITS

This project has been realized with the excellent and committed work of members of BASEbeijing including project managers Andrew Norskog, Richard Tursky, Daniel Weisman, Elizabeth Yarina, Jason Zhao, Professor James Lowder and his group from the University of Buffalo, students from Mary-Ann Ray and Robert Mangurian's Fall 2008 "China Inside Out" seminar at the Taubman College of Architecture and Urban Planning, including project manager Walter Raymond Alexander Hobocienski. This investigation into Beijing's urban villages has been generously supported by the University of Michigan's International Institute's Experiential Learning Fund, the Office of the Vice Provost for Research, Center of Chinese Studies and Taubman College of Architecture and Urban Planning, and by a grant from the Graham Foundation for Advanced Studies in the Fine Arts.

NOTES

1 The urban village phenomena is common to most large developing cities worldwide.
2 China has perhaps two to four million rural villages – with populations of about 200–500 inhabitants.
3 Normal – housing, office, shopping, parks. Abnormal – airports, historical sites, aggregation of shops forming "illegal" markets.
4 Capital Steel was initially established in 1919, developed in the Mao era, and greatly expanded in the Deng Xiaoping era. Currently, the facility is being closed down and moved further from the city for environmental reasons.
5 Note that Beijing's and China's urban villages are not "shanty towns." The brick and reinforced concrete constructions are substantial, and extremely well constructed. Although the buildings do not have building permits, they are planned, designed, and certainly structurally sound.
6 We experienced this first-hand in our Caochangdi residency in May and June 2007 (the year before the Olympics and one year after the New Socialist Countryside mandate within the Eleventh Five Year Plan) when there was an explosion of infrastructure construction having to do with

storm and sanitary sewers, natural gas lines, and road and sidewalk improvements.

7 Speech by Chen Xiwen, Deputy Director of the Office of Central Financial Work Leading Group, February 14, 2006.

8 The floating population is housed in the following ways within China's cities. Most large-scale construction sites have "built-in" dormitories for the construction workers. Many migrant workers live in middle-class housing as *ayi* – live-in nannies, housekeepers. Large factories (especially in south China) provide dormitories for the migrant workers that include meals. All other members of the floating population are housed in urban villages.

9 See http://chinafacttours.com/facts/china-agriculture.html.

10 For references to this plan, see the following:

Dong, Guang Qi. "Wu Shi Qi Nian Guang Hui Li Cheng – Jian Guo Yi Lai Beijing Cheng Shi Gui Hua de Fa Zhan," *Beijing Gui Hua Jian She* 9 (2006): 13–14.

Lu, Lu. "Xin Zhong Guo Yi Lai de Cheng Shi Gui Hua," *Beijing Dang Shi* 1 (2005): 18–21.

Su, Feng. "Cong Beijing Qi Ci Cheng Shi Zong Ti Gui Hua Kan Shou Du Jian She de Zong Ti Si Lu," *Beijing Dang Shi* 2 (2008): 21–22.

Shi, Wei Liang. "Beijing Cheng Shi Gui Hua de Hui Gu yu Zhan Wang," *Zhong Wai Fang Di Chan Dao Bao* 3 (1999): 7–8.

Wang, Jun. "Beijing Cheng Shi Gui Hua Fang an Lue Lan (1949–1993)," *Liao Wang Xin Wen Zhou Kan* 14 (2002): 18–20.

11 Unpublished.

12 BASEbeijing is the authors' architectural laboratory attracting students from American, European, and Chinese schools of architecture.

13 *Caochangdi: Beijing Inside Out* (2009), Beijing: Timezone8, was produced at the authors' BASEbeijing in Caochangdi, at the Taubman College of Architecture and Planning at the University of Michigan, and at Studioworks Los Angeles with the help of over 50 students, including project manager Darien Williams.

14 Albeit, this population makes up only a small percentage of the overall population of Caochangdi's 10,000 residents.

15 *Vanity Fair*, December 2007.

3 ROTTERDAM 1979–2007

From ideology to market communism and beyond

MICHAEL SPEAKS

INTRODUCTION

From the post-war reconstruction period until the end of the 1960s, architects played a leading role in rebuilding the city of Rotterdam and planning its future development. Van den Broek and Bakema, Groosman, Maaskant and Van Tijen and Bakker, among others, built a new modernist city following the outline of Witteveen's Basisplan, transforming the rubble created by the German bombs into the foundation of a new metropolis. From the late 1960s and continuing into and through the 1970s, however, the power of architects and the ambition to build a new world city and port was greatly diminished and made subservient to national and local political agendas that purported to democratize – but instead politicized – the building and planning process, especially in the inner-city neighborhoods, which became the focus of intense sociological analysis, community organizing, and small-scale building activity. Consultants displaced architects as politics displaced city building in a nation-wide city-renewal program whose largesse was disguised by the small, neighborhood scale of its implementation. In Rotterdam, as in other cities in the Netherlands, "building for the neighborhood" became more important than building for the city, as the *cul de sac* and the conversation pit became architectural emblems of a society and a decade whose transformative energies were smothered by coziness and provincialism.

The call by the Rotterdam Arts Council for "inspection" by international critics in 1979 put the question of architecture and building for the city back on the agenda, and led, only a few years later, to the first in a series of Architecture International Rotterdam festivals. The emergence of AIR – whose name alone seemed to encourage the city to exhale the stultifying air of provincialism and breath deeply once again the fresh breezes blowing in from the port and across the continent – promised a more metropolitan approach to architecture, the city, and its future development. Breaking with the 1970s obsession with the small scale, AIR focused attention on the city as a whole and significantly, on the port and its infrastructure. These efforts, however, were accompanied by other trends driven by the changing nature of the global economy and the rise of greater competition among nation-states and indeed among cities. Beginning in the 1980s and picking up pace through the 1990s, the politicization of architecture that dominated Rotterdam in the 1970s was slowly but steadily displaced by the marketization of architecture. This occurred, most notably, through the privatization of housing, and through the use of architects and architecture to create a new marketing image of the city that would enable it to compete more effectively for tourist dollars and for service and new knowledge-based industries. Many now believe the pendulum has swung too far as the image of Rotterdam seems to have become more important than the reality of Rotterdam. As one city of Rotterdam marketing campaign puts it: "Rotterdam is increasingly to architecture what Paris is to fashion or Los Angeles to entertainment." While other cities have used architecture to help create a new branded identity, Rotterdam has gone one step further by making architecture itself the brand and in so doing seems to have lost sight of building the housing as well as the industries necessary to maintain and grow the city – not only for outsiders who may be attracted by "the city of architecture" but also for those who already live and work there.

It is this situation that seems to have made AIR allergic to the successes of its own past initiatives and has led them to draw up a new selection of buildings for inspection. But unlike in 1979 when there appeared to be a dearth of new and exciting architecture and a need for such a review, Rotterdam is now filled with new architecture, new architects, and new architectural institutions, including the NAi, the Berlage Institute, and 010 Publishers, to name only a few. Rotterdam is home to many of the so-called "Superdutch" architects who emerged to become stars of the international architectural world in the 1990s. And, of course, Rotterdam is the home of OMA, headed by Rem Koolhaas, arguably the most important architect in the world today. All this leads one to wonder, "Does Rotterdam really need three international inspectors to evaluate the quality of its architecture?" Obviously, AIR thinks so, and I am honored to be chosen as one of the inspectors. But rather than make an analysis that handicaps each of these buildings – a useful endeavor if your intention is to create an architectural scorecard that shows Rotterdam in an architectural deficit, as was the case in 1979 – I prefer instead to let the buildings selected for inspection by AIR narrate their own story – about the past, the present, and perhaps even about the future of the city of Rotterdam.

HOUSING IDEOLOGIES, HOUSING MARKETS

No two buildings draw the line between the 1970s and what was to follow more dramatically than the first and second on our inspector's list. The first is the timid, inner-city social Housing Project at Gouvernestraat (1976–1980), dressed in happy, structuralist-colored pajamas and ready to be tucked into bed. Nestled inside an enclave on a street I have walked past on many occasions without ever noticing or finding cause to enter, the feeling there is one of constriction and constraint, despite the architect's attempt to introduce light and air by setting back the houses from the street. The tenant we visited there was nice and was pleased with her apartment and neighborhood, despite the fact that she did not seem to know or have reason to get to know any of her neighbors. She lives there, it seems, not because of the neighborhood, but because it is cheap and convenient. The second building is Carel Weeber's famously shaped social-housing revolt, the Peperklip (1979–1982). One of the first housing projects built in the harbor area, this massive, reptilian superblock makes its presence known and felt, even when viewed from the safe distance of Google Earth. Built of pre-cast concrete with colored façades that aggressively refuse to distinguish individual apartments one from the other, nothing says the end of the 1970s like this rationalist, harbor-scaled beast marked with the inscription "De Peperklip Anno 1980."

If the Peperklip bolts from the cozy corners of the inner city for the tough, open spaces of the harbor, DKV's Agniesebuurt Housing Complex (1984– 1988) illustrates a different, more generational and stylistic break that saw a number of then-emerging Dutch architects return to a modernist design idiom that had been largely abandoned for the nineteenth-century flavor of 1970s inner-city renewal. Unlike in America, where avant-gardes like the "New York Five" were also resuscitating Modernism, here primary forms and geometries took up residence in a real neighborhood – next to a train line. Choosing against the normative perimeter block and instead for one tall and another slightly-less-tall slab with room for businesses below, allowed the architects to open up the site for a public square out front, which, the day we visited, was filled with children playing and people from the surrounding neighborhood. I first saw the DKV building some years ago in Hans Ibelings's *Modernism without Dogma* (1991), an exhibition catalog that featured a group of emerging Dutch architects who favored a pragmatic, non-ideological approach to modernism. The work of Mecanoo was also featured there, and like the work of DKV, was derided as "schoolteacher modernism" – as architecture that looked modern but lacked an agenda.

Mecanoo designed one of the first social-housing projects in Rotterdam built in this idiom, the Social Housing Project for Young People at Kruisplein (1989–1993). And they brought this same pragmatic, neo-modern approach to the suburban housing project we visited in Ringvaartpas Area (1989– 1993). There the landscape is idyllic and the housing and public spaces are extremely attractive, so we were surprised to hear complaints from several residents about how the neighborhood was changing due to newcomers moving there from the inner city. One can only imagine that this has something to do with the trend in Rotterdam to develop more market-rate housing in the old inner-city neighborhoods and the perception of residents in suburban areas that their neighborhoods will degrade as social housing is squeezed out of the inner city, leaving residents there no choice but to find housing in the suburbs. The large social-housing corporations, which control much of the housing stock in Rotterdam, were privatized in the early 1990s, effectively transforming them into developers-on-the-make with staggeringly large property portfolios and an eye fixed on the bottom line. This explains why in many cases they now choose to replace their older social-housing properties with new market-rate housing, a strategy consistent with – though not necessarily connected to – the demand in the last few years from certain quarters in city government that the burden of social housing now be shared more equitably between city and suburb. We visited one such property, Spaans Water Housing on Spanjaardstraat (1999–2002) in the Bospolder neighborhood, among the last of the old neighborhoods to be targeted for renewal. Designed by Putter Partners, it is a smart, no-nonsense, brick-clad housing block of four varying unit types, and just one among a number of new market-rate rentals and owner-occupied housing projects in the neighborhood. It is hard to imagine that only a few years ago this neighborhood was crime-ridden and drug-infested. If current political and developmental trends continue, someday in the near future this will be the case in all the old neighborhoods of Rotterdam making them safe and truly "livable" – but for a price.

As housing continues to be privatized and held in the hands of increasingly powerful corporations and developers, what was once a guarantee made by the municipality and the state is rapidly becoming a lifestyle choice for those who can afford it and a matter of increasing hardship for those who cannot. We heard just such a story of hardship from a tenant living in one of the housing blocks on the Rotterdam Waterworks site, who, though he had lived there for many years, could not now afford to purchase his own apartment, which, it seems, will soon be put on the market for sale. He will have to move, but where? At the same time, it is now possible to return to the nineteenth century if you choose to live in the brick, gable-roofed De Compagnie superblock (2000–2005), designed by Hans Kolhoff and built in the Zuidkade area of the Kop Van Zuid. But unlike with the 1970s version of the nineteenth century, in this twenty-first-century version the city is not likely to subsidize your rent. It is also possible to choose to live on the other side of the River Maas in the newly revitalizing Laurensquarter in De Hofdame (2003–2007), designed by Klunder Architects, a deceptively (rather than ostentatiously) large brick-clad complex located just next to St. Laurens Church. Or, you might choose to live just across the market square in the Bosch Haslett designed City Building (2003), a glazed, futuristic volume-fold that wraps a historic bank building designed by J.J.P. Oud. Here, in these new buildings, history and geography are collapsed and made available in new combinations with each suggesting a different lifestyle choice represented in the shape and disposition of the building and in its menu of hidden amenities.

Even getting old is now a lifestyle choice, as is made clear by the architects Arons and Gelauff, whose theme for the senior housing project they designed in Ijsselmonde was "What do you mean gray?" referring, one presumes, not only to the hair color of seniors, but also to the drabness associated with senior housing. Their De Plussenburgh Residential Complex (2004–2006), with interiors and landscaping designed by Petra Blaisse of Inside Outside, is anything but gray and is in fact the most hip senior housing I have ever visited and one of my own personal favorites among all the buildings we toured. The interior and exterior public spaces are exquisite and the building's slab towers – one turned upright and one on its side – provide an economical and aesthetically pleasing solution to the brief as well as a frame to showcase the multicolored glazed façade and undulating balconies. It is a choice I would happily make now, long before retirement age. De Plussenburgh, like the other buildings mentioned above, is a choice available in a marketplace seemingly absent the ideological struggle evident in Weeber's blunt disavowal of the sentimental 1970s or in DKV's and Mecanoo's housing projects, critiqued as "schoolteacher modern" but clear in their conviction about the superiority of a non-ideological, pragmatic modernism to the ideologically charged historicist agenda of nineteenth-century city renewal. Now, even those soft ideological distinctions no longer exist because the market has effectively removed ideology – though not politics – from the housing equation once and for all and replaced them with a menu of individual housing choices. If in the 1970s architects designed housing blocks that were statements of ideological belief, and in the 1980s and 1990s they designed housing blocks that were statements of non-ideological belief, today they design housing-block choices unattached to either ideology or belief.

CAPITALIST TOOLS: TOWERS, SHOPPERS, POSEURS, AND CREATIVES

The end of the 1970s also brought to an end the antipathy toward "capitalist development" expressed by powerful city officials like Rotterdam Alderman Mentink, who, it is said, proclaimed in the late 1970s that the 26-story Shell office building addition would be the last capitalist erection to occur in the center of Rotterdam. Shooting up and out of the old Rotterdam Stock Exchange, seemingly in defiance of such proclamations, the World Trade Center (1983–1986) literally and figuratively reconnects the financial ambitions of pre-war Rotterdam with what in the 1980s was becoming an increasingly interconnected global marketplace. Along with Wim Quist's Willemswerf Office Building (1983–1989), the World Trade Center initiated a rush to build office towers in the city that would have seemed impossible only a few years earlier. That said, nothing refutes Mentink more forcefully than the auspicious presence of the Nationale Nederlanden Headquarters (1986–1991), once heralded as the tallest building in the Netherlands and located in the center of the city at the corner of Weena and Stationsplein. Nothing, that is, more forcefully than the promotional use for marketing purposes now made of Piet Blom's Cube Houses (1978–1984) – commissioned by Mentink as part of the effort to build small-scale, dense city dwellings – to project the image of a cool, cosmopolitan Rotterdam.

If the tall office building signals from on high the return of capitalist development in the form of banking and business services, then the Beurstraverse Shopping Center (1991–1996), a below-grade pedestrian shopping mall designed by Los Angeles shopping mall guru John Jerde, heralds the emergence of a new, 24-hour, consumer-driven urbanism. Segregating shopping as a distinct urban activity by connecting, in American shopping mall fashion, two anchor shopping areas – the Lijnbaan and Hoogstraat – and then making the entire area accessible through an existing underground metro stop at Beursplein, Jerde dramatically increased pedestrian traffic density by drawing in shoppers from all over the city and surrounding areas. Some of that traffic spills onto the nearby Schouwburgplein (1990–1997), a marvelous floating urban stage set designed by landscape architect Adriane Geuze, before being drawn, like fireflies to a lantern, into Koen van Velsen's Megabioscoop (1992–1996) to catch a movie in one of its seven theatres. Along with the City Theatre (1982–1988), designed by Wim Quist, and the Concert Center de Doelen (1955–1966), they form an entertainment area that is as much part of consumer-driven urbanism as the French fries which can be had at the Kees Christiaanse-designed Snackbar Bram Ladage (1990) before popping into the Donner Bookshop on the Lijnbaan for a book or magazine.

But the ultimate break with the 1970s occurs with the development of the Kop van Zuid, and 1996, the year Ben van Berkel's Erasmusbrug was completed, is perhaps the most significant for it was in that year that the center of the city – and the world's attention – moved out from its former location into the old harbor areas of south Rotterdam. Just as Jerde had crossed underneath the Coolsingel to join two mid twentieth-century shopping anchors, so had van Berkel crossed over the Maas to connect the twentieth-century urban economy of material things to the emerging twenty-first-century urban economy of immaterial things. The year 1996 saw the beginning of construction for Peter Wilson's new Luxor Theatre (1996–2001), lifted like a little seed of culture by the winds of economic change from its former location in the city center and planted on one of the most important intersections in the new Kop van Zuid development. There the Luxor joined the storied Hotel New York (1901/1919), former office quarters of the Holland America Line, to form new "lifestyle" anchors situated on either end of the Wilhelminapier. Soon after, these lifestyle anchors were enhanced by a complement of cafes, bars, clubs, and just this year, by the completion of the Rotterdam Fotomuseum in Las Palmas designed by Benthem Crowel (2001–2007). Such cultural amenities were the fuel that in the 1990s drove the engine of an emergent "experience economy" in which it was argued that designed "experiences" added value not only to products but also to the quality of urban life itself, transforming normal business or personal activities – lodging in a hotel – into multilayered user experiences replete with signature furnishings, nostalgia services such as old barber shops, and water-taxi rides across the harbor, all of which were then and are still today on offer at Hotel New York. What one consumed was not so much a tangible thing as an intangible experience.

While "experience" was one feature of a new, immaterial economy that began to emerge in the late 1990s, without question the most significant economic transformation occurred with new developments in telecommunications, logistics, and security, all of which found their place on the Wilhelmenapier. As the port grew larger and more complex and moved farther out towards the North Sea – enabled, among other things by automation and new, decentralized means of communication – it was nonetheless important to secure a fixed strategic location in the old harbor area for the Rotterdam Port Authority. The location chosen was the Wilhelmenapier and there soon followed Norman Foster's World Port Center (1995–2000), an office tower and center of port operations, logistics, and communications, situated on the end of the pier next to Hotel New York. Though the tower has other commercial office spaces, its primary tenant is the Port Authority who chose also to locate their Emergency Coordination Center in the crow's nest at the top of the building. From there it is possible to control, though not see, all operations of what is still one of the largest and most complex ports in the world and the real driving force of all current harbor development. Foster's World Port Center is matched on the other end of the pier by another tower devoted to immaterial, twenty-first-century commerce, the KPN Telecom Headquarters (1997–2000), designed by Renzo Piano. Once part of a telecommunications giant that controlled the Dutch mail, KPN is today the largest fixed line and mobile telephony provider in the Netherlands and one of the largest in Europe. Now joined by the Montevideo (1999–2005), a luxurious, self-contained "vertical city" designed by Mecanoo, these early arrivals on Wilhelmenapier will soon be surrounded by a veritable cornucopia of new luxury mixed-use towers with names like New Orleans, San Francisco, Boston, Philadelphia, Baltimore, Chicago, Rotterdam, and Havana, all of which will contribute to an impressive skyline that has already outgrown its old moniker, "Manhattan on the Maas."

Another, recently completed building, the Bruggebouw (2000–2005) office building designed by JHK Architects with West 8 for the global food giant Unilever just up-river at Nassaukade, has added its "bridge-building" profile to this skyline. The impressive structure straddles an existing, non-working factory, leaving it and the surrounding area available to be developed in the future as housing. The design is a striking and clever one that preserves an old harbor factory and its surrounds; gives employees a work environment that is open, playful, and conducive to creativity; and provides the company a much-desired new building-logo. Due to the sensitive nature of the work conducted there – product research and development – we were restricted from visiting the building in person, though we did view it from our tour bus and from as many vantage points across the river on the north side as we liked. (I saw interior images online and in a company brochure.) Like the new skyline itself, and like the other corporate giants and real-estate heavyweights gathering on the south bank of the river, the pose struck by the Bruggebouw as it hovers over the old factory and warehouses is somewhat aggressive, if not vaguely predatory. The building lays claim to an increasingly valuable water frontage from which it can project its image, unobstructed, back onto the city on the other side of the river and from there out into the world. And yet, Bruggebouw's visage does not match the menacing stare of the Peperklip, the old neighborhood tough around the corner who needed to be tough just to survive the 1980s and 1990s. Rather, its look is that of the bohemian newcomer – striking a cocky, stylized pose while nervously looking about – who seeks the "street cred" gained from living in a tough, harbor neighborhood. For Unilever, moving to the harbor was ultimately a corporate lifestyle choice that enables them simultaneously to project the image of an edgy, creative, environmentally sensitive company while at the same time using the frisson created by living in the harbor to stir up the creative juices of its employees – the lifeblood of a global giant in need of constant innovation.

Creativity has also been on the minds of city officials and developers all over the Netherlands and in particular on the minds of those in Rotterdam since the publication and dissemination of Richard Florida and Charles Landry's ideas about the importance of a new, putative "creative class" for urban development. It is hard to imagine a development in Rotterdam, or anywhere, for that matter, which conforms more closely to the "creative class" recipe than in Lloyd Quarter, a former dock area located on the north side of the river, and the next stage of harbor development to occur after the Kop van Zuid. Financed with public and private development money, the area seeks to attract creative industries including multimedia production and digital post-production companies, as well as television and film-related industries. The emphasis here – unlike at the Kop van Zuid – is on small start-up companies who are sought not only for the economic value of their actual work output but also for the economic value of the communities – both physical and online – they form. The architect Robert Winkel of Mei Architects has played a key role in transforming many former industrial buildings in the Lloyd Quarter into new studio spaces, hotels, and housing for these communities. At 25KV building (1996–2000), Winkel has rather deftly converted a former power station into a wonderful new venue for media studios. By sheering away the concrete façade and replacing it with a 2-meter-thick glass wall, Winkel was able to break open this dumb concrete box to create a veritable temple of twenty-first-century workplace transparency. The space between the building and glass façade is fitted with a steel frame hung with toilets, cupboards, and meeting modules, effectively pushing all but the most private activities (the toilet walls are not transparent) into clear view from both inside and outside the building. Winkel also renovated the ultra-cool Hotel Stroom on the other end of the pier and is in the process of converting a mammoth warehouse across the street into apartments. Just across the quay on the Mullerpier there is another massive housing development, planned by KCAP, which includes 13 residential complexes designed by KCAP, de Architecten Cie and Neutelings Riedijk, among others. There is great variety in housing options in these attractive, dark brick-clad tower blocks and low rises, though when we visited there were very few people on the street and it seemed not such a large percentage of the apartments were filled. There is, in addition to these developments, a television station under construction behind Schiecentrale and a number of attractive apartments and small studios now opening in other industrial buildings scattered along the pier.

The real attraction in the Lloyd Quarter, however, is the Shipping and Transport College (2000–2005) designed by Neutelings and Riedijk, among the most thrilling buildings I have visited in years. Its shape and color-patched corrugated skin give the impression of a stack of shipping containers topped with a huge window that overlooks the harbor and creates, as a consequence, a literal and figural metaphor for port management and education in the harbor. The building, which brings together under one roof a number of maritime-related schools from around the city, is fresh without being campy, and no-nonsense without being a bore. On the inside, a series of brilliant orange escalators feed more than 2,000 students through the 16 stories of stacked educational program. All others use lifts. With cafeteria, bookshop, recreation facilities – including a climbing wall and basketball court – and a distinctive, cantilevered auditorium on top that can be rented for non-college functions, it is easily the densest, most heavily trafficked piece of real estate with the greatest variety of program on the pier. To risk using a cliché, it is rather like a small city. And yet, however excellent a building, it is not a city, but rather the home of a part-time community, distinct even from the other part-time communities – media, arts, hotel, housing – being nurtured in the Lloyd Quarter. Students, faculty, and staff are drawn to the College from all over Rotterdam and indeed from all over the Netherlands and Europe, just as "creatives" are drawn here to work and others are drawn to the wonderful housing on both Lloydpier and the Mullerpier across the way. But none of these part-time communities overlaps with the others to create a single, full-time community, nor do any of them seem to have any real connection with the neighboring area of Delfshaven, an area that could surely benefit from the economic infusion promised by so-called "creative class" developments.

If the Lloyd Quarter fails – and it has really only just begun – it will not be a failure of architecture but a failure to create a real, working community. Just like those responsible for the city-renewal campaign in the 1970s, those responsible for the Lloyd Quarter have created a seemingly ersatz community which does little more than burnish the image of Rotterdam – portrayed in the 1970s as a cozy, small-scale, neighborhood city, and now as a "creative" city eager to compete in the global marketplace. City renewal produced no real neighborhoods – only a cozy feeling – and it seems the Lloyd Quarter is not likely to produce a real creative community – only the look of one. Like the office towers, shopping malls, and entertainment facilities built in the city center in the 1980s, and like the twenty-first-century city built on and around the Kop van Zuid in the 1990s, the Lloyd Quarter is the result of an approach to city development that treats architects, architecture, and the city more like products than producers. Since the end of the 1970s the city has – quite rightly – pursued strategies to make Rotterdam more competitive in an increasingly competitive global marketplace. It has done so, however, by marketing the city to those who consume its various products, from business services to housing, and it has used architecture as a primary source of attraction. It seems, though, that the city simply traded in a political vanguard that touted Rotterdam as "the city of neighborhoods" for a marketing vanguard that now touts Rotterdam as "the city of architecture." But this top-down, consumerist approach has built-in limitations that make it ever more difficult for the city to control its own future development when it owns or controls fewer and fewer of the assets and products it markets and sells. As marketization and technological transformation – the two engines of globalization – do the heavy lifting of moving public goods and services into the hands of the private sector, city government, whether in Rotterdam, Los Angeles, or Hong Kong, necessarily plays a diminished and continuously diminishing role. Without sufficient resources to provide necessary housing or jobs, and unable to redevelop blighted neighborhoods, cities are forced, as was Rotterdam, to develop strategies like the *Groeibriljanten*, or "growing diamonds," that encourage entrepreneurial action initiated by local communities. There have also occurred in Rotterdam projects of "collective private commissioning," like the one that took place at Spangen, where 30 apartments were given away in an effort to encourage the new owners to join together and renovate the block. These entrepreneurial, public–private development projects, which produce both social and real capital, point to an alternative to marketing the city – even a creative city – as a product. But these initiatives can have only a limited effect unless they are deployed more comprehensively and more radically.

MARKET COMMUNISM?

The only way forward, it seems, is to expand – not contract – and radically democratize marketization. Carel Weeber has proposed that all the social housing given to the housing corporations in the late 1980s now be given to the tenants who occupy them. This is indeed a radically democratic approach that would immediately transform those living in housing corporation property into homeowners. It is also not likely to happen. The future of marketization is instead now in the hands of the housing corporations who, unlike the city, have the properties and the means to engage in large-scale urban developments that include housing as well as schools, health care, and other "public" amenities. But there is a lot to be learned from Weeber's radical speculation. Indeed, the basic assumptions of this audacious project are now being tested in a limited way by Rotterdam-based architect, Dennis Kaspori, who, since 2003, has worked with Weeber on "Wilde Wonen," a plea in the form of a book (1998) and a website to democratize housing ownership in the Netherlands. Along with the artist Jeanne van Heeswijk, Kaspori is now working on a project in Amsterdam that seeks to discover the desires and needs of tenants so that they can be translated into new programs and requirements for a housing block that, if all goes well, will ultimately be given to them. This information is gathered by a "caretaker," who lives with and works for the tenants for three months doing small jobs and learning, in the process, how they live and how they want to live. The idea is that when the block is turned over to the tenants – and this ultimately depends on the housing corporation that owns it – the tenants will become collective members of their own housing corporation. It is an interesting and promising speculation.

Kaspori has also been researching and developing an online decision market, "The Rotterdam Index," a virtual stock market exchange that allows anyone who signs up to use virtual currency to buy and sell properties in Rotterdam. The website, which is sponsored by several housing corporations, also includes a discussion forum and news reporting by participants from the neighborhoods. Ultimately, when the Index has enough players, it will generate market intelligence that enables users, especially those new to the market, like first-time home buyers, to make decisions about where to rent and where to buy. The Rotterdam Index is an example of Kaspori's attempts to develop new models of inclusive urbanism, as he calls them, models that involve residents, in particular, who are often left out of normal design and planning discussions. As housing corporations slowly displace the city as planners of entire communities, such negotiative strategies will become increasingly important. The market-based intelligence created by the Rotterdam Index and by projects such as "The Caretaker" will become crucial as corporations seek to use cultural and other public amenities to meet the requirements of tenants and to enhance the value of their portfolios – there is no reason these should be mutually exclusive concerns. Nor is there any reason that housing corporations will not ultimately make new social housing part of their portfolios, but that will happen only if social housing is a portfolio asset rather than a liability. One way of ensuring this is to give those who live in social housing a greater stake in its design and more real and cultural capital in the form of neighborhood identity and job opportunities, and this is precisely what Kaspori is now trying to instigate with his provocative agenda.

I viewed one of his projects in the first and last building I visited on our official tour, the Kunsthal (1988–1992), by Rem Koolhaas. The project, "Face

Your World," another developed with van Heeswijk, is an interactive game that allows participants to understand and interact with their urban world through design. The game, which is played on proprietary software set up on two banks of eight computer stations, was used in Amsterdam to involve 600 residents and 50 youths in discussing and designing a local park that will ultimately be built. The "Face Your World" workshop in the Kunsthal involves local youngsters in an interactive design project for the Museumpark, the redevelopment of which is now at an impasse due to competing interests among the many stakeholders. The interactive nature of the game allows them to speculate and discuss with each other and with stakeholders possible design solutions that could break through the impasse. Kaspori is also working with Rotterdam-based philosopher Henk Oosterling and van Heeswijk on "Skill City," a project that redefines creativity by arguing that Rotterdam needs to develop the creative potential of those living in the city rather than developing districts devoted to attracting a creative class from outside the neighborhood and the city. They seek to bridge the efforts to develop creative-class enclaves, like at the Lloyd Quarter, with a more inclusive, cultural- and entrepreneurial-based infrastructure that treats skilled labor as a form of creativity. To their credit, they see the merit of Florida's arguments and the potential for projects like the Lloyd Quarter, but they argue these only address one form of creativity. As Kaspori remarked when I spoke with him at the Kunsthal:

> Rotterdam is a labor city and it should consider labor as a form of creativity. Creativity is not just a matter of design, architecture, cinema and new media. Creativity can also be seen in the work of people who have skills, of people who know how to make things.

Kaspori will unveil a series of "Skill City" pilot projects in the next year, including "Freehouse," a center to encourage local cultural and business entrepreneurship. These projects – of which there will be at least four – are similar in spirit to the restaurant Gemaal in Afrikaanderplein in South Rotterdam, where we lunched one day during our long bus tour through the city. There, area youth are trained by a famous Rotterdam restaurateur to cook and run the restaurant using only ingredients from the local market across the street. It is a truly sustainable entrepreneurial endeavor. The excellent food and atmosphere attract diners from all over the city who are made aware of the potential of this down-market area and who contribute to providing locals a marketable skill.

What is exciting about the restaurant, and indeed about all of Kaspori's work, especially in comparison to the creative-class strategy used at the Lloyd Quarter, is that it returns us to an indigenous, Rotterdam-based model of creativity documented in Patricia van Ulzen's excellent study, *Imagine a Metropolis: Rotterdam's Creative Class 1970–2000* (2007). There, she reminds us that in the late 1970s, long before Richard Florida penned a single sentence about the creative class, a group of former TU-Delft students, including 010 Press founders Hans Oldewarris and Peter de Winter, as well as Gerard Hadders and Rick Vermeulen of the graphic design firm Hard Werken, created a community of cultural entrepreneurs at the Rotterdam Waterworks site that would ultimately save those splendid buildings and transform them into the epicenter of a creative network that was in large measure responsible for building a new, metropolitan Rotterdam from the ground up. Theirs was indeed an ethic of hard work and their labors in this former harbor area created the foundation for much that came after, including the first AIR manifestation in 1979. As their example shows, the task of building the city is not one that can be accomplished with architecture alone, though it is a process that can be greatly enhanced by architects and architecture.

CONCLUSION

The 1970s were indeed depressing. The early 1970s saw the publication of the Club of Rome's *Limits to Growth* (1972), the infamous study that predicted dire consequences for the world economy due to the combination of rapid population growth and limited resources. Just a year later, in 1973, many of those fears seem to be confirmed with the OPEC oil crises that sent gasoline and other petroleum product prices soaring. By the end of the 1970s, however, the world economy was beginning to recover, and in many places the foundations for a new economic paradigm – globalization – were being put into place. In 1978, Deng Xiaoping initiated liberal reforms in the Chinese economy, unleashing one of the most powerful engines of economic growth in history. And in 1979 and then in 1980, Margaret Thatcher and Ronald Reagan undertook reforms to deregulate industries and liberate financial and capital markets from the remnants of Keynesian strictures. These and other events also marked an important transition from the nation-state to what political scientist Philip Bobbitt calls the market-state. Bobbitt, in his magisterial study, *The Shield of Achilles: War, Peace and the Course of History* (2002), convincingly argues that for the last 30 or so years we have seen the gradual emergence of a new form of state that has arisen as a result of increased global competition and the global integration of commodity and financial markets. The market-state is a dynamic state that no longer provides jobs and housing guarantees but rather seeks to provide its citizens with the opportunities necessary to obtain them. "The market-state is, above all, a mechanism for enhancing opportunity, for creating something – possibilities – commensurate with our imaginations."[1] Taking various forms – mercantile, entrepreneurial, managerial – the market-state is found almost everywhere in the world today, and the Netherlands, especially in the 1990s, became one of the strongest examples in Europe.

The impact of the market-state on cities like Rotterdam can be seen in the architectural traces left by the city's attempts to respond to its challenges – the office boom and build-up of shopping and entertainment both in the inner city and on the Kop van Zuid in the 1980s and 1990s; the new "creative-class" strategies initiated in the 1990s at the Lloyd Quarter and elsewhere, coupled with new market-rate housing intended to provide this new class suitable homes. And, even though it provides a less tangible signature for us to read than do buildings and infrastructure, the market-state has had an even more profound impact on cities like Rotterdam: The end of planning as we know it. *The Architecture Yearbook in the Netherlands 2006/07* published an image still taken from a "tongue-in-cheek" VPRO television documentary featuring Rudi Stroink of TCN Properties attempting to purchase the village of Warmond that illustrates very well the paradoxical situation cities now face. The caption reads, "And if all goes according to plan, we'll float Warmond on the stock exchange…and every Warmonder will be able to buy a share in their own town." Though humorous, this image nevertheless portrays the new reality of the market-state. The simple fact is that cities no longer have the ability to plan but must instead act as partners in ventures with developers and housing corporations, the only real actors with the resources necessary to engage in large-scale development. And yet, such market-oriented actors cannot afford to plan, at least in the conventional sense: they have neither the authority of the municipality nor the motivation to put their investments at risk in long-term, large-scale ventures when market conditions can change and leave them and their investors – in Stroink's and Weeber's scenarios the citizens themselves – holding losses. Planning, then, must take new, hybrid forms and become, like the *Groeibriljanten*, stimulative and empowering, not regulatory and punitive. Plans must make strong interventions with real consequences, but they must also be responsive to changing market conditions. Toward this end, the city of Rotterdam should encourage experimental developments where citizens become truly invested – both in their housing and in their jobs. With the aid of urban market intelligence provided by aggregators like Kaspori's "Rotterdam Index," Rotterdammers would then be able to disinvest, sell, and reinvest elsewhere, if they choose. When these things begin to happen, Weeber's and Stroink's visions will not appear so utopian after all. Market communism anyone?

NOTE

1 See Philip Bobbitt, *The Shield of Achilles: War, Peace and the Course of History* (New York: Knopf, 2002), especially chapter 10, "The Market State."

4 MEGAHOUSE

HITOSHI ABE AND MASASHIGE MOTOE

MEGAHOUSE is a lifestyle proposal for inhabiting the entire city as if it is one enormous "house".

Figure 4.1 Key image.

MEGAHOUSE is a lifestyle proposal for inhabiting the entire city as if it is one enormous "house."

There are always many empty rooms in the city, as neither office buildings nor apartment buildings are being completely utilized. The provider here

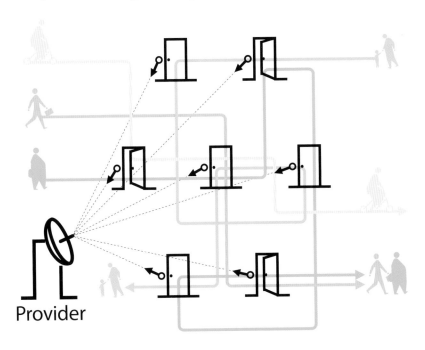

Provider

Figure 4.2 ZapDoor network.

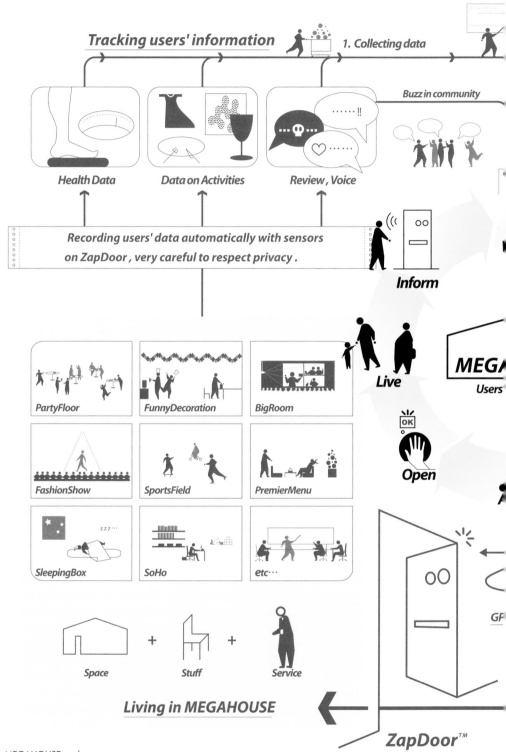

Figure 4.3 MEGAHOUSE ecology.

Analyzing logs

3. Archiving information

Ad tailored to user

Biometrics

Media Archive

User Tracking DB

Users' account services

Get Account

Market Information

Recommend

Feedback

Book

Online   or   **Megahouse Station**

Anytime Anywhere

Real Store , VR fitting . Concierge

Select

BrandRoom   CharacterHouse   EventBox

Basic   **Premier Menu**

×

Ad Rate

Info

Pay   Rental Fee   Info

User   **Megahouse Provider**   **Owners**   **Sponsors**

Rent Out   Provide

Space   Stuff   Service

Business Model

Unused Resources , New Items

Basic Graphics : Asao Tokolo (TOKOLO.COM)

Bring   **Fit**   **Open**

Seamless & Realtime Biometric Recognition

Figure 4.4 ZapDoor function.

FedEX Slot   **Media Archive**   **Monitoring Behavior**

collects and rents those empty rooms that permeate the entire city, then equips them all with a centralized management system called ZapDoor.

Users who have a contract with the provider can find, reserve, and use a particular room that fits their objectives. These rooms are available to the users for differing time-spans, from a short-term use of several hours to a long-term occupation of several months. Fees may be paid by various different methods. The application system is similar to that of a hotel.

As ZapDoor furnishes rooms everywhere in the city, these rooms collectively constitute a "house" for the users. Users inhabit the entire city like a dwelling, walking between many rooms. This "house" is dispersed and embedded throughout the entire city, and is overlaid at different time periods. A condition is born wherein the entire city may be used like a big "house." Produced by the ZapDoor network, this new condition of urban dwelling is the MEGAHOUSE.

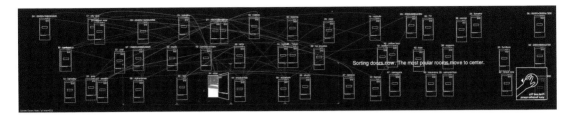

Figure 4.5 MEGAHOUSE exhibition.

Figure 4.6 MEGAHOUSE exhibition.

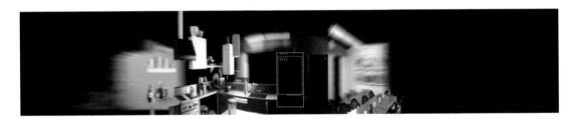

Figure 4.7 MEGAHOUSE exhibition.

Figure 4.8 OroshiMachi District, Sendai. First trial site of MEGAHOUSE system.

The ZapDoor is furnished with various sensors such as cameras and displays for biometric recognition, using fingerprints, retina prints, and faces. All of the ZapDoors are connected to the provider server via a digital network, and the locks are remote-controlled. Just by substituting the doors of existing vacant rooms with ZapDoors, these rooms can become part of the MEGA-HOUSE network.

Users register as MEGAHOUSE residents by recording their biometric information in advance. If users access the system from mobile phones or computer terminals, they will be introduced to appropriate rooms that respond to their objectives in terms of location, fee, equipment, and design. The user books the room that they prefer. The user is guided to the reserved room by GPS navigation software.

Although the design of each room is different they have a shared style, so ZapDoors can be visually recognized. If a user touches a doorknob, biometric confirmation is carried out, and the door will open if it is the correct user. It can then be used as if it is your own room. In technological terms, the technical elements required for implementing ZapDoors are already in use. What we are proposing is nothing more than integrating existing technical elements into a new way of using technology and an alternative way of using urban space.

MEGAHOUSE is also a thought experiment that inscribes the multiple relationships between technology and urban lifestyles in our surveillance society, with its loss of a sense of place and its ambiguity of boundaries between private space and public space.

PROJECT CREDITS

MEGAHOUSE project is realized in collaboration with Shingo Abe (motion graphics), Shohei Matsukawa/000studio (application programming), and Tohru Horiguchi/Tohoku University (research). W0W is a visual design studio based in Tokyo and Sendai doing production work for promotion videos and visual installations. W0W collaborate with Abe and Motoe in the MEGA-HOUSE installation in making motion graphics.

5 BORDERLAND/BORDERAMA/ DETROIT[1]

JERRY HERRON

Figure 5.1 View from Pedestrian Bridge, Cochrane Street.

DETROIT LOOKS JUST LIKE A CITY...

...especially at night, from my apartment downtown, with its floor-to-ceiling glass: that's when Detroit really *does* look like a city; friends have come over to dinner, 28 floors up, sitting around my table, and inevitably one of them turns toward a window and remarks, as if arriving at some kind of original insight, which of course it is for the person making the observation, who has just now noticed the altogether astonishing fact that despite what you might expect, what people know and say about this place, and what the person about to be delivered of the insight also probably thought up until this very instant, a person now baffled into a state of startled recognition: "Detroit looks just like a city!" The conversation stops, maybe, for a few seconds, while the other guests glance toward the windows, the vast grid of lights arrayed across the night-time landscape out toward the dark, invisible horizon. And it's not the first time you've been witness to such a discovery, not if you have lived here any time at all. The other guests nod polite agreement: Yes, Detroit *does* look just like a city. And then they go back to eating their dessert.

But it's *not* a city, not when the sun comes up and you can see the place for real. It *was* a city once, that's clear, or at least Detroit seems to have been a city, given all the physical evidence left behind in maybe the most moved-out-of metropolis ever invented and then evacuated by Americans – houses and factories, theaters and schools, streets and whole neighborhoods now walked away from on so spectacular a scale that you can't fault other people when they register amazement. "It is a remarkable city," Rebeca Solnit wrote in *Harper's* magazine, "one in which the clock seems to be running backward as its buildings disappear and its population and economy decline." Her wonderment is precisely rendered, if not precisely news:

> This continent has not seen a transformation like Detroit's since the last days of the Maya. The city, once the fourth largest in the country, is now so depopulated that some stretches resemble the outlying farmland and others are altogether wild.... Between the half-erased neighborhoods are ruined factories, boarded-up warehouses, rows of storefronts bearing the traces of failed enterprise, and occasional solid blocks of new town houses that look as though they had been dropped in by helicopter.[2]

Detroit looks just like a city, except it's not one any more. But instead of truly vanishing, like those old Mayan cities of Mesoamerica, it persists in a death-in-life existence, and that is what lends the place an uncanny relevance and makes it so persistent an object for journalistic last words, none of them, of course, ever being the last word. Detroit may be emptied out, then, but it is hardly over, nor will it be any time soon, precisely because of the questions that this city/not raises. What could have happened here? Does it have anything to do with the rest of America? Such questions are particularly pressing just now, as the world's population – at some point in 2008 – supposedly crossed a border never yet traversed by humans with the majority of us now becoming urban for the first time in history.

And that is just where Detroit's relevance lies, because it is not only the busiest border crossing in this country – literally – thanks to the volume of Canadian–American trade that passes through here by water and rail and highway, but the busiest border in another, perhaps more crucial sense. Detroit sits precisely at the border of city and not-city; its condition renders the conflict between the natural world and the built environment in a specially forceful way, as Solnit points out. Here, the fearful energy released by a city in decay raises questions not only about the economic and governmental system that produced Detroit (and America), but the humanity of citizens so transformed by urbanism that they can visit upon each other all the miseries and cruelty locally deployed. It's enough to make a person wonder, and especially to make Americans wonder, and maybe the rest of the world wonder too, as we all verge on a global urbanism and the city/not opposition achieves such universal relevance. We wonder how so much that is valuable, in both material and human terms, could be so quickly and violently squandered. And we wonder at the cost – the waste and cruelty, and what the city has to do with it all, and what this place might portend.

BORDER AND BORDERAMA

So the dispatches keep arriving from the border of city and not-city. But unlike the Mesoamerican parallel that Solnit points to, Detroit's vanishing is not some distant historic event; it is an ongoing condition, compounded in its spectacular oddity by the simultaneous re-birth of certain parts of town. Here, the border is always shifting and re-defining itself, although the opposition remains consistent. On one side, the entropy and violence that un-build the city and return it to some pre-urban state – the ruined neighborhoods and inner-city prairie that writers and tourists never fail to be struck by, "an urban void nearly the size of San Francisco" as Solnit puts it.[3] And on the other side, the energy and capital investment that define the parts of town that never went away, and what is more baffling still, the parts of the city that are growing and re-developing.

"It's remarkable, really," according to Mary Kramer, publisher of *Crain's Detroit Business*, "Despite the political turmoil in Detroit and the economic turmoil throughout Southeast Michigan, our reporters found new angles for this third annual 'Living and Investing in the D' supplement." Kramer then goes on to enumerate the good-news items – urban gardens, revitalized neighborhoods, downtown comeback, plans for light rail, etc. – all played out against the backdrop of corruption and political bungling.[4] Her piece is aptly titled "Optimism amid Turmoil," and that is surely the story of "the D," and the two cities that simultaneously occupy this historically conflicted real estate. That the two – city and not-city, life and death – should be so obviously and perhaps necessarily linked is a discomfiting prospect, with the resulting metropolis being apparently like no other, although maybe the border between Detroit and everything else is not so clear or fixed as it is made to appear in popular representations.

And here is a truly chilling possibility, that Detroit is linked causally somehow to the rest of America, that this mix of rot and revival, violence and reinvigoration is a condition inherent to ourselves that the city only exacerbates. Maybe Detroit is the cost Americans pay for being who we are. Consider the facts, which is what the *Wall Street Journal* invited:

> Detroit is 81% black and, according to the Census Bureau, one-third of its residents live below the poverty line. The nuclear family is all but non-existent in the city. In 1960, 25% of black residents were born to single mothers. By 1980, that number had climbed to 48%. Today, over 80% of Detroit's black children are born to single-parent households. Just one in nine black boys is raised with a father.
>
> According to academic research, over 50% of black men in Detroit are high-school dropouts. In 2004, 72% of those dropouts were jobless. By their mid-30s, 60% have done prison time. Among black dropouts in their late 20s, according to a University of California, Berkeley, study, more are in prison (34%) than are working (30%).[5]

The article refers – inevitably – to violence and murder as well, noting that a Congressional Quarterly report (based on FBI statistics) rates Detroit "America's most dangerous city." "Some have said that Detroit is in the throes of committing cultural suicide," the writer, Henry Payne, concludes. "It may be more accurate to call it a cultural homicide."[6] Not that any of this isn't true about the city, and there is no reason to doubt the facts being reported. The question is how those facts are being applied to construct a border that will separate Detroit from everything else in this country. Is this really a singular case – the case of a city committing cultural suicide or homicide? Or is it a case of something broader and more generally shared – a city being done in by the racialization of poverty and crime in America, with this place only making more visible things that exist – homicidally – across our culture? In this context, it's not the actual border that counts, but the way the border gets represented, as a means of separating things we want to believe from things we want to believe aren't relevant because they apply to somebody else.

Think of it this way, then. Detroit is not so much a border as it is a "borderama," a spectacle contrived to perform culturally relevant work. I am poaching here on the performance-art term of Guillermo Gómez-Peña, and his staged interventions, the point of which is to make conscious the otherwise unconscious functioning of the borders we construct.[7] And Detroit is surely like that – not the place, but the things done with the place, in the name of entertainment or news, or both, from broadcast television to Hollywood films to the *Wall Street Journal*. The borderama spectacle of America's city/not is never far from the public consciousness.

Figure 5.2 New Casino, Pine Street.

I am using the term *spectacle*, of course, in the sense suggested by Guy Debord, who remains an unimpeachable guide when it comes to borderama:

> Understood in its totality, the spectacle is both the result and the project of the dominant mode of production. It is not a mere decoration added to the real world. It is the very heart of this real society's unreality. In all of its particular manifestations – news, propaganda, advertising, entertainment – the spectacle represents the dominant *model* of life. It is the omnipresent affirmation of the choices that have *already been made* in the sphere of production and in the consumption implied by that production. In both form and content the spectacle serves as a total justification of the conditions and goals of the existing system. The spectacle also represents the *constant presence* of this justification since it monopolizes the majority of the time spent outside the production process.[8]

The spectacle buys us into where and who we already are. The actual borders here are ones potentially dangerous to cross, as the statistics make clear – borders between "good" and "bad" parts of town, neighborhoods that are safe, and those where things go violently wrong. And those borders implicate problems that Americans may generally share, or at least share the fear of, problems that result from "choices that have *already been made* in the sphere of production and in the consumption implied by that production," as Debord says. So if Detroit represents choices *we* have already made, then how to live with the results? How to understand ourselves in relation to real and troubling things which are unavoidable? We spectacularize our visits to the city/not site of our anxieties, which is the reason Detroit is so consistently in the news, which is not really news at all. Who needs to be told that this place is old and poor, black and dangerous, depopulated and scary? Nobody. But who needs reassurance? All the rest of us, of course, who make periodic borderama excursions, the point of which is to afford us the comforting assurance that Detroit is what the rest of America is in recovery from, and that such recovery is available as elective choice. We want to believe that where you are is all a matter of choice, and that everybody is free to choose, so that stupid and destructive choices are all the fault of the person doing the choosing. This may be a lie, but it is no less powerful for that.

THE PARIS OF SOUTHEASTERN LOWER MICHIGAN

I have a t-shirt with that phrase imprinted on it: "Detroit, the Paris of Southeastern Lower Michigan." It was a gift from a friend, who left town several years ago, fed up with his most recent home invasion, after the alarm went off in the middle of the night, the police arriving, checking things out, with nothing taken but a TV set, and the post-traumatic family gone back to bed, when they hear something downstairs because the burglar has come back to finish the job, figuring correctly that the alarms would now be disabled and the family duly chastened so they'd keep out of the way. So the thief finished his work, the police returned after the fact, and next morning, my friend decided it was time to go, leaving me the t-shirt as a kind of legacy. It's like other shirts that people here wear occasionally, imprinted with various city/not slogans advertising a certain stubborn pride in our various negative claims to fame, such as being the sometimes murder capital of the United States. We indemnify our catastrophes with an in-your-face self-captioning. "Beware," goes the admonition, per a recent t-shirt sighting, "I have friends in Detroit." We're already partying at the borderama even before the news crews and reporters arrive to "discover" our most recent calamity.

But we were not always that way, which is important to keep in mind. For a long time, Detroit really was America's great success story, as an article in *Fortune* magazine explained in 1956:

> The community's great $4.5-billion auto industry makes and sells a product that every American loves; the industry's 400,000 workers are among the highest paid in the world; and all in all, U.S. capitalism seems to stand out in its finest colors and in its greatest genius in the manufacturing area around Detroit.[9]

"It is a company that helped lift hundreds of thousands of American workers into the middle class," the *New York Times* wrote, 53 years later, on the day when GM declared bankruptcy. "It transformed Detroit into the Silicon Valley of its day, a symbol of America's talent for innovation."[10] That transformation was spectacular in its dimensions. In 1890, Detroit was the fourteenth largest city in the United States, with a population of 205,876 and a size of 22.19 square miles. It was a prosperous if modest place, with a diversified economy based on timber and railroad cars, cigar manufacturing and stoves, locomotives, pharmaceuticals, and marine engines. By the 1920 census, following the birth of the moving assembly line and the Model T, Detroit had become the fourth largest city in the country, with a one-industry economy and a population of 993,675 – over four times what it had been only 30 years before – and a size of 79.62 square miles. The city population peaked around the 1950 census, at just under two million, almost twice what it had been in 1920, by which point Detroit had achieved its present size of 140 square miles. And then, just as the city reached its historic high of population and prosperity, people immediately began to leave, as the rush to suburbia began, with the population today estimated at less than 900,000, the lowest it's been for almost 100 years.

The interesting thing about this demographic rocket ride, with an ascent and descent perhaps more rapid than any other city in this country, is that it suggests a kind of one-off urbanism inherent to this place, certainly, and perhaps to American city-making generally. The city – *this* city – was never meant to be like other cities, especially European cities, with a population achieving a certain size and density and then remaining there, for generations; Detroit was always on the way to becoming something else, with a population that no sooner peaked than it began immediately to shrink. The riot of 1967 was still almost two decades off when this ex-migration began, so that wasn't the reason. Not that there's a single or a simple explanation. But one thing is clear. The people who came here never intended to stay. And it is this prospect of improbable – but indicative – human behavior that has been making Detroit significant almost from the beginning.

We were one of the stops on the tour of Alexis de Tocqueville, the young French aristocrat, who was sent by his government in 1831, along with a partner Gustave de Beaumont, to investigate the penitentiaries of the then still new United States, on the assumption that the French might learn something from our supposedly more rational and humane system of incarceration. There's an easy irony to be found here in the fact that America is still the world's leading jailor, with more of our citizens living behind bars than in any other country, but it's an open question whether anybody would still consider us to be a model. It's not the study of prisons that made Tocqueville's fame, however, but his two-volume investigation, *Democracy in America* (1835, 1840). He landed in the United States at a particularly rambunctious time, as Jacksonian democracy was in full sway, with its populist enfranchisements and expansionist bravado. We presented a good test case, in other words, for a cultivated European whose own country was in the midst of revolutionary transformation, and who found himself – like a great number of others – wondering if a people could really govern themselves democratically.

To that end, Detroit presented an interesting case study. The population when Tocqueville arrived was just over 2,000. The city at that point was more than 100 years old, having been founded in 1701 by a French entrepreneur, Antoine Laumet (1658–1730), who preferred the self-invented title, sieur Antoine de Lamothe-Cadillac. Nothing much had been produced in Detroit during a century and more of existence, except for the periodically bloody conflicts between French and English troops and their Native American surrogates. But the place held a special significance for Tocqueville, much the same as it does for tourists today. "We were curious to see entirely savage country," his partner Beaumont wrote, "to reach the farthest limits of civilization."[11] What the two men found, however, was more contradiction than pure manifestation. As they approached Detroit by river on the afternoon of July 22, 1831, they were greeted with a paradigmatic sight. On the Canadian side of the straight where Detroit is located, a Scottish Highlander in full uniform; on the American side, two Indians in a canoe, naked, with painted bodies and rings through their noses.[12] That symbolic opposition still rules, 200 years later, over the city and city/not spectacle of Detroit.

But it's not metaphors I'm after. And here Tocqueville's report has come honestly by its enduring interest to Americans. He recognized early on an exceptional feature of our national character – one that he thought bore the potential to become our un-doing; that feature is *individualism*, a new word that Tocqueville did not invent, but applied skillfully, to describe us:

> Individualism is a reflective and peaceable sentiment that disposes each citizen to isolate himself from the mass of those like him and to withdraw to one side with his family and his friends, so that after having thus created a little society for his own use, he willingly abandons society at large to itself.
>
> Selfishness is born of a blind instinct; individualism proceeds from an erroneous judgment rather than a depraved sentiment. It has its source in the defects of the mind as much as in the vices of the heart.
>
> Selfishness withers the seed of all the virtues; individualism at first

dries up only the source of public virtues; but in the long term it attacks and destroys all the others and will finally be absorbed in selfishness.

Selfishness is a vice as old as the world. It scarcely belongs more to one form of society than to another

Individualism is of democratic origin, and it threatens to develop as conditions become equal.[13]

Associations, he thought – our collective belonging to other than individual causes – would save us from the dangers inherent in individualist democracy. Otherwise, there could be little hope for the American experiment:

Thus not only does democracy make each man forget his ancestors, but it hides his descendants from him and separates him from his contemporaries; it constantly leads him back toward himself alone and threatens finally to confine him wholly in the solitude of his own heart.[14]

This dangerous tendency he noted, almost 180 years ago, is surely no less an explanation of Detroit and the bafflement that visitors register, when confronted with the catastrophic results of a people accustomed to dwelling in the solitude of our own hearts.

As to the urbanism that results, there's a wonderful passage in a letter Beaumont wrote, following his visit to Detroit. In it, he recounts an experience he and Tocqueville had when they entered the shop of a Mme de Moderl to buy some mosquito netting:

While she was giving us what we asked, my eyes happened to encounter a little print posted in her store. This print represents a very well dressed lady and at the bottom is written: *Mode de Longchamps 1831*. How do you find the inhabitants of Michigan who give themselves the styles of Paris? It's a fact that in the last village of America the French mode is followed, and all the fashions are supposed to come from Paris.[15]

City and not-city were alive here, then, in that shop, in "the last village of America," which also contained news of the latest Paris fashions – presumably because citizens needed such information in order to maintain an appropriate sense of who they were here in the Paris of southeastern lower Michigan.

That exceptional, American condition is what sets our cities apart, like the people in them, as Witold Rybczynski points out in his study *City Life*; it's what Beaumont noted in that Detroit shop, the distinctive way in which our individualism deployed itself:

the United States is the first example of a society in which the process of urbanization began, paradoxically, not by building towns, but by spreading an urban culture. Here is an important distinction, and perhaps also another reason for the ambivalence that marks American attitudes toward the city: there never was a sense of cities as precious repositories of civilization. Because urban culture spread so rapidly, it lost its tie to the city, at least in the public's perception.[16]

Figure 5.3 Urban Prairie with Old Silos, Orleans Street.

And that, Rybczynski says, is why our cities are not like Paris – not because Americans are a society of bunglers who can't imitate correctly, but because we were never trying to build Paris in the first place: "[I]f our cities are different – and they clearly are – it may be not only because we build them differently and use them differently but also because we imagine them in a different way."[17] And there is surely no more different-seeming city than Detroit – America's greatest city/not.

But all of our cities are – to a greater or lesser degree – cities/not, in the terms Rybczynski suggests; they are not places where most of us want to live. As *U.S. News* points out, "Without immigrants pouring into the nation's big metro areas, places such as New York, Los Angeles and Boston would be shrinking as native-born Americans move farther out."[18] We are metropolitan but not urban. When *Money* magazine posts its yearly list of "best places to live," they are not cities, typically, but small towns, such as Middleton, WI, with a population of 17,400.[19] Served by elaborate, high-speed transportation and communication networks, Americans don't need cities the way other people seem to, any more than those residents of Detroit in 1831 needed Paris in order to keep up with the latest styles. We proceed by spectacular means toward the fulfillment of our exceptional individuality. And most of the time, it seems – both to ourselves and to others – as if we were all along intending something entirely different, something unrelated to actual conditions on the ground, which are not our doing, really, but somehow self-generating. That kind of forgetting is perhaps comforting, even necessary. But it comes at an extraordinary cost.

HENRY FORD AND THE FORGETTING MACHINES[20]

I doubt that the founder – I mean Henry Ford – ever read Tocqueville, or any other writer who might be mistaken for a historian – but he surely enough understood that Frenchman's strictures about individualism and its potential for organizing humans into the greatest productive force ever assembled on this Earth. And that achievement was based on a clearly articulated theory. "History is more or less bunk," Ford said to a reporter for the *Chicago Tribune* in 1916. "It's tradition. We don't want tradition. We want to live in the present, and the only history that is worth a tinker's damn is the history we make today."[21] A history reinvented each day is no history at all, of course, at least not in the usual sense of that term, with all it implies about the narrative chain of cause and effect that binds the present inextricably to the past. And that belief in necessary cause and effect is precisely what Henry Ford is calling "bunk." We want to live in a kind of perpetually self-renewing *now*, which residency would have come as no surprise to Tocqueville and what he thought democracy had in store for us: "Thus not only does democracy make each man forget his ancestors, but it hides his descendants from him and separates him from his contemporaries..."[22] That forever present condition of the individual is precisely what Henry Ford depended on to create a modern industrial work force – not people enmeshed in tradition or each other's affairs, least of all union affairs, but individuals unfettered from the past, whom machine-made prosperity would turn into believers in Ford's evangel. What he built, then, both the cars themselves and the factories that produced them, might be thought of as forgetting machines – industrial works that became so successful as to make Ford's point about the "bunk" of history seem self-evident.

As is often pointed out, Ford's genius lay not in great acts of invention – unlike his hero Thomas Edison. Ford's genius was for putting together things that others had thought of. And by the time he began work on the moving assembly line in 1913, the ground in this country, literally, had been well prepared for his insights. The history of America – which was written by those who arrived here, rather than the native peoples or people brought forcibly here, who mostly couldn't write and whose records, like their history, were destroyed – *that* history is a history like Ford's. It's a centuries-long exposition of mapping and re-mapping, as if the land the newcomers confronted were a blank slate, endlessly renewable, for the purposes of drafting whatever propositions seemed best at the time. And whatever got in the way was reduced to bunk, with the city – *our* kind of city – being both ideal and justification for all the forgetting on which this vast project depended.

Where "nothing" existed before, then, we were free to plan as we saw fit, getting it right this time, in a way that the old world, mired in history and tradition, could never do. Our cities in particular came into being first as designs – as contracts with some higher ideal that entitled us to do whatever it took. Thus liberated from history, these idealizations had imbedded within them their own inevitable undoing. Nothing real can ever live up to ideal standards of perfection, so that all our cities in that way have been cities/not – forgetting machines always already sabotaged by history. But that would come later. With each new map of forgetting came the exhilaration and freedom of Henry Ford's "bunk." The plans of colonizers would vary, with French, Spanish, Dutch, and British models each having their own distinctive features. But one crucial element is common to all these national projects, and that is the erasure of any existing history that might otherwise need to be accommodated. The mandate of a higher purpose – whether God or king or profit, or some combination of all three – rendered invisible the claims of natives and their ways of organizing themselves, including the great city plans of Meso-america. In that sense, the settlements that resulted are each a "city on a hill," to use a phrase from the gospel of Matthew, applied famously by John Winthrop, Governor of the Massachusetts Bay colony, in his sermon, "A Model of Christian Charity," delivered while he and his fellow colonists were on their way to the new world in 1630. Winthrop was a puritan, intent on creating a model here that would become an example for the purification of the old world, specifically the English church. "We shall find that the God of Israel is among us," he wrote,

> when ten of us shall be able to resist a thousand of our enemies; when He shall make us a praise and glory that men shall say of succeeding plantations, "the Lord make it like that of New England." For we must consider that we shall be as a city upon a hill. The eyes of all people are upon us…[23]

This designer project would carry us forward, variously on this continent, through war and strife on to the Declaration of Independence and Constitution and beyond. In each iteration, the supposed superiority of the design entitles the designers to certain unalienable rights to make bunk out of other people's history (as well as their own), with results both disastrous and sublime, from the genocidal elimination of native peoples and the enslavement of others to the creation of a republic that remains a city upon a hill, albeit one of frequently conflicted purpose. But a "beacon" nevertheless.

In this connection, Henry Ford is merely extending the great design project that brought us here. He has applied to individual life the kinds of forgetting technology that inform our national agenda. He literally re-tooled the city upon a hill for a new kind of mobility. The cars he built, and the roads created to serve them, radically re-mapped the historical cities that had existed before, as if exposing some heretofore unrecognized design fault, which revealed as bunk – or city/not – the claims of old ways of living and moving through the world. Similarly, to do his work and buy his cars, Ford required a new kind of re-designed individuals. And this, perhaps, is his greatest insight. "Henry Ford had once been an ordinary automobile manufacturer," E.L. Doctorow writes in *Ragtime*, where he imagines Ford's feelings as he watches the first Model Ts rolling off the assembly line:

> Now he experienced an ecstasy more intense than that vouchsafed to any American before him, not excepting Thomas Jefferson. He had caused a machine to replicate itself endlessly…. Ford established the final proposition of the theory of industrial manufacture – not only that the parts of the finished product be interchangeable, but that the men who build the products be themselves interchangeable parts.[24]

Ford was a master designer of forgetting machines. The cars allowed owners to forget their place in the old order of things, and to value mobility for its own sake – a mobility that the "five dollar day" now made available to Ford's workers as well, who became "themselves interchangeable parts."

Ford's labor force was variously monitored for acceptable, standardized behavior, both inside and outside the factory, with prompts provided by a manual that laid out the terms of eligibility for employment and participation in the profit-sharing plan that was the basis of the "five dollar day." The title of the Ford manual gives a clear indication of the project at hand, *Helpful Hints and Advice to Employes [sic] to Help Them Grasp the Opportunities Which Are Presented to Them by the Ford Profit-Sharing Plan*. The scope of Ford's oversight, through the agency of the "sociological department," was comprehensive, extending into all aspects of life, from job performance to domestic arrangements, addressing such topics as banking, home economy, insurance, education, mastery of English, and use of a toothbrush. The proposal was couched in the most blandly paternalistic terms:

> The Ford Motor Company hopes through its profit-sharing plan, to help uplift humanity, and make better men of its employes [sic]; raise their moral standard through better surroundings, and foster habits of thrift, to provide against sickness or any misfortunes that may befall them or their families.... Almost every country on the globe is represented among the army of workers in the Ford Plant, there being no less than 53 distinct types of nationalities among its employes [sic]. The task of acquainting and getting each employe [sic] imbued with the idea and spirit of the Company in this work is therefore a large and slow one.[25]

Whatever the variety of "distinct types of nationalities" before, each man now became an interchangeable, standardized product, empowered by Ford to make something individually of himself. And the proof of that design lay in the results – a level of prosperity heretofore unimaginable to all those willing to submit, although the price of submission, day to day, could be extreme. " 'It's worse than the army, I tell ye – ye're badgered and victimized all the time.... A man checks 'is brains and 'is freedom at the door when he goes to work at Ford's.' "[26] Thus the testimony of two workers talking to Edmund Wilson when he visited the Ford assembly line in 1932. As their statements make clear, the forgetting involved was always more virtual than real, at least in the lives of individual humans, but there could be no disputing the larger results produced by the forgetting machines and the Fordism they brought forth on a national scale. The kind of city that results and the life it imposes on those now trapped inside it are another matter.

BORDERAMA, THE TAILFIN, AND THE RETURN OF THE REPRESSED

I remember as a little boy an advertising campaign created by Chrysler Corporation for their 1957 model lines. "Suddenly, it's 1960!" the ads breathlessly proclaimed.[27] My dad managed a car dealership, so I came naturally by my personal interest in things automotive. But it was more than that. This proposition had immediate relevance to Americans' situation generally, it seemed to me. It was the same year the Soviets launched Sputnik; we were trying to get ourselves into the future – first. Just imagine: a consumer purchase could provide the precise time travel we were struggling to achieve, offering a three-year jump on the next guy. Not surprisingly, the ads, like the cars, were a huge success. And also examples of a self-demolishing potential built into our cities and the economic system that supports them – a potential referred to by the economist Joseph Schumpeter as "creative destruction":

> The opening up of new markets, foreign or domestic, and the organizational development from the craft shop and factory to such concerns as U.S. Steel illustrate the same process of industrial mutation – if I may use that biological term – that incessantly revolutionizes the economic structure *from within*, incessantly destroying the old one, incessantly creating a new one. This process of Creative Destruction is the essential fact about capitalism. It is what capitalism consists in and what every capitalist concern has got to live in.[28]

So, Amazon drives the neighborhood book store out of business, just as the iPod renders your Walkman obsolete; and similarly, extrapolating from Schumpeter, the tailfins on the 1957 Plymouth Belvedere – "the only car that dares to break the time barrier" – made the body style of your serviceable '49 Ford seem embarrassingly old-fashioned by comparison. As J. Bradford DeLong points out, commenting on Schumpeter's theory, capitalism is consequently and inherently unstable; it is always producing winners and losers on both small and large scale, together with disproportionate inequalities in wealth, and it is these inequalities that are incompatible with democracy:

> Capitalism ... inevitably generates these mammoth inequalities through creative destruction. The combinations of market economies and political democracies that we see today in the richest countries in the world were, Schumpeter thought, unlikely to be stable. No country that wanted to see rapid economic growth could afford to remain a political democracy for long.[29]

He imagined, in the economic sphere, an inherent tendency toward instability and self-destruction analogous to what Tocqueville saw politically, as the tendency of individualist democracy: "individualism at first dries up only the source of public virtues; but in the long term it attacks and destroys all the others and will finally be absorbed in selfishness."[30] Play this out historically, and what you end up with is the city/not of Detroit, a place that only *looks* like a city, but for all intents and purposes has exhausted all remnants of civic virtue, just as it has been reduced economically to rustication.

But cities are always being torn down and built up, from ancient times to today, and in all parts of the world. What makes ours exceptional, and perhaps none more exceptionally representative than Detroit, is the historical mandate we have granted ourselves in this country. We are in pursuit of a design, with the city (upon a hill) being only a means to an end rather than an end in itself, so that our cities, more than any others, are subject to a kind of intentional un-doing that sets us apart. "[T]here is something fleeting about the American city," as Witold Rybczynski points out,

> as if it were a temporary venue for diversion, a place to find entertaining novelty, at least for a time, before settling down elsewhere ... the permanence of residence that was and is the stable foundation of European cities has always been absent in America, and accommodation to this transience has had an effect on the way that cities evolve and are altered.... Sometimes the past is impatiently discarded, sometimes it's resurrected, sometimes it's ignored, but throughout the making and unmaking of cities, there is evidence of a constant striving to correct and improve, of an attempt finally to get it right.[31]

Our kind of city – deprived of any virtuous, public sphere, and subject to the ongoing disruptions imposed by a capitalist economy – is inherently a city/ not, with some places – the so-called cities that work – merely being better at disguising their true nature than Detroit, which is the most unabashed of American sites.

In this context, then, the city as a whole is a gigantic forgetting machine, the purpose of which is to prepare people to forget that they ever needed it in the first place; residents find the city useful, even necessary for a time, "before settling down elsewhere," as Rybczynski says. It is not where we live any more, at least not the majority; the old central city hasn't been a destination

Figure 5.4 Old Train Station, Dalzelle Street.

for almost 40 years, having lost out to suburbia by the 1970 census, the culmination of a seemingly inevitable convergence of forces. Henry Ford built the cars and the consumers to drive them, and the federal government paved the highways and created the Federal Housing Administration, all of which are informed by the same design principle, which is the built-in obsolescence of the city.

So the downtown department store buys suburban land and develops the first shopping center, with money financed by the largest bank in town. The city votes to tear up the old trolley tracks in the name of modernization. Downtown firms realize the problem clients have with parking and relocate to the edge city. Factories need to modernize and expand, the old vertical structures no longer being practical, so they too move out. "Levittown" beckons, metaphorically speaking, and people follow. And it all takes place in the name of a superior design, in the same way the tailfin taught people to think themselves into the future, to "break the time barrier," and discover the undesirability of their homely car model from only a year or two before. Pretty soon, the evidence is clear for all to see, proving we were right to take off, as the city tax base shrinks, the schools decline in quality; the downtown department store gets shabbier and shabbier and finally closes, with only the suburban incarnations surviving, and the old neighborhood turns out to be a place where nice people don't think of living any more.

We're still seeking that city upon a hill, in other words, it's just not located where it used to be, so that perhaps the most distinctive feature of American city-making is the border between city and not-city. The uncanny representations of Detroit are no accident, therefore. Things that might otherwise seem unthinkable – the wholesale abandonment of urban wealth and with it the abandonment of people trapped inside the city who are exposed to unprecedented levels of poverty and violence and all the ills of a systematic and vicious racism – are made to appear spectacularly inevitable here, and also irrelevant precisely because they *are* here. Detroit is a site both to confront our problems and also to get over them. Not a real place, but an ongoing borderama that marks the boundary between real and not-real, things with consequences and those that will have no consequences. In that space, we are allowed to forget – opportunely – the spectacularly repressed truth that the way the rest of us live is the way we choose to live, and that the cost of our individual happiness is one we are willing to impose upon others. In the city/not, anything goes, and everything can be seen no matter how frightening because none of it seems to matter. If it did, wouldn't somebody have done something about this national disgrace?

LEARNING FROM DETROIT

What is there to learn from Detroit?

- Everything we have forgotten as Americans, including things forgotten by the people still stranded here, whose predicament is no less puzzling to themselves, perhaps, than the luck of those others who have managed to escape. To quote another popular local t-shirt: last person to leave, turn out the lights. And we did leave Detroit, both literally and figuratively, even the people who remain behind. That's the one thing everybody in this conflicted and self-absorbed country of ours has in common: we *all* don't live in Detroit.

- This single fact defines us by virtue of our being so collectively and willfully wrong to think that we can ever leave Detroit. The city/not is by no means a thing of the past. On the contrary, it is the city where all of us still live, no matter how far from downtown – or Detroit – our residence might be.
- Our history, then, is a history of forgetting how to remember what brought us to where we are, with the city still calling the shots – the place where perhaps "nobody" lives, but everybody lives in relation to.

So, that's what there is to learn from Detroit, and the general abandonment that this place inspires. But it's not as if we didn't leave a trail behind, on our way out of town. The urban landscape is cluttered with dereliction – modern equivalents of those vine-covered Mesoamerican temples that nobody remembers the sacred meaning of. But with this important difference: those forgotten sites were no longer inhabited at the point of discovery; our cities, on the other hand, *are*. Not that we all still believe in the city, quite the contrary, but at the same time, we can't seem to abandon the *habit* of belief, the wanting to understand *what this all means*, even if it turns out to mean nothing, which defines our agnostic predicament and gives rise to the spectacular anodynes of borderama.

The situation is a lot like the one Robert Venturi described when he set out to learn from Las Vegas, another of America's great misread and written-off places:

> the order of the Strip *includes*; it includes at all levels, from the mixture of seemingly incongruous land uses to the mixture of seemingly incongruous advertising media.... It is not an order dominated by the expert and made easy for the eye. The moving eye in the moving body must work to pick out and interpret a variety of changing, juxtaposed orders...[32]

Venturi concludes this thought with a quotation from August Heckscher's *The Public Happiness*, "Chaos is very near; its nearness, but its avoidance, gives ... force."[33] And the same might be said about Detroit – a place distant in many ways from Las Vegas, but not so far away in the terms Venturi is suggesting. The confrontation of city and city/not defines a condition where a mixture of seemingly incongruous elements converge; it is surely not a sight made easy for the eye, which is where the quotation from Heckscher seems particularly apt. In Detroit, "chaos is very near," and that is what keeps bringing visitors back; "its nearness, but its avoidance" (for people elsewhere) is what defines the special power of this place. By being so visibly and chaotically not a city, Detroit makes real the possibility that people might agree on what "the city" is, and how it might still be relevant both as ideal and as a way of life. The border of city/not is a site where necessary work is getting done, then; it defines an order both materially and symbolically; and this is where the contradictions inherent in capitalism emerge in a particularly vivid way, just as Schumpeter imagined they would.

As to what we can learn from Detroit, it comes back to the caution that Tocqueville registered when confronted with democracy on a national scale – something democracy brought out among Americans, that he feared might afflict his own countrymen, inasmuch as they seemed headed in the same direction we had already taken: "individualism at first dries up only the source of public virtues; but in the long term it attacks and destroys all the others and will finally be absorbed in selfishness."[34] It is possible to learn from Detroit a paradigmatic lesson about individual responses to the chaotic conditions of our cities, and the "avoidance" that keeps us able to believe in our essential goodness, even if that belief is finally to be purchased by the confinement Tocqueville feared, each man a prisoner, "wholly in the solitude of his own heart." Not as if he is the only one to posit such a result. "It is in the city," Lewis Mumford wrote, "the city as theater, that man's more purposive activities are focused, and work out, through conflicting and cooperating personalities, events, groups, into more significant culmination."[35] Take away that collective "theater," and man's more purposive activities are imperiled. Jane Jacobs feared just such a loss when confronted with the willful destruction of neighborhoods and the loss of "associations" as Tocqueville would have said, which she saw represented by the urban sidewalk, with the vast design projects of Robert Moses and their emphasis on the private automobile, posing an immediate threat. "It is questionable," Jacobs wrote, "how much of the destruction wrought by automobiles on cities is really a response to transportation and traffic needs, and how much of it is owing to sheer disrespect for other city needs."[36] That disrespect is evidence of the forgetting machines having done their work, exhausting any belief in the importance of things shared, preparing the ground for the creatively destructive working-out of capital as exemplified in the private automobile – an engine not of necessity, but "selfishness," to use Tocqueville's word.

Jacobs and Mumford provide two classic examples, among many others, of what might be called our history of forgetting, with what we have forgotten being the theater of associations that once made cities and city life seem worth preserving. But we followed another path, a distinctively American path, out of the city and out of the kinds of associations the city stood for. And that has made all the difference, with the experiences we have encountered along the way being variously recorded and analyzed from David Riesman's *The Lonely Crowd* (1950) to Robert Putnam's *Bowling Alone* (1995), each responding in one way or another to the cost of our collective acts of forgetting what came before. And that might be where the story ends, rather hopelessly, if it were not for Detroit. Our spectacular history of forgetting how to remember the past really is our history, and that history makes us exceptionally who we are. But that is not all we are, or might aspire to being, which brings me to an equally spectacular, operatic final example – one made possible only because of the potential for vernacular learning that exists in America's greatest city/not. I'm talking about Eminem's film, *8 Mile* (2002, directed by Curtis Hanson).[37] The film takes its title from the ultimate city/not border, 8 Mile Road, which separates Detroit from its affluent northern suburbs. And it's the borderland defined by this paradigmatic separation where differences of race and class in particular are acted out with particular force.

The film stages, literally, the urban theater where those differences will either get resolved, or else render city life impossible, with violence and drugs always being the ready alternative. There is one scene that makes this point with particular vividness and intelligence. It follows an earlier sequence when Eminem's character, Rabbit, chokes in a rappers' stand-off; he simply can't get the words out. Subsequently, he must reclaim his voice performatively, and the place he chooses to do this is one of the most spectacularly over-produced sites in Detroit – the ruined auditorium of the Michigan Theater, designed by C.W. and George L. Rapp of Chicago, and completed in 1925, one of downtown's premier movie palaces. "It is beyond the human dreams of loveliness," as the *Detroit Free Press* exclaimed at the opening.[38] By the 1970s, creative destruction had had its way, with audiences abandoning downtown movie palaces for the supposed superiority of the suburban multi-plex. Then an inventive real-estate developer saw an opportunity to turn this derelict theater to use and hacked into the by-then decaying interior to create a parking garage, leaving decorative elements intact, including the shredded curtain on the stage. The whole place has an eerie aspect to it, like images from the sunken *Titanic*, except unlike that wreck, the Michigan Theater – just as Detroit – is a wreck that is daily re-inhabited by commuters. This spectacular, if unintentional, rendering of the city/not loses its power, however, through familiarity, at least for the people who live here, and the uncanny prospect of the city/not begins to seem "natural," which is the aim of the forgetting machines as elements of Debord's spectacular apparatus.

And therein lies the genius of Eminem's operatic incursion. He reclaims the space of borderama spectacle for the purpose of personal testimony and critique; he populates the now cliché site of the Michigan Theater parking garage with "real" people and real confrontation that pits white against black, suburban against urban. And he dramatizes brilliantly and complexly the questions of association and ownership and responsibility that make the borderland of city/not such a perilous and potentially deadly place to live, and also the place where we will either reclaim our history – like Rabbit's voice – or else lose it forever. As the crucial sequence begins, he and his friends drive up the ramp and into the Michigan Theater parking garage, where Rabbit will triumph over his former stage-fright to deliver a particularly smart and raunchy rap. "You better recognize me like I look familiar," he demands. And that's the challenge delivered here, against this spectacular backdrop – the demand for recognition, and the caution that he only looks familiar. But he's not, any more than the city he lives in – a place that gets treated like it looks familiar thanks to the forgetting machines and the spectacular apparatus that serves them, none more spectacular perhaps than the Michigan Theater itself and the way it has been overproduced to the point of cliché. But always in the now-familiar photographs, the set is empty, or else populated only by cars. Like the city it stands in for, no people are present, since nobody really lives there any more. And that is Rabbit's point: people do live here and they have plenty to say, but not what you might expect, and surely not what you'd like to hear, and one thing is for sure, you better listen: you better recognize me like I look familiar; you better recognize me in spite of my looking familiar.

Rabbit will triumph in the end, although not in the way that romantic stereotypes would suggest; he wins the climactic rappers' contest, but not the girl. And at the moment when victory is his, he doesn't sign a big recording contract or even go out on the town with his pals; instead, he just returns to work at the factory where he's employed. Which is just as it should be because that victory over stereotype is enough; it un-does the work of the forgetting machines and makes real in the urban theater of association the testimony of an individual about the inadequacies of borderama spectacle as a way of knowing anything real. What is probably most important, and hopeful, of all, he does this with art. Violence is always circling around the plot and breaks out periodically, but in the end it's not violence that wins, but – literally – song. It's a romantic proposition, but one that Marshall Mathers' own life makes seem real enough.

CITIES FOR EVERYBODY

Last year was it, supposedly – 2008 – when the world's population for the first time became urban, with more humans now living in cities than anyplace else. But what will that mean, and will it make a difference? Maybe it will mean nothing. That, arguably, is the "flat world" prospect advanced to much effect by Thomas L. Friedman, on the assumption that globalization renders residence insignificant. "Place, according to this increasingly popular view, is irrelevant," as Richard Florida points out. But as he also suggests, "It's a compelling notion, but it's wrong." Florida has his own version of the future to sell:

> Today's key economic factors – talent, innovation, and creativity – are not distributed evenly across the global economy.... In today's creative economy, the real source of economic growth comes from the clustering and concentration of talented and productive people.... Because of the clustering force, cities and regions have become the true engines of economic growth.... And cities and their surrounding metropolitan corridors are morphing into massive *mega-regions*, home to tens of millions of people producing hundreds of billions and in some cases trillions of dollars in economic output. Place remains the central axis of our time – more important to the world economy and our individual lives than ever before.[39]

If he is right, then the city – now morphed globally into mega proportions – defines the once and future border between the past and what is yet to come, between limitation and limitless prosperity. Which leads to the question of what this will mean to the people living inside these places. How will urbanism meaningfully assert itself, or will it, *can* it?

Anticipating this moment, Rem Koolhaas wrote in *S,M,L,XL* about the economy of scale at stake here, and the challenges imposed by the sheer scope of the task of representing:

Pervasive urbanization has modified the urban condition itself beyond recognition. "The" city no longer exists. As the concept of city is distorted and stretched beyond precedent, each insistence on its primordial condition – in terms of images, rules, fabrication – irrevocably leads via nostalgia to irrelevance.[40]

But this is an old story, as anybody from Detroit knows – an old story that has now become new again. How to apply "city" in relation to unprecedented conditions? That's the question. Where to look historically for sources of meaning and intelligence, when the essence of Detroit's success and also undoing – from five-dollar day to "arsenal of democracy" to post-urban dystopia – has been the precise outmoding of precedents, or the expectation that there should be any, at least not when this place is involved. "'Model city? Bah!'" Henry Ford said to a reporter from the *New York Times* in 1915. There were no models, according to Ford: "'I say pay the workingman what he is entitled to and the model city will come as a matter of course.'"[41]

The scale and the speed at which the Fordist experiment succeeded in Detroit (like its inverse when the city seemed almost overnight to collapse) present precisely the dilemma pointed out by Koolhaas, when memory leads only to nostalgia and irrelevance, because there is – apparently – no precedent, there is only the present. The world's population now seems headed toward a condition like that, which is precisely the origin of Detroit. We will live in cities/not – vast "mega-regions" where "the concept of city is distorted and stretched beyond precedent." Just like home – a place where lots of people may dwell close together, but where it's arguable whether any of them is a "citizen," in the old-fashioned sense of belonging that Mumford thought essential to the city as "theater." So, if we're all going to end up living in Detroit, what will that mean? Perhaps the borderland of city/not will define new openings for knowledge and inquiry. I can imagine an archaeology of abandoned forgetting machines becoming specially relevant, with history being written not so much narratively as photographically and in a site-specific way. That possibility already exists on the web, with such sites as The Fabulous Ruins of Detroit,[42] and in the remarkable work of the photographer Corine Vermeulen, whose images accompany this chapter. Our place in the world, as citizens, becomes one defined by particular responses to images, rather than kinds of belonging dependent on actual residency, which is the proposition that Vermeulen is urging in her photographs – just as Eminem does in *8 Mile*. But this belonging will not be defined by nostalgia – a feeling sorry for ourselves that we feel sad about a history that we have forgotten. Instead, I can imagine a kind of knowing, operatic response to the past with that active, sight-specific ensemble of feeling supplanting the narrative record. We are humanized by a resulting aesthetics of loss, and loss is more.

EPILOGUE: DETROIT, JUNE 1, 2009

I read the news today, not in the local papers because there weren't any; the *News* and *Free Press* home delivery is all electronic on Mondays, so when I opened the front door of my apartment, the only real paper waiting for me was the *New York Times*. "After Many Stumbles, the Fall of an American Giant," the headline proclaimed, with the story, of course, being about the bankruptcy filing of General Motors.[43] There's a graph at the top of the page showing the decline in vehicle production, with various images punctuating the seemingly inevitable "fall." And there, just above the fold, is an old black-and-white photograph that really got to me. It shows a woman, stylishly dressed, standing next to a shiny new car, talking to her friend who is behind the wheel of that improbably tall automobile. "Sunnier Days," the photo caption reads, "The 1941 Oldsmobile four-door sedan from G.M., a car that, among other G.M. models, embodied the spacious and expanding quality of American life at the time."

My dad sold Oldsmobiles, not here in Detroit, but in the little West Texas town where I spent my childhood. My grandfather was a Packard dealer before that. I grew up hearing stories about "the boys from Detroit." I imagined this place from afar, where giants walked the Earth. And they did. Those giants made us rich, relatively speaking, more than any working person ever thought possible; the cars that drove it all "embodied the spacious and expanding quality of American life," just as the *Times* said. That spacious and expanding quality of life seems lost to us now, and not just here, but everywhere in America. We've been given hard lessons to learn, about the limits that history has finally imposed on our desires. We're not who we imagined ourselves to be, only a few years ago, back when my wife's father thought to

Figure 5.5 Skyline and General Motors Headquarters, Atwater Street.

look after his daughter by leaving her a portfolio heavy in GM shares, the value of which today is zero.

I read the paper, drink my morning tea and wonder what this all means. Through the plate-glass window in my living room, I can see GM World Headquarters, and the city around it, a city/not of contradictions so confounding, and also so distinctly American, that the impulse to look away is compelling, to go back to what I was doing. But what *was* I doing? I can't seem to remember. I can see abandoned housing projects and new condominiums, I look over the tree tops of Lafayette Park, where I live, with the largest collection of Mies Van Der Rohe buildings in the world; there's Ford Field to the left, where the Detroit Lions play football, and Comerica Park, which is home to the Tigers, Comerica Bank having decamped for Texas leaving their stadium behind; and church steeples – St. Josephat's, St. Albertus, Sweetest Heart of Mary; and the old city market with its vast sheds; there are burned-out houses and downtown skyscrapers, one in particular with its see-through empty floors, the sunset poking through each evening, creating a kind of impromptu, urban Stonehenge; and the freeways that paved the way to exurbia with edge city clumps of mirrored glass high-rises punctuating the horizon; and new casinos, four of them, offering the gullible a chance to spin flax into gold, 24/7.

Maybe it's not so much a question of *what* this all means; maybe it's more a question of *how* to make meaning here, how to take responsibility for seeing this spectacular place in a way that doesn't trivialize or misrepresent the lessons to be learned. Not that I have the answer, because I don't. I've made some suggestions, and maybe that's the best any of us can do. One thing for sure, though, we can't afford to look away. And that is the insight Vermeulen registers in her remarkable photographs and their way of seeing that is at once beautiful and also confrontational. These panoramic images represent an understanding that demands response – "the mixture of seemingly incongruous land uses ... the mixture of seemingly incongruous advertising media," as Venturi put it.[44] Freed from the blight of nostalgia, these unsentimental pictures make clear at once all the work that memory must now do. Which reminds me of a possibly apocryphal story about Ralph Waldo Emerson and Henry David Thoreau, and the exchange that took place when the older man confronted the younger one about spending a night in jail for reasons of conscience. "Henry, why are you in there?" Emerson supposedly asked, or words to that effect. "Waldo," Thoreau may have answered, "why are *you* not?" I don't care if the story is true. That's what I feel like saying to people when they ask me why I am here in this place that only looks like a city. This is what I want to say to them, Why are you not?

NOTES

1 All the images in this chapter are from a series, "Your Town Tomorrow," by the photographer Corine Vermeulen, www.corinevermeulen.com (see "Your Town Tomorrow" photo series).

2 Solnit, R. "Detroit Arcadia: Exploring the Post-American Landscape," *Harper's Magazine*, July 2007: 66.

3 Ibid., p. 67.

4 Kramer M. "Optimism and Turmoil," *Crain's Detroit Business: Living and Investing in the D*, 24, no. 32a: 2.

5 Payne, H. "Cross Country: Murder City," *Wall Street Journal*, December 8, 2007: A10.

6 Ibid.

7 Gómez-Peña www.pochanostra.com.

8 Debord, G. Statement 6, *The Society of the Spectacle*, available online: www.bopsecrets.org/SI/debord/1.htm.

9 Holli, M. *Detroit* (New York, St. Martin's, 1976).

10 Maynard. M. "After Many Stumbles, the Fall of an American Giant," *New York Times*, June 1, 2009, sec. A: 1, 12.

11 Brogan, H. *Alexis de Tocqueville: A Life* (New Haven: Yale University Press, 2006): 170.

12 Ibid., p. 169.

13 Tocqueville, A., *Democracy in America*, ed. and trans. Harvey C. Mansfield and Delba Winthrop (Chicago: University of Chicago Press, 2002): 482–483.

14 Ibid., p. 484.

15 Beaumont, G., in G. Pierson, *Tocqueville in America* (Baltimore: Hopkins, 1996): 284.

16 Rybczynski, W. *City Life: Urban Expectations in a New World* (New York: Scribner, 1995): 114.

17 Ibid., p. 27.

18 "Without Immigrants," *U.S. News* 2007, available online: www.msnbc.msn.com/id/17954186.

19 "Best Places to Live," *Money* 2007, available online: http://money.cnn.com/magazines/moneymag/bplive/2007/index.html.

20 For another discussion of Ford and the "forgetting machines," see Jerry Herron, "Detroit: Disaster Deferred, Disaster in Progress," *The South Atlantic Quarterly* 106.4 (Fall 2007): 662–682.

21 Lacey, R. *Ford: The Men and the Machine* (Boston: Little Brown, 1986): 238n.

22 Tocqueville, op. cit., p. 484.

23 Winthrop, J. "A Model of Christian Charity," in *The Norton Anthology of American Literature*, ed. Nina Baym, vol. 1, 5th edn. (New York: W.W. Norton, 1998): 225.

24 Doctorow, E.L. *Ragtime* (New York: Random House, 1974): 112–113.

25 *Helpful Hints and Advice to Employes [sic] to Help Them Grasp the Opportunities Which Are Presented to Them by the Ford Profit-Sharing Plan* (Detroit: Ford Motor Company, 1915): 9–11.

26 Wilson, E. "Detroit Motors," *The Edmund Wilson Reader*, ed. Lewis M. Dabney (New York: Da Capo Press, 1997): 205.

27 For a sample of the advertisement, see www.plymouthcentral.com/57Belvedere1.html.

28 Schumpeter, J., from *Capitalism, Socialism and Democracy*, quoted in Thomas K. McCraw, *Prophet of Destruction: Joseph Schumpeter and Creative Destruction* (Cambridge, MA: Harvard University Press, 2007): 351–352.

29 DeLong, J.B. "Creative Destruction's Reconstruction: Joseph Schumpeter Revisited," *The Chronicle of Higher Education*, December 7, 2007: B9.

30 Tocqueville, op. cit., p. 483.

31 Rybczynski, W. *City Life: Urban Expectations in a New World* (New York: Scribner, 1995): 33–34.

32 Venturi, R., Denise Scott Brown and Steven Izenour, *Learning From Las Vegas: The Forgotten Symbols of Architectural Form*, rev. edn. (Cambridge, MA: MIT Press, 1977): 52–53.

33 Venturi *et al.*, op. cit., p. 53.

34 Tocqueville, op. cit., p. 483.

35 Mumford, L. "What is a City?" quoted from *The City Reader*, ed. Richard T. LeGates and Frederic Stout (London: Routledge, 1997): 185.

36 Jacobs, J. *The Death and Life of Great American Cities* (New York: Modern Library, 1993): 441.

37 *8 Mile*, prod. and dir. Curtis Hanson, 110 min., Universal Pictures/ Imagine Entertainment, 2002, videocassette.

38 Ferry, W.H. *The Buildings of Detroit* (Detroit: Wayne State University Press, 1968): 324.

39 Florida, R. *Who's Your City: How the Creative Economy Is Making Where to Live the Most Important Decision of Your Life* (New York: Basic Books, 2008): 9–10.

40 Koolhaas, Rem, "The Generic City," in *S,M,L,XL*, ed. Rem Koolhaas and Bruce Mau (New York: Monacelli, 1995): 963.

41 "What Ford Plans For New Tractor," *New York Times*, September 12, 1915, sec. X: 10.

42 See www.detroityes.com/home.htm, or also www.100abandonedhouses. com.

43 Maynard, op. cit., pp. 1, 12.

44 Venturi, op. cit., pp. 52–53.

6   RUBBLE IN THE SAND

A CONVERSATION BETWEEN
JOHAN VAN SCHAIK AND
SIMON DRYSDALE

Johan van Schaik is a co-director of Minifie van Schaik Architects whose work includes residential, educational, public, and urban projects. He is a lecturer at RMIT University's School of Architecture & Design and has traveled and worked in Abu Dhabi, Al Ain, and Dubai.

Simon Drysdale is an architect currently practicing in Melbourne, delivering high density residential and commercial projects. He has worked and traveled extensively in the Middle East, with a particular emphasis on Gulf Cooperation and Persian Gulf regions.

JvS: *In the introduction to her book* From Trucial States to United Arab Emirates, *Frauke Heard-Bey attributes the late colonization of the UAE to the water's edge being very difficult to approach from either side. Approach from the sea passage was blocked by large mangroves and approach from land was hindered by the desert. How does this edge play a role in the current state of urban issues in the UAE?*

SD: In the undeveloped arid environment there's a more level playing field for potential edges between landscape architect and architecture. This is an interesting problem in a very interesting place where large and dedicated

Figure 6.1 The Dubai dry docks from above (Photo Credit: Google Earth).

Figure 6.2 The Ajman Corniche
(Photo by Simon Drysdale).

funds are available. The most obvious location for amalgamation of landscape and architecture is the waterfront. Like the reveal on a door, this is
where two planes intersect in an interesting spatial phenomenon. This phenomenon is acutely visible from Google Earth but less obvious as experience.

JvS: *It was only once this edge became engineered that it became accessible.
Do you think there is mileage in a discussion regarding the hard edge
versus the soft edge?*

SD: Mangroves have been going through a renaissance of late. Their contri-
bution to the visual realm has more credential and they're seen to prevent
creep from tides and indicate a healthy ecology. There are now large
chunks of the Middle East which identify with eco-tourism and mangroves
are seen as a visual signature for this trend.

I think engineering is a key term that you raise, in this case dredging. If
you want to follow waterfront development you follow dredging companies. There's a parallel between waterfront architecture and dredging.
The companies are predominantly from the Netherlands and they tend to
signal forthcoming development. Dredging is interesting because it's carto-
graphic in a very physical way.

JvS: *You have spoken in the past of the idea of greening the desert, to spend
oil money to colonize the desert. Are mangroves part of this?*

SD: Not in the *image* of green. Mangroves occur naturally while the mandate
to green the desert is often about overcoming nature. This is one of the
greatest challenges of working in the area and also one of the most interesting. A paradigm shift in building type resulted from the elevator overcoming gravity, and in the same way a shift in type follows the overcoming
of the desert through planting. I would even make an analogy between
greening the desert and parting the waters.

In Australia, we clear the edge of the freeway to prevent people from
wrapping their cars around tree trunks and to make the freeways traversable

Figure 6.3 Abu Dhabi
mangroves from above
(Photo Credit: Google Earth).

Figure 6.4 Yas Marina under
construction (Photo by Johan van
Schaik).

Figure 6.5 Yas Marina under construction from above (Photo Credit: Google Earth).

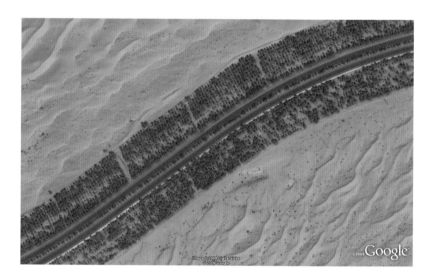

Figure 6.6 Planting along the Abu Dhabi to Al Ain freeway (Photo Credit: Google Earth).

during a fire. In the UAE by contrast, the threat comes from the steady creep of sand into the lanes of traffic and grids of olive trees are planted to abate this.

There has been a massive amount of speculative development in the UAE so it's littered with beautiful failures, magnificent failures. Some of my favorite examples are the unfinished resort hotels on islands only accessible by boat, only used by locals and not by the expatriate or tourist community.

It is interesting that the tourism or resort type is often the building type that most challenges this overcoming of nature. There's the inland approach where you camouflage yourself within the landscape then there's the water's edge development which is about the conquering gesture and then there's the obscure hybrid which is quite often the beautiful failure.

JvS: *So these types of things are not really the slick over-marketed towers of Dubai's financial real-estate boom and its architectural symptoms. How do these resort types fit into this financial real-estate bubble? Are they part of this real-estate bubble or are they just capitalizing on the populations traveling through on business who just happen to have high disposable incomes?*

SD: Both. There's a demographic which is independent tourism but increasingly the hotel-resort is taking on a more conventional model of serviced apartments, a model which is totally geared toward the expatriate professional community. This is evident in the format of the floor plan which does not correspond to the cultural conditions that the indigenous community would expect or be familiar with. That said, the younger Emirate population are usually highly educated and well traveled.

JvS: *Let's get back to cities, and how their extents are defined. Are they defined geographically? Or is it more that the city is an idea, and once this is established anything that fits within this idea is part of the city, whether it be geographically contiguous or not?*

SD: What you have with Dubai is a lamination. There's an urban format all about infrastructure which is completely dysfunctional and then on top of this there's a final veneer which is an image of a global city. Underneath this it's all chipboard – the substrate. This is different from other cities and

Figure 6.7 Billboard along the Dubai to Abu Dhabi freeway (Photo by Johan van Schaik).

91

it comes down to a comparison between a functional city and a more organic phenomenon.

Abu Dhabi is a much more zoned city with large industrial areas, sports suburbs, residential suburbs, a downtown, and then a ring of resort and entertainment/cultural areas. At a diagrammatic level it's more organized and easily understood.

Al Ain, Umm al-Quwain, RAK, and Ajman are far more familiar to me, having experienced large tracts of regional Australia. The city's edge is defined and it's quite often a signature of rubble, urban rubble. Rubble often appears ad hoc at a glance but it can also be a form of urban camouflage. It's where the ragged landscape collides with infrastructure. You end up with car lots, factories, some housing, farms, waste processing. These forms flag the boundary of the city, if you can really call it a boundary. The image of a metropolitan city is more often a line or a fence.

JvS: *Do you think it would be productive to say that the whole of Abu Dhabi is in fact rubble?*

SD: Well that's something that really pokes you in the eye when you arrive there. Building forms are losing their magnitude through age. A lot of them are being demolished. There are empty sand allotments in the center of the city. But there's still a sense of procession which is not evident in a lot of other cities in the UAE. I don't feel at ease saying that I entirely agree with your statement. Abu Dhabi has a real sense of boulevard or avenue as you enter the city, which you don't experience in other UAE cities. Actually, you don't have it in Dubai either.

JvS: *OK, you don't buy the idea that in the case of Abu Dhabi and Dubai the whole city is rubble, but clearly neither is a metropolis. Can we have a conversation about what exists between these two things?*

SD: This is exactly where the power of an architectural vision kicks in – where rubble is recompiled into something which is a metropolis. This is where the role of the architect, the planner, and the vision maker is strongest.

JvS: *There is the quote "And the future is no more uncertain than the present";[1] I think it's a Walt Whitman quote. I'll check. How does this compare with Australian cities?*

SD: In Australia, for example, the edge of Melton (Victoria) is a hard line. You go through a development and then there's an agrarian bit and then there's a little more settlement and then you get the edge of Melton and it's literally a hard line that goes all the way to the horizon. This is the edge of the suburb. This strikes me as being unnatural. It's a fantastic diagram, but unnatural.

JvS: *This discussion about how the limits of a city are defined is very fertile in terms of a post-Google Earth understanding of the city. It's a discussion about what it means to perceive things more from above. This means that the geographical limits of the city as they appear in plan form a greater part of your mental map than previously. What do you think?*

SD: The Google Earth phenomenon is very interesting when you think that five years ago getting aerial photography was difficult and expensive and now it is a free desktop application. There's now Google Moon, Google Mars, Google Sky, and soon Google Earth Ocean.

Figure 6.8 View of Abu Dhabi sky line from the fish markets (Photo by Simon Drysdale).

This type of aerial mapping highlights post-war techniques of camouflage. It has become what the abacus was to the sailor or the compass to the modernist.

JvS: *How do you think the instant availability of aerial photography has affected the way cities in the UAE have developed over the last few years?*

SD: An external consultant will often use Google Earth as a tool for proving a concept. Urban planning, urban development, economic planning, architecture, and master planning consultants rely heavily on this tool simply because it's possible to accurately superimpose global examples. This has given development in the UAE an encyclopedic nature.

JvS: *So it's an enabling tool for fly-in fly-out consultants?*

SD: Absolutely. Also, clients have their own aspirations and have a tendency to suggest things like "we want this to be like Paris" or "we want this to be like Venice."

JvS: *So Google allows consultants to instantly demonstrate this superimposition of known cities onto proposed sites?*

SD: Yes. You can understand a lot by examining an aerial photograph. Scale by comparison, internal planning by reading roof form, topography by examining drainage, levels of access, floor area, car parking arrangement.

As a design tool, Google Earth is a unifying standard and protocol. It has become a shared language and incorporated into standardized methodology. We can move easily from plan to perspective to speculation. This methodology imitates the process of the urban development professional in defining a brief.

JvS: *Is it possible then to construct an argument something like this: The way that cities have developed in the UAE recently is particular to the proliferation of fly-in fly-out consultants and the speed at which they can now work due to the availability of online aerial photography?*

Figure 6.9 The American University of Sharjah from above (Photo Credit: Google Earth).

Figure 6.10 The American University of Sharjah architecture school forecourt (Photo by Johan van Schaik).

SD: I think there's a unique digital context in the UAE. There's access to a vast amount of information to validate an argument presented to a client and this is integral to the successes and failures that have occurred in the UAE. Take musical "mash-ups" which will use the beat from one song and overlay the lyrics from another or Machinima gaming technology which lets you reconstruct a film narrative within the limitations of the gaming software and, say, make a new episode for an existing television series. I think a lot of development in the UAE follows these trends. It's like super-saturated post-modernism.

Google Earth is limited by its inability to "test consequence" or generate the "mud map." But there's inherent speculation in the method. It's common enough to find base satellite images that are almost two decades old that you then overlay with a contemporary proposition. For the urban professional it can be like working on the set of the television series *Life on Mars* where "déjà vu" is part of your professional operations.

JvS: *The easy access to aerial photography then basically allows for urban scale sampling?*

SD: Absolutely, and I think that is where things can often go wrong. Madinat Jumeirah, which is a reconstruction of an old town, is symptomatic of this condition. The boats there, the "arboras" designed to be like the boats in the Dubai Creek, travel around in just two feet of water. Only these two feet of water are necessary for the marketing of the resort.

JvS: *There's nothing new about this sort of phenomenon, or a fascination with it is there?*

SD: Yes, but compare it with Las Vegas where this happens at an urban level, like a film strip. In the UAE it takes place on a site-by-site basis and each site has no relation at all to any other, like a series of unrelated frames.

JvS: *Surely this is not really a result of Google Earth techniques but more to do with a shortcoming in the scale of the ambition?*

SD: No, not really. The mash-up is non-linear: you have old town simulation in Madinat Jumeirah and over the road you have Wild & Wet World then around the corner is the Burj Dubai, a seven-star hotel. Any representation of this in an urban planning diagram would demonstrate madness.

JvS: *It's difficult to see freeways from Google Earth. A freeway is a long thin line and Google Earth is displayed in the dimensions of a screen. Once you get zoomed in enough to see the detail of the lanes, cars and trees, then you lose a sense of the line. You can pan, but in doing so you very quickly lose your point of reference and a sense of how far you've panned. It's very difficult, for example, to pan back to the spot you started from, but very easy to zoom out and then back in to the same spot.*

SD: Well, there is always Street View for that.

JvS: *Street View is designed for looking at buildings and landmarks beside the road, not the road itself. So once you leave urbanized areas, street view on freeways tends to drop off. Also, Street View is not yet available in the UAE.*

SD: I think you're right about the scale of roads. If you look at Abu Dhabi from Google Earth you might find yourself looking at a road that you think that you understand then you realize that this "mark" you're looking at on the road is in fact a *car* and there are *thousands of* them. This suddenly distorts the understanding you have of the scale of the place, even after visiting there.

The other thing that's really interesting about freeways is that in the UAE the entire length of the freeways is flood-lit. This was a very foreign experience for me. In Australia, the rural night-time driving experience is mainly lit by headlights.

JvS: *Why are the freeways in the UAE so highly engineered, while other pieces of infrastructure lag behind?*

SD: *Confessions of an Economic Hit Man* describes how external consultants fly into developing countries and plan massive transport infrastructure. This causes land values to skyrocket and the country can borrow more. The infrastructure artificially inflates the land value and the country is tied to debt they can't afford. Inverse leverage follows, where the debt is forgiven in exchange for a percentage of natural resources, most often oil.

JvS: *I have this image then of surveyors pegging out a thin line across a sea of sand dunes which then becomes a highly engineered freeway. Is this how it happened?*

SD: While the freeways were part of a larger economic plan, it wasn't surveyors who laid out the road so much as the Sheik himself. He walked the line of what is now Sheik Zayed Road with bulldozers grading behind him as he walked. There's a wobble where he corrected his direction at one point. You can see it from the air. There's no logic to this kink in the surrounding geography, it's explained through the story. The line is most visible from above but Google Earth provides no insight into its history.

JvS: *The freeways that form the triangle of Abu Dhabi, Dubai and Al Ain are highly lit and linear. Does this night-time connection exist at all between cities in Australia?*

SD: No. The far-off glow of the Australian city when approaching it from the road at night is a very poetic experience. The experience relies on the blackness of country roads. Night in the UAE is often an over-illuminated structural diagram. So the poetic experience of approach is replaced by the flight in at night.

JvS: *How different is the experience of this when traveling along these roads by car?*

SD: Well, the frequency of lights on UAE freeways is phenomenal. They are at a domestic scale, every 100 meters or so. And they whip past you as you travel along them at speeds up to 180 kilometers per hour with the driver munching on a sandwich, steering with his knees and talking at a high pitch on his mobile phone.

JvS: *So the speed at which we experience certain environments is another thing that can't be perceived by observing the world via Google Earth?*

SD: Sure, yes.

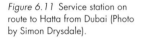
Figure 6.11 Service station on route to Hatta from Dubai (Photo by Simon Drysdale).

JvS: *I'm interested in these gaps between the possibilities and the shortcomings of Google Earth urbanism. For instance, if you looked closely at these*

freeways by day, you might be able to see the shadows of the light poles but to do so would require you to zoom in very close indeed, thus obliterating context. Could you describe some other gaps?

SD: Google Earth photographs are taken on different dates, from different angles, at different times of the day, in different weather conditions, and at different resolutions. These are then stitched into what seems to be one long seamless image. Naturally, it's not possible to photograph the entire surface of the planet in a single shutter opening. In Melbourne, for example, parts of the Docklands in the center of the city have been completely redeveloped but none of this is currently shown in the Google Earth image.

JvS: *Perhaps we could put together a list of its limitations?*

SD: Temperature is something that's very hard to imagine when you're not experiencing it directly. And it can't be seen. Humidity too. Although symptoms can be observed in geology and flora. It's the experience of leaving an aircraft after landing and hitting a wall of 38 degrees Celsius heat at five in the morning.

JvS: *It's a sauna you can never leave.*

SD: Absolutely. Also there's the importance of micro-climate or understanding how to design with the natural attributes that are available, like wind and water.

Figure 6.12 View of Reem Island from the Beach Rotana hotel at 4.30 am (Photo by Simon Drysdale).

Figure 6.13 View of Reem Island from the Beach Rotana hotel at 1:00 am (Photo by Simon Drysdale).

JvS: *So we can add wind to the list. How does water get added to the list?*

SD: Proximity to the coast creates a certain climatic and sensory experience that's not visible. Humidity, breeze, smell ... the sense that you're next to a large expanse of ocean.

It's often very foggy and you don't expect a desert to have fog. Fog produces some of the most dramatic experiences in the UAE. Enormous car pile-ups and dramatic sunsets or sunrises. But through Google Earth everything just disappears under fog and is edited from the database.

JvS: *I'm also interested in the gap between the image of UAE cities and the experience of them caused by the rate of development outpacing the Google satellite.*

SD: The classic example of that is trying to get around Dubai using Google Earth or Google Maps. I've heard stories of people being unable to enter their homes or workplaces because the road to their basement car park has moved without notice. It's a very strange urban quality.

Google Earth in the UAE can also be a powerful tool for collecting evidence. For example, observing the housing conditions for some expatriate workforces. It's also a useful local tool for waste management. I was lucky enough to meet a consultant who was advising the Abu Dhabi municipality on how to deal with their waste. She told me about the large plastic-covered waste dunes on the edge of the city where they throw untreated domestic, industrial, and medical waste. These are inaccessible but visible from Google Earth. So desktop aerial photography lets us bear witness,

Figure 6.14 Overflow at the Al Mafraq water treatment plant (Photo Credit: Google Earth).

albeit remotely, to the social conditions of workers or the implications of crude waste-management practices.

JvS: *I think it's interesting that alongside the view from above of The Palm, The World, and all the other images with which the UAE chooses to represent itself there is evidence of the thinness of this image.*

SD: An interesting parallel is the brine bloom which floods into the ocean from the desalination plant. The salt levels in this brine are extremely high and very damaging to the ocean and coastal ecologies, yet populating and greening of the desert relies on the creation of fresh water. Oddly enough this bloom appears beautiful from above, until you realize what it is.

Luxury glimpses have been widely distributed through UAE marketing but until five years ago you would have had to work for a government organization to have access to knowledge about the *consequences* of these luxuries. Now even the mildly curious can see both.

JvS: *To your knowledge are there areas that are blacked out for security reasons?*

SD: Anything to do with military is scrambled.

JvS: *It's odd, is it not, given that this advertises the exact location of anything sensitive? There's such an abundance of information visible so the bits that are blocked out are unique. It's a bit like walking down the street and screaming at the top of your lungs "Don't look at me!" and expecting this to work as a form of camouflage.*

SD: The other thing about Google Earth is that there are a number of blogs which discuss how to hack it.

I think it's interesting that a fascination with the contraband is built in to the value of Google Earth. You're witnessing something that's a privileged view.

JvS: *Do you think that these tools are used in the UAE by local government, authorities, etc.?*

SD: Oh, without a doubt. I have presented to clients in the UAE entirely using Google Earth, building a case for a particular design by showing precedents and the client has taken hold of the controls and taken us on whole alternate journey. On many occasions this has opened up liberated discussions about the project.

NOTE

1 Whitman, W. (1860) *Leaves of Grass*, New York, p. 32.

7 DENSITY OF EMPTINESS

JASON YOUNG

1

The metropolitan experience of congestion confirms at the level of experience our expectations about the city and its attendant built density. Having one's visual field lined at its edge with buildings that preside over it reaffirms our anticipation for what the city will provide. Buildings standing close together, with a proximate relationship to the street, facilitate the propinquity suggested in the terms *urbanity* and *urbanism*. The central city has historically been the site within which urbanism provides this closeness. Space flows here, but it does so inside the frame of reference made by a multitude of buildings working together and forming a sense of congestion. Significantly, the horizon is absent from these urban experiences. The visual field does not extend out and draw the horizon inward. The resultant experience features a complex and frenetic *vertical* edge condition. A sensation of being subsumed by the built density of the city, by its formal and material presence, is followed by a mental shift toward anonymity. In this vertical congestion there is an invitation to quietly assume one's role within a collective public. The mental and physical dynamic of the crowd accentuates this sense of being subsumed by the city, but it does so after the perception of being crowded is initiated by the city's material density.

One could speculate that it is something like this feeling in cities that makes them so appealing to the disciplines of architecture and urbanism. To be sure, those seeking urban experience almost always look to the city in this paradigmatic sense. And what of those curious moments when the city fails to deliver? Or, in the same spirit, what do we do with these urban experiences when environments other than the dense central city provide them? The city is urbanism's most exemplary formation, to be sure, and quite possibly the only urban form disciplines can fully anticipate. Instead of intellectual work that labors to *discipline* the wildness of urban space, wrangling it into compliance with dominant images of the city as it used to be, one might also take on the failure of the city for how it forces disciplines to rethink conceptions of urbanism and cities alike. This chapter explores these questions and also the degree to which the spatial and experiential strangeness of Detroit makes giving credit to the conditions on the ground in the city and responding to them more troublesome, more unnerving, and more alluring.

Figure 7.1 Photograph of
Detroit by Erich Mendelsohn,
from *Erich Mendelsohn's
"Amerika": 82 photographs*
(Minneola, NY: Dover, 1993).
Used with permission from
Dover Publications.

2

I am looking at a series of published photographs of Detroit taken by the German architect Erich Mendelsohn during his travels to America in the 1920s.[1] The images effectively confirm the expectations for a city and its material density along with capturing the particular vitality of Detroit at that time. In Mendelsohn's photographs of Detroit, one is struck by the activity all around. The streets are lined with three- and four-story buildings. Taller buildings are under construction. Intersections are bustling with automobile and streetcar traffic. Sidewalks and crosswalks are full of pedestrians. Trolley-car cables visually pull the sky toward the ground. Advertising vies for the eye of the urban citizen. There is profound complexity in each of the images. Significantly, there is no horizon line evident in any of his photographs of Detroit. The ground plane is dense with ongoing activity and the built residue of previous activity. The material density within the frame of each image is compelling in the consistency of its effect. This is made more remarkable given the rather diverse visual content across the overall collection of photographs. At that time Detroit was a burgeoning industrial city. The automobile was just beginning to hint at its progressive arc. Henry Ford's famous eight-hour, five-dollar workday had contributed to both the promise of the city and its crowded streets. The agents of industrial modernity were in full force. Each Mendelsohn photograph can be read as a memory of Detroit many today would like to have had. To be sure, Mendelsohn's images are read today as instruments of nostalgia, as prompts for remembering and contemplating a past that contained an idea for the future that may have seemed viable, if not vital and nourishing. In the photographs we see the modern city as it used to be before the onset of what Jerry Herron has termed the "expectable oppositions" that we struggle with today: "*then* versus *now*, industrial power versus postindustrial failure, white versus black, suburb versus city."[2] Mendelsohn's 14 photographs of Detroit, first published in 1926, make a compelling argument for the density of the ground plane. The images present construction sites, crowded constellations of billboards, trams, and tightly cropped streetscapes. The images are heavy at their lower edges, suggesting that while the city's vertical dimension is clearly under construction it is still the ground plane that registers its metropolitan effect. Looking through the entire collection of Erich Mendelsohn's photographs makes the logic of his travel itinerary clear. With photographs from New York, Buffalo, Chicago, and Detroit, it appears that Mendelsohn was captivated by the dense urban growth of American industrial modernity. Looking back at the time of his travels, we can imagine that the material density of the city offered Mendelsohn a sense of endless, self-replicating possibility and promise.

Some 80 years after Mendelsohn, I found myself with a similar itinerary. I follow his path, yet my interest is, necessarily, in the post-industrial American city and its waning sense of fullness. The Detroit I drift through is subject to much different pressures. If Mendelsohn found a city setting its stage for explosive growth, I found a city under erasure. Despite the frequent articulations of fear and suspicion thrust upon the Detroit I traverse, both Mendelsohn's and my iteration of the city share a sense of the new, the expectancy of

Figure 7.2 Photograph of
Detroit by Erich Mendelsohn,
from *Erich Mendelsohn's
"Amerika": 82 photographs*
(Minneola, NY: Dover, 1993).
Used with permission from
Dover Publications.

Figure 7.3 Photograph of Detroit by Erich Mendelsohn, from *Erich Mendelsohn's "Amerika": 82 photographs* (Minneola, NY: Dover, 1993). Used with permission from Dover Publications.

a situation that is unfolding and offering a fresh sense of what we might expect. Perhaps Mendelsohn felt the same sense of discomfort with Detroit (and with the other sites) that we feel today when we try to make sense of a city under erasure.

3

Despite losing over 50 percent of its population, Detroit still feels materially congested.[3] In the city, my visual field is bound by a dynamic sense of overlap. In the downtown, activity on the ground plane is scarce but the visual sense of crowding is quite strong. The central business district confirms the metropolitan experience of space that I briefly described at the beginning of this chapter. I attribute this to the radial organization of the streets, which were laid out by Judge Augustus Woodward in 1807. Woodward, influenced by L'Enfant's plan for Washington, DC, imagined a series of streets emanating

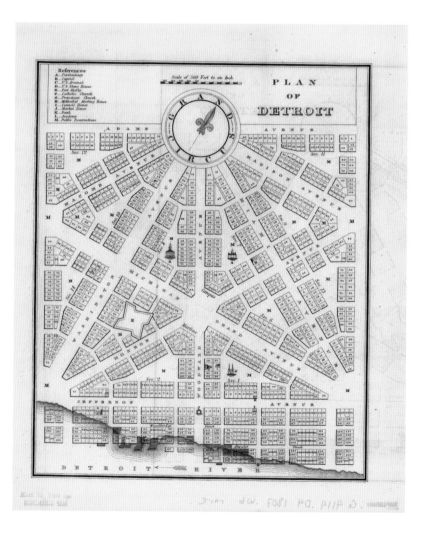

Figure 7.4 Woodward Plan of Detroit, drawn in 1860. Courtesy of the Harlan Hatcher Graduate Library, University of Michigan.

from a network of nodal points.[4] Like most master plans, the Woodward Plan was not materialized to the extent of its original vision. Instead a small fragment of the radial plan was built very near the edge of the Detroit River, marking the core of the downtown business district to this day. It is the radial organization of the downtown streets that guarantees a sense of metropolitan density in Detroit. Buildings following the radial logic of the street strike dynamic, off-grid relationships with buildings on the next block. The frenetic condition of the bound visual field is intensified in the downtown core of Detroit as one building visually collapses on another and another. Even during the early 1990s, when building vacancy rates were at an all-time high, the city still looked full, dense, congested.

But there are a number of aspects to experiencing Detroit that unsettle this exemplary city-space experience. The city delivers its material density on cue, but it is a confounding sense of fullness; provisional, tentative, fading … There is a strange formal confusion between the formality of *front* and the utility of *back*. The dismantling of one building has thrust the back elevation of another forward into the role of façade. Shorter buildings intermingle with taller buildings in very abrupt and unapologetic ways. The blocks that are filled with buildings are not uniformly filled. One gets the sense that the ebb and flow of the region's economy is registered here in the varied massing and size of buildings sharing the same block. As buildings were built up and torn down in this part of the city, the radiating spatial organization of Woodward's plan persisted. Tapered, wedge-like shapes lend an object-quality to even the most unassuming buildings. The buildings that would otherwise recede and be simply understood as *urban fabric* hold space here in unexpected ways. The narrow side of these wedge buildings often construct the space of the street in radically different ways than the opposite, wider side of the tapered mass. The buildings that capture the gaze of the viewer display a profound material sobriety resulting from a sustained period of time with little or no maintenance. The architecture here is gritty, tough, and robust in its material quality. As one moves across the grain of the radial streets, there is a vague sense of symmetry from one block to another lending to the experience a quality of disorientation. It is easy to get lost even though this city demands your attention at all times. The sensation of material density appears to be the manifest aim of Woodward's Master Plan. It is hard to imagine that Detroit would *feel like a city* if not for the Woodward Plan's radial logic.

Detroit exerts the material density of urbanism in a distorted manner. I cannot help but to associate the box constructions of Joseph Cornell with Detroit's material sobriety, their contents being reminiscent, if not vaguely symbolic, of a private order that we can participate in but are unable to fully understand.[5] Joseph Cornell, the American surrealist, exerts a definitively strange object-quality in the interior of his nostalgic boxes. The intensity of the contents and the corresponding sense of density he achieves through bricolage strike an analogous relationship with Detroit's complicated material density. The experience of box and city alike never fully develops in the narrative sense. Rather, both set up a sense of expectancy and fullness only to then yield to an overwhelming sense of loss: the loss of narrative continuity; the loss of the city as something culturally important and worthy of maintenance; the loss of an

Figure 7.5 Detroit: material congestion resulting from the radial logic of Woodward's plan.

economy that seemed strong enough to preclude anything other than its own predominance; the loss of viable forms of social diversity long associated with urbanism; the loss felt when the city does not deliver what is expected of cities. For Joseph Cornell, the empty birdcage summons the bird. The absence is made present by our own sense of reconciliation with the power of the voided

Figure 7.6 Detroit: unbuilding has thrust these building backs into the role of façade.

contents. Cornell's longing for *what could have been* serves as a mantra for making our own nostalgic sense of Detroit. And in Detroit, the material density, the fullness of the city, seems to present a trope of what we expect from congestion and from metropolitan experience. Detroit's material density is a confounding one.

Figure 7.7 Detroit: buildings in off-grid relationships collapse into the visual field.

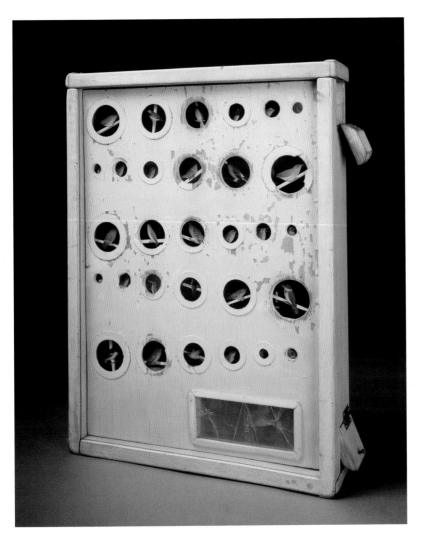

Figure 7.8 Joseph Cornell, American, 1903–1972, Untitled (Forgotten Game), c.1949, Box Construction, $21\frac{1}{8} \times 15\frac{1}{2} \times 3\frac{7}{8}$ in, Lindy and Edwin Bergman Joseph Cornell Collection. Reproduction, The Art Institute of Chicago.

4

But there is another density in Detroit. It is the density of emptiness. Even as the radial outlay of the Woodward Plan confirms our expectation that the city is dense and crowded, there are large, horizontal clearings resulting from multiple building teardowns in the same area of the city. These vacant landscapes are the product of Detroit's other legacy – that of unbuilding. In the early 1990s it was apparent that "unbuilding [had] surpassed building as the city's major architectural activity."[6] Within Detroit's figure–ground relationships there is a profound confusion between the oppositional terms. At the scale of an inner-city residential block, *ground* and *figure* are in the process of inversion. At the scale of the city itself, large grounds have formed through a systematically ad hoc process of divestment, abandonment, and collapse. Historical outdoor civic spaces, operating as exterior urban rooms, have seen

Figure 7.9 Detroit: large clearing in the city.

their power to preside over the city usurped by large unauthorized clearings, holes in the concept of city fabric. In these clearings, the Mid-Western prairie makes an assault on the hardness of the city's ground plane. Vision rambles uninterrupted across the ground, stretching to the horizon and violating the bound nature of the urban frame of view. This feeling of horizontal openness in the city is oceanic. Its vastness is due primarily to its shocking presence alongside the more canonic urban evocation of congestion. There is a power to these areas of the city; one that is not unlike the experience of the vast horizon line in the rural countryside, or the expansive view of the ocean as seen stretching out infinitely from the shoreline. One feels humbled by the expanse of nature, but also animated and empowered by one's position in the world.

These territories of profound emptiness confirm at the level of bodily sensation what Ignasi de Sola-Morales has termed *terrain vague*. "The relationship between the absence of use, of activity, and the sense of freedom, of expectancy, is fundamental to understanding the evocative potential of the city's terrains vagues."[7] De Sola-Morales provides the descriptive analysis of these clearings, torn as they are from our routine, visual occupation of the city. We do not see ourselves reflected in these rogue landscapes. We do not understand the absence of utility found there, and we have trouble understanding what went terribly wrong to lead to these spaces – these holes – in the city. All of this leads us to a sense of powerlessness and, at the same time,

Figure 7.10 Detroit: terrain vague adjacent to downtown.

a sense of urgency and impending action. But the action is not ours; it is not at our volition. It is an unaccountable, *vague* action taken upon us, perhaps against our will. This is the density of emptiness. It inverts the promise of the industrial city as Mendelsohn experienced it. If Mendelsohn's photographs exert optimism at all, which they do, it is optimism for a future of promise and plentitude. His is a commitment to the city in all of the exuberance of that time. Mendelsohn's Detroit is important in that it exemplifies the belief in progress embedded within industrial modernity. For us, it is easy to bear witness today to the power and the plenitude that the industrial age of modernity has thrust upon us (and also to its volatile inversions). We are sur-rounded by its trappings – the spoils of its success and the struggles associ-ated with its obsolescence. Detroit, like no other place, never wavered from its belief in the progress of modernity, even as its messy endgame became predictable.[8] Over-committed to industrial systems of production and the spatial configurations necessary to make the promise of modernity a reality, Detroit stands today as an unprecedented merging of the *expectable opposi-tions* between front and back, figure and ground, inside and outside, pres-ence and absence, and between density and emptiness. In Detroit, the future seems imminent just as the present overwhelms us with questions regarding how such empty space is possible deep inside the congested city. Turning to the past for answers only makes the questions more gnawing, and the space of the city even more eerie.

5

Formally and spatially, Detroit is remarkable precisely for its mutual presentation of material density and emptiness. As the distinctions between figure and ground become blurred, Detroit presents an opportunity to rethink the disciplinary use of figure/ground analysis as a tool of urban inquiry. One would have to embrace the technique of analysis while overcoming the predisposition that the articulation of figures set against a ground will (only) offer continuities and discrepancies in the *urban fabric*. More specifically, one would have to get past the idea of urban fabric altogether and look instead at the ways in which buildings are spatially charged, how objects hold the space around them, and how the space around buildings stage the object quality of the building. Detroit space recommends that the project of maintaining the clarity between the terms "figure" and "ground" may have run its course; that we might want to take stock of the indirect value of something offering less clarity. In other words, there might be a spatial possibility that is relationally ambiguous. Further, we might pursue the possibility of accounting for both material density and emptiness within spatial fields and buildings alike, celebrating the waning contrast between the terms.

In her book, *The Optical Unconscious*, Rosalind Krauss discusses a Klein Group diagram that seems quite useful for understanding the context of waning spatial contrast between figure and ground. The square organization of the diagram juxtaposes the contrasting terms "figure" and "ground" against one another across the top horizontal axis and then again across the bottom horizontal axis, expressed here as negatives ("not figure" and "not ground") (see Figure 7.11). Of this organization Krauss writes,

> [t]he graph's circumference holds all the terms in mutual opposition: figure versus ground; ground versus not ground; not-ground versus not figure; not-figure versus figure. Its diagonal axes yield, however, to mirror relations, or rather mirror restatements ... with figure in this case being the "same" as not-ground.[9]

Krauss's interest in the diagram can be linked to this re-statement, or re-writing of the oppositional terms and the implications the Klein Group has on distinctions she makes between vision and perception within modernity. In the context of Detroit space, the graph is particularly useful given that it explores a vital relationship between what might otherwise only be understood as oppositional terms. The terms juxtaposed around the periphery of the diagram are "both preserved and cancelled"[10] toward a re-approximation of the oppositional character of the binary logic of figure/ground. Krauss explains that "what the rewriting made clear ... is that for every social absolute – marriage, yes; incest, no – there is its more flexible, shadow correlate: the kind of maybe, maybe of the not-not axis."[11]

The *maybe, maybe of the not-not* condition put forward by Rosalind Krauss aptly captures Detroit's eerie spatial language, and the "shadow correlate" might be as close to an optimal spatial vocabulary as we are likely to find in contemporary examples of urbanism. In other words, we are seeing

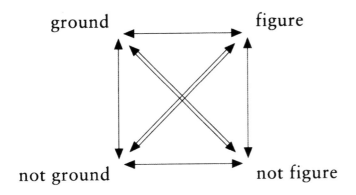

Figure 7.11 Rosalind Krauss, *The Optical Unconscious*, diagram, p. 14 (© 1993 Massachusetts Institute of Technology, by permission of MIT Press).

urban space move more and more toward the open specificity of ambiguity.[12] The notion of a double movement of cancelation and preservation is an important conceptual orientation to contemporary urban experience generally, but even more so given the tendency for architects and developers to over-specify the status of nostalgic authenticity within redevelopment and new development alike. Culturally, the attractiveness and popularity of newly activated urban spaces is often predicated on the same conceptual organizations that make those spaces feel fake and contrived. The public's willingness to occupy city spaces seems based on those spaces being suburban in character. This follows the recognition that in contemporary urbanism the predominant urban subjects along with their sense of power and agency are mostly being constructed within suburban typologies of space. This is true for suburbanites and city dwellers alike as the mass media emits persuasive messages that the city is derelict, dangerous, and site of rogue behaviors. This message is accompanied by their attempt to forge strong, vivid images of a post-city lifestyle that orients cultural *desire engines* toward so-called suburban ideals. Renovating and re-activating derelict city space is akin to suburbanizing it, thus rendering it acceptable terrain for occupation at the same time that the wildness and openness of that space is deeply sacrificed. As one of the complexities of post-city urbanism, this is something to understand and harness within contemporary urban thinking, not something to dismiss. Krauss's invocation of cancelation and preservation is an apt precept for a post-city practice of urbanism.

Two points seem important here. First, it is easy to understand the dilemma faced by architects and planners alike. Dissatisfaction with the city's stubborn refusal to deliver the historically stable metropolitan experience of congestion and anonymity leads efforts to bring the city back into conformance, which mostly falsifies the experience of the city and thereby communicates to its occupants that its success is a contrivance. Second, the ambiguity of Krauss's description of the preservation and cancelation of what were previously understood as oppositional terms and ideas might be more the rule than the exception when it comes to anticipating the conditions with which we might work within contemporary urbanism. While I am primarily drawn to Krauss's Klein Group for its potential for thinking about the physical, spatial quality of Detroit, I am eager to connect her interest in relational ambiguity to larger problems of post-city urbanism. Paradoxical and challenging, the sort of double thinking set up by Krauss's diagram, along with the spatial and conceptual potential of the double negative as a working method might serve well our disciplinary work on urbanism.

6

Giorgio Morandi, the Italian still-life painter, produced a number of paintings that could serve to illustrate the shadowy correlate space posited by Krauss's diagram, and in doing so help develop some of the projective potential the Klein Group holds. Painting serial compositions of bottles and other vessels perched on his studio table, Morandi's work can be seen to oscillate between a concern for the objects in his compositions and an infatuation with the spaces between them. Deploying various painterly strategies, Morandi curiously awakens something powerful in what one might understand at first glance to be quotidian domestic objects.[13] Manipulating the viewer's point of view in relationship to the edge of the table top (which acts as the horizon line); flattening the depth of the painting by collapsing the figure of one bottle onto another; painting light as it falls across the surfaces of the bottles such that the object is made both present and absent through the same gesture; sequestering the range of color within the painting so that the background, foreground, and middle ground differ only in terms of tonal variation; and making low the level of contrast between the figural objects and the background such that there is ambiguity between them – such are the techniques and effects within Morandi's still-life paintings that recommend them as an

Figure 7.12 Morandi, Giorgio (1890–1964), *Still Life with Vases* (© ARS, NY).

important reference to the *kind of maybe, maybe of the not-not*. I'd like to describe one Morandi painting in particular as emblematic of the strong relationship between his work and the Klein Group diagram introduced by Krauss; and taken together, to the eeriness of Detroit space.

Still Life V. 295, painted in 1941, seems to be worthy of some reflection here, as the contents of the painting are pertinent to the relationship between Krauss's murky double negative and Detroit's strange spatiality. In the painting, Morandi has narrowed the range of color and intensified the role of shadow and light such that there is a strong sense of flickering, or oscillation between figural objects and the space between them. It is, interestingly, impossible to discern whether he is painting the space between things or the things themselves. The table top and the background have been endowed with the same tone and color, rendering the difference between them minimal, if not non-existent. Likewise, the surfaces of the objects in direct light have been painted the same as the background resulting in the objects being rendered present, but only conditionally so. The second bottle from the left captures my attention (see Figure 7.13). Here it appears as though this bottle has been embedded between figure and ground. The crenulations of its surface have been invaded by the background of the painting. It is as if Morandi has eviscerated this object with the space between objects. The result is a deeply ambiguous and troubling status for the object and the space around the object alike. Lowering the contrast between the thing and the space it holds has resulted in a beautiful manifestation of Krauss's shadowy correlate. Here we are presented with a *not-not bottle* and a *not-not background*, the two enveloping one another in a struggle of co-dependence, and in doing so perpetuating a simultaneous cancelation and preservation. Paradoxical and charged with a liminal status of form/anti-form, this *not-not condition* challenges the clarity and discreteness associated with figures or objects. It is easy to understand this *failed bottle* in the context of the painting, and its value here is that it corroborates the role ambiguity might play in establishing a very specific spatial effect.

Figure 7.13 Morandi, Giorgio (1890–1964), *Still Life V. 295* (© ARS, NY).

In Detroit a city block marked with the cadence of repeating single-family houses, all closely knit by finger-like spaces between them, can be reminiscent of Morandi's row of bottles sitting on the table top. Remove all the houses except one, and you will see an entropic urban space, no doubt, yet one that is relatively clear and easy to understand. In fact, many of the well-known images of Detroit's vacancy present an image much like the one I am invoking – the lone remaining house in a space that was previously full of serially repeating units, all roughly of the same size and character. Images like this effectively represent the shocking reality of a city under the pressure of globally mobile capital along with a cultural willingness to walk away from the project of city (for those who can afford to). While such an image is problematic due precisely to the inversion of the city it represents, this image (by now the most familiar way to "see" Detroit) is one wherein the logic of figure/ground is still intact and paradigmatically strong. Even though we are shocked and captivated by such spaces of vacancy, these spaces stop short of delivering the shadowy correlate appearing due to the loss of contrast between figure and ground. We are challenged by the inverted spatial syntax brought on by large clearings that strand single objects (frequently those that are derelict and ruinous), but that syntax is still classically defined by the relationship between an object and its spatial field. Far more disturbing and pressing are those de-simplified spatial relationships that are defined by in-between, liminal, and oscillating not-not conditions.

Developing the analogy between an urban block and what we find in Morandi's *Still Life V. 295* allows us to articulate what is truly exceptional about Detroit's eerie spatiality. Imagine the same city block defined by the repetition of houses and spaces between. Now, remove one house from within the row of houses along the street. The removal results in new open space, or ground that is roughly equivalent to the figures that define it. Or, stating it differently, there is now an absence that is roughly equivalent to a presence. This initiates a flickering relationship between the terms, as both figure and ground have now gained equal footing. The two terms/conditions are suddenly equivalent by virtue of their shared spatial dimensions. The result is a spatial scrimmage between the two. The interchangeability of figure and ground, the loss of contrast between the terms, and their propensity to flicker back and forth stages the breakdown of the classically positioned object in space. The object and its space begin to be confused with one another just as the failed bottle in Morandi's painting presents such a physical and spatial confusion. Morandi's failed bottle is a painterly conceit and is presented effortlessly in the pictorial space of the painting making it seem more direct and easier to intellectually process than the complex spaces of urbanism. While this sets its value in the context of this chapter, the relationship between the painting and the city is more provocation than it is a straightforward question of scale. As was introduced earlier in this chapter, the dual action of preservation/cancelation is both a spatial and cultural phenomenon in the city, given the degree to which urban modes of behavior, or subjectivities, are largely constructed through suburban typologies of space and experience. Complicating the translation from Morandi's painting to the space of the city is the assertion that we do not necessarily anticipate, nor cultivate this sort of profound confusion from urban buildings because we mostly define cities through the sanctity of contrasting systems and the clarity that contrast affords. It is this contrast and clarity that Detroit upsets so profoundly with its proliferation of *maybe, maybe, not-not conditions*. The resultant breakdown or collapse of the classically positioned object in space might be the most pressing architectural issue aggravated both by cities like Detroit and the horizontally contested forms of urbanism emanating from them.

7

In an effort to extrapolate on the collapse of the classically defined object in space, I want to compare the 1748 Nolli plan of Rome[14] and a plan drawing of Rome published in Edmund Bacon's book, *Design of Cities*,[15] and begin to consider the ways in which contemporary American forms of urbanism might present a radical dissolution of "urban fabric." For Nolli, the dense fabric of compressed blackened, or figured, buildings held the significant civic spaces of the city (squares, piazzas, prominent interiors) together, granting the exceptional spaces of the city the sense that they had been carved out of a dense tapestry or fabric composed of buildings whose primary task as figures was to yield to the continuity of the ground and not make objects of themselves. In Edmund Bacon's drawing of Rome, all of those background buildings have simply been omitted in order to emphasize the processional character of the civic monuments and to make his point that without the massiveness and compression of its incremental growth, Rome would have likely yielded a much more chaotic urbanism.[16] For me, the Bacon drawing deftly shows a much more recent phenomenon of object buildings set among a distinct lack of urban fabric (as traditionally defined). Looking at the two drawings together and thinking of them as an historical progression (admittedly a misreading of Bacon's intentions), one imagines that it is the nature of fabric that has changed from dense, continuous, and compressive to something much more sparse and spatially sporadic. In Bacon's drawing, the very idea of fabric ceases to exist and one reads the drawn buildings as floating in a vastly open space that is only barely held in place by the buildings themselves.

This strikes an uncanny (and unwitting) resemblance to contemporary horizontally dispersed urban patterns while recommending the possibility that the language of figure/ground urbanism could be opened to a wider range of interpretive results; a range that supersedes the predisposition of continuous and dense urban fabric and looks more closely at how buildings consume and are consumed by their spatial fields and patterns of both density and emptiness. It is possible that both Morandi's failed bottle and Krauss's interest in the double negative (the not-not condition) come together with Detroit's dual presentation of density and emptiness to suggest that what might first be seen as a singularly interesting phenomenon in one particularly extreme American city is in fact a view into a much larger quandary involving ways of conceiving of and acting spatially within post-city contemporary forms of urbanism. The Edmund Bacon drawing closely resembles a suburban spatiality within which disaggregated buildings sit in the ether of a mostly undifferentiated field of space. The majority of suburban buildings are acutely unaware of the

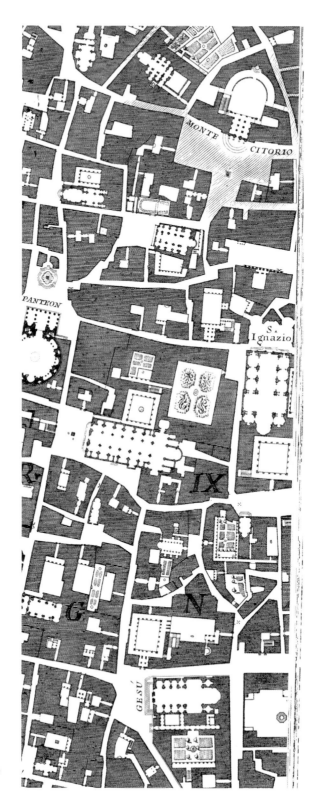

Figure 7.14 *Pianta Grande di Roma*, Giambattista Nolli, c.1748. Partial view. Courtesy of the Harlan Hatcher Graduate Library, University of Michigan.

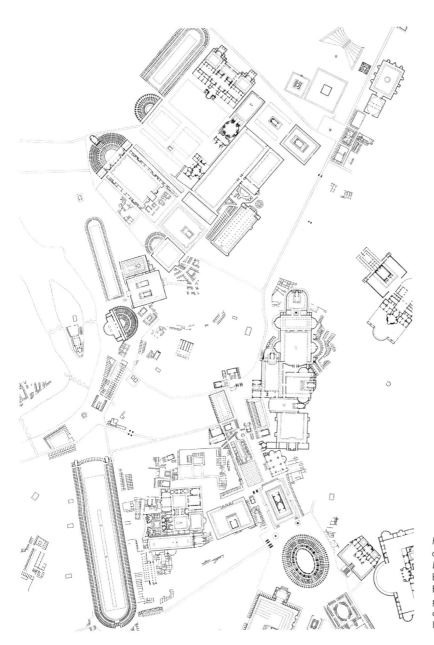

Figure 7.15 Drawing of Rome, drawn by Alois K. Strobl, from Design of Cities, by Edmund Bacon (© 1967, 1974 by Edmund N. Bacon. Used by permission of Penguin, a division of Penguin Group (USA) Inc).

role they play as spatial objects that first articulate a loose horizontality then lose themselves in the generic sense of that space. Still, we might look again at the radical alteration of "fabric" from something that is compressive, tight, and materially full toward that same condition now eviscerated by speed (in many senses) and marked with a strange sense of distance.[17] Musing at Bacon's drawing in this frame of mind suggests that the white space surrounding the drawn figures might be retroactively described as a not yet knowable, nor drawable, *medium* or *plenum* (and not a "fabric") within which communication, digital transactions, wireless fidelity networks, and other flowing information have replaced the compressive solid/void character of built urban density. We might consider the absence of the city, rendered white in his drawing, as an early representation of an urban medium that both distinguishes built objects from one another and also renders the comparative terms of their relationship unknowable in classical terms of figure/ground. The relationships between built objects might be understood as preserved in the same step that cancels them. Perhaps a new medium for urban architecture has emerged alongside newly formed modes of subjectivity and civic behavior in an age defined by detachment, ubiquitous surveillance, increasingly irrelevant institutions, and deeply personal forms of *publicness*.[18]

Detroit space, then, presents a particularly legible and challenging model for what this new urban medium might be when it is played out in the same geographical territory that *used to be the city*. The anticipation for economic growth and cultural wealth, easily associated with the sense of exuberance and optimism in Mendelsohn's photographs of the sites of industrial modernity, has now been replaced with the rhetoric of failure and abandonment, just as the open spaces of the city now stand as an inverted symbol of wealth and plenitude currently amassing *somewhere else*. As we try to cope with this massive inversion, Detroit offers us the opportunity to think beyond the concept of urban fabric. We might see the loss of contrast between figure and ground as a call to arms, so to speak, toward a new way of considering the role cities play in the formation of our ideas about urbanity. Developing this assertion, we might also consider the likelihood that the traditional city is not the exemplar of this new urban medium. In this sense, the market-driven processes of urbanism have used speed and digital processing to burn holes in the concept of the city, and thus have decimated the formal preoccupation of "fabric" in places like Detroit. There might be spatial lessons in the horizontality of suburban or perimeter urbanisms useful when dealing with cities like Detroit that wrestle with the mutual construction of density and emptiness, but that is largely an exploration for another time. It is worth noting, however, that the terms and concepts, "urbanism" and "city," might be undergoing a similar inversion as are "figure" and "ground." Namely, that the pre-eminent urban form – the city – might now be an obstruction or blockage within our disciplinary attempts to conceptualize and participate in the far more contested and entropic condition of urbanism that we see before us today.

8

In 1968 Robert Smithson proposed that "[w]hat is needed is an esthetic method that brings together anthropology and linguistics in terms of *building*." His interest in "pavement, holes, trenches, mounds, heaps, paths, ditches, roads, terraces, etc.," sponsored his concern for finding new strategies for art-making that do not simply critique earlier art practices.[19] In light of its paradoxical density of emptiness, Detroit offers itself as an analogous site for thinking similarly about urbanism. Here, urbanism could be understood as having freed itself from its own expectant forms. The separation of the terms "city" and "urbanism" would parallel the trajectory of other dualities such as "figure" and "ground." While not traditionally viewed as oppositional (as is the case with figure and ground) "urbanism" and "city" would, nevertheless, effect change upon one another as they reposition themselves. Perhaps Detroit's alluring spatial texture is prompting us to reconsider urbanism from outside the confines of its precedent forms. The profound emptiness in Detroit might be seen as urbanism's attempt to tear at its historically dominant site, the city proper. Terrains vagues, after all, are "where the city is no longer."[20]

Following Smithson, the notion of a *boring* strikes me as an apt metaphor for the way in which emptiness and material density coexist in Detroit. It is as if emptiness is simply an excavation out of the surrounding material congestion in the city. It is like a hole, bored out of a material that it is not.[21] Emptiness perforates density, countering the mental effects of congestion with a *fullness* and a sense of expectancy all its own. This double-thought density, the density of emptiness, could prove to serve our generation as well as the predominance of a material density, of congestion in the city, served Mendelsohn's. But the possibility for this to be true seems contingent on shifts in attitude and in practice. Maybe our disciplinary strategies are too well rooted in congestion? Or, maybe they rely too heavily on their own disciplinary precedents? Perhaps we are disarmed by our tendency to try to solve the problem of emptiness? Confronted with a city that fails to deliver material density in its conventional sense, maybe we should ask if our disciplinary tendencies are limited to simply reinstating what the city used to be, insisting on clarity in the face of something far more wild and demanding.

NOTES

1 Mendelsohn, Erich, *Erich Mendelsohn's "Amerika": 82 photographs* (Mineola, NY: Dover, 1993).
2 Herron, Jerry, *AfterCulture: Detroit and the Humiliation of History* (Detroit: Wayne State University Press, 1993), p. 204.
3 According to the US Census Bureau Detroit's population shrank from 1.8 million in 1950 to 951,270 in 2000.
4 Ironically Woodward's Master Plan both established congestion as its aim and tended toward a decentralized city. The dispersed network of nodes and radial connectors was preferred to a centralized organization. For more on Woodward's Plan, see Dunnigan, Brian (ed.), *Frontier Metropolis: Picturing Early Detroit 1701–1838* (Detroit: Wayne State University Press, 2001).
5 For more on Joseph Cornell, see McShine, Kynaston (ed.), *Joseph Cornell* (New York: Museum of Modern Art/Prestel, 1990).
6 Hoffman, Dan, "Erasing Detroit," in Daskalakis, Georgia, Waldheim, Charles, and Young, Jason (eds.), *Stalking Detroit* (Barcelona: ACTAR, 2001), p. 101.
7 De Sola-Morales Rubio, Ignasi, "Terrain Vague," in Davidson, Cynthia C. (ed.), *AnyPlace* (Cambridge, MA: MIT Press, 1995), p. 120.
8 This is one of the major themes in *Stalking Detroit*. See Daskalakis, Georgia, Waldheim, Charles, and Young, Jason (eds.), *Stalking Detroit* (Barcelona: ACTAR, 2001).
9 Krauss, Rosalind E., *The Optical Unconscious* (Cambridge, MA: MIT Press, 1993), p. 15.
10 Ibid.
11 Ibid., p. 14.

12 Open specificity is one of the interesting provocations in the book *snooze: Immersing Architecture in Mass Culture*. See Studio Sputnik, *snooze: Immersing Architecture in Mass Culture* (Rotterdam: NAI, 2003).

13 For more on Giorgio Morandi, see Bandera, Maria Cristina and Miracco, Renato (eds.), *Morandi 1890–1964* (Milan: Skira Editore, 2008).

14 The *Pianta Grande di Roma* was etched in 1748 by Giambattista Nolli and is now known widely as the "Nolli Map."

15 Bacon, Edmund N., *Design of Cities* (New York: Penguin Books, 1976).

16 Ibid., pp. 84–91.

17 The role of speed and distance in contemporary urbanism is one of the major themes of Lars Lerup's book, *After the City*. See Lerup, Lars, *After the City* (Cambridge, MA: MIT Press, 2000).

18 The implications of a provocation such as this are beyond the scope of this chapter. However, it is worth considering the degree to which urban subjectivity is but one consequence of a complex cocktail of cultural imperatives. Such recognition helps substantiate the notion that there is a new urban medium far surpassing the solid/void relationships of an "urban fabric."

19 Smithson, Robert, "A Thing Is a Hole in a Thing It Is Not," in Flam, Jack (ed.), *Robert Smithson, The Collected Writings* (Berkeley: University of California Press, 1996), pp. 95–96.

20 De Sola-Morales, op. cit., p. 120.

21 Smithson, op. cit.

8 ANTISEPSIS

LI SHIQIAO

At the turn of the twentieth century, Adolf Loos was deeply enthralled by the impact of plumbing in architecture; it is as if architecture was no longer driven by classical sensibilities of harmony and proportion perpetuated since the Renaissance, but by a deceptively simple technological scheme, the supply and drainage of water. For Loos, plumbing enables daily washing, which had a great cultural significance; "an increase in the use of water is one of our most critical cultural tasks."[1] He called for a return to the love of water for the Austrians, who had been misled by the fear of water in the over-cultivated Latin culture epitomized by the French; the English and the Americans embraced the ancient Germanic love of water and had no fear of either dirt or water, which was the cultural root of their success. "There would have been no nineteenth century without the plumber."[2] Loos's sentiment was not entirely contrived; since the mid nineteenth century, great advances in medical research led to tremendous improvements in public hygiene in urban centers in Europe. Public health has been a crucial concern particularly for the "laboring population" since the mid nineteenth century; Edwin Chadwick's report on sanitary conditions in England (1842), and the subsequent Public Health Act (1848) and the establishment of a Board of Health, is a well known example.[3] Central to these improvements were the design and construction of sewage systems, something that deeply impressed one of the earliest Japanese visitors to Europe, Nagayo Sensai, in 1872; in Berlin, he also witnessed, in amazement, the development of new hospitals, laboratories, and the beginning of a national public health bureaucracy.[4] Ancient attitudes toward dirt and washing seem to be confused – oscillating between holiness and defilement[5] – but the nineteenth century put forward a clear message: dirt and disease are inextricably connected. Loos was not alone in turning this long-standing nineteenth-century concern for public health into an architectural discourse; Le Corbusier brought a much more emphatic aesthetic and moral expression of public hygiene in architecture. The foyer sinks at Rufer House (1922) and Villa Savoy (1929) are attempts to aestheticize the inevitable architectural consequences of the act of cleansing the body.[6]

Since Loos's pronouncements, hygiene in architecture has developed in two directions to become what might be described as the architecture of bacteria and virus control. The first direction is centered on whiteness in the early twentieth century; whiteness seems to have emerged from the visual act of bleaching, the physical and metaphorical removal of dirt as an antiseptic practice. The second appears to be rooted in the medical procedure of disinfection; the result of this in architecture is the homogeneous surface. While plumbing reinvents the layout of habitable spaces through the creation of daily washing rituals for all, antisepsis impacts on surfaces, which disturbs and reorders traditional aesthetics of the surface – classical or modernist – in architecture. The antiseptic surface is thin and sealed, which deviates from the traditional "thick surface" (*poché*) fundamental to texture and depth.[7] The thin surface is generating its own aesthetic realm, therefore can no longer be easily dismissed as "untruthful"; it is combining the Baroque impulse for decorated surfaces with the logic of antiseptic procedures to create a new age of surface effects. Through a powerful alliance with the ubiquitous electronic screen which focuses tremendous intellectual energy on surface effects, the thin surface has acquired an extraordinary strength in contemporary design. Skin and wrapping, rather than depth and tectonics, are much more attractive architectural propositions today. This way of looking at architecture, in turn, points to its own pioneers and their manifestos – those of Florence Nightingale and the Center for Disease Control and Prevention instead of Alberti and Le Corbusier – which present, without intellectual pretension and with starkness, some of the most important forces shaping a new hygienic architecture for our age.

The new form of hygienic architecture is being reformulated in Asian cities for several reasons. Asian cities in the past decades have demonstrated a particular vitality resulting from a blending of Western architectural and urban

Figure 8.1 Kowloon Station, Hong Kong.

planning principles and a range of indigenous sensibilities. Founded as a place for global trade initiated by distant powers, Hong Kong is perhaps one of the best examples of a multicultural society in which all cultural practices have undergone transformation in response to practical demands of trade; it is relatively removed from the aesthetics of ideological constructs. Hong Kong is also an exceptional example of a city of high density, which has cultivated an urban culture – its internalization and aestheticization of proximity, noise, sociality, and efficiency – that optimizes the high-density urban environment. In these senses, Hong Kong is not a compromise because of its density; in the Chinese urban context, it points to an urban future for countless Chinese cities, one that is not rooted in classical sensibilities of the "country house" (or the ideal villa) but in the necessity of sharing scarce resources together. Hong Kong's creation is a tribute to the diligence of the engineers and bureaucrats of urban hygiene in all its aspects, plumbing and antisepsis; Hong Kong's endeavors to improve its public hygiene standards, unlike those in Japan and Korea, is particularly remarkable and revealing because its notion of "public hygiene" does not seem to be indigenous, and the notion of "public" itself was grounded in private social circles. This chapter traces Hong Kong's aesthetic developments rooted in the practices of antisepsis that contribute to its distinct architectural and urban characters. Through Hong

Figure 8.2 Entrance door handle, foyer, Hong Kong Arts Centre (Photo by Esther Lorenz).

Kong, we can perhaps gain glimpses into future cities: the hygienic roots of ancient rites are now combined with modern medical knowledge to give rise to a new architecture that is yet to be described.

WHITENESS

Like many modern cities embodying the heritage of urban hygiene, Hong Kong has many white or off-white surfaces. This, not very long ago, would have seemed rather strange for a Chinese city; whiteness is a state of "depletion" in the traditional Chinese cosmological conception of "five colors" (*wuse*) – blue, red, yellow, white, black – which are connected to the ever-changing "five elements" of the universe. For this reason, red is often used to celebrate life at its sanguine prosperity (weddings) while white is used to indicate the depletion of life (funerals); in the ancient tradition of colors, whiteness was carefully avoided on general occasions unless it was used to form a set of five colors. The Chinese intellectual tradition conceives whiteness in the visual arts as the surface of the "unexplained," which, when arranged skillfully, is highly valued. This whiteness in the visual arts is better understood as "richness in nothingness," particularly in painting and calligraphy; it is always intentionally "left blank" (*liubai*), and not "painted white," as a way of developing artistic and philosophical space. The white walls in the private gardens in southern China should probably be seen in this context. The Western construction of whiteness, however, was perhaps first centered on its quality of potentiality rather than depletion; whiteness seems to present maximum potential in its purity (weddings) while blackness, one could argue, indicates its exhaustion (funerals). The whiteness of the bedroom Loos designed for his 19-year-old wife in 1903 perhaps blended the potentiality of whiteness and that of the youthful female body. The second focus of the meaning of whiteness lies in its status as defiance to nature. The existence of its purity is precarious; this fragility, like that of the body in combat and knowledge in contest, is pregnant with enormous intellectual and aesthetic content. The extraordinary labor to sustain whiteness – as well as power, virtue, truth – seems to have become the ground for distinction: divinity, virginity, intellect, and social and economic class. The potentiality of whiteness, in the Western intellectual context, could indeed be seen to be the "mother and nurse" of all other architectural possibilities;[8] whiteness in architecture could be seen as "the thin white line between architecture and decoration" which gives rise to the discipline of architecture.[9]

The moral and aesthetic potentiality became crucial in Le Corbusier's formulation of a theory of the superiority of whiteness in architecture, which contains three aspects. First, whiteness is honesty.

> Whitewash is extremely moral. Suppose there were a decree requiring all rooms in Paris to be given a coat of whitewash. I maintain that that would be a police task of real stature and a manifestation of high morality, the sign of a great people.[10]

Second, whiteness is a material form of equality. "Whitewash is the wealth of the poor and of the rich – of everybody, just as bread, milk and water are the wealth of the slave and the king."[11] Third, whiteness provides intellectual power, an "unfailing imperative which is the sense of truth and which recognizes in the smoothness of ripolin and the white of whitewash an object of truth."[12]

> The Stadium, like the Bank, demands precision and clarity, speed and correctness. Stadium and bank both provide conditions appropriate for action, conditions of clarity like that in a head that has to think. There may be people who think against a background of black. But the tasks of our age – so strenuous, so full of danger, so violent, so victorious – seem to demand of us that we think against a background of white.[13]

These arguments were powerful and became widely accepted by those who wished to depart from the mediocrity of Beaux-Arts architecture in the early twentieth century. One of the most extraordinary examples is the exhibition houses by 16 architects at Weissenhofsiedlung in 1927, which were constructed with a common directive of white exterior walls. Over a century, the white wall has become so common that one would generally associate "modern architecture" with white walls.[14]

Whiteness in Hong Kong has a very different trajectory, which may explain the fact that the whiteness in Hong Kong is more often "off-white": lightly colored surfaces; there is a general absence of moral and aesthetic intentions in the use of whiteness, and there is an absence of policing the purity of whiteness. In this sense, Hong Kong's use of whiteness is perhaps closely connected to a different architectural practice influenced by Florence Nightingale's *Notes on Hospitals* in 1863. Although generally ignored by architectural historians perhaps for its lack of interest in architectural discourses, this "architectural treatise" is extraordinary precisely because of this lack of interest in academic debates in architecture, and because of its tremendous influence in the construction of hospitals throughout the world. Nightingale's treatise resulted from her experience and achievement at the military camp hospital at Scutari during the Crimean War (1853–1856). As a volunteer nurse, Nightingale arrived at the British military camp in 1854 to discover that ten times as many soldiers died of infections such as typhus and cholera than from battle wounds; there was an unacceptably high mortality rate. After several improvements in drainage and ventilation instigated by her, the mortality rate dropped dramatically. Reflecting on this and other experiences, she began her treatise on hospital design: "It may seem a strange principle to enunciate as the very first requirement in a Hospital that it should do the sick no harm."[15] The reality in hospitals at the time made it crucial for her to make this point. Nightingale shows that the mortality rate in 24 London hospitals in 1861 was over 90 percent while that in 25 county hospitals in country towns was just below 40 percent.[16] She argues that this was due to the poor hygiene conditions in London, and cleaner air and better ventilation in county hospitals. Nightingale's campaign in hospital hygiene brought a new focus on the connection between health and hygiene; her highly influential principles of hospital design demonstrated dramatically the benefit of sensible designs, and these principles are equally applicable in the design of other buildings in cities, particularly in the context of polluted nineteenth-century European urban centers.

Nightingale was a believer of the miasma theory of diseases, which approximate closely the modern germ theory. She believed that the sick exhaled substances which were "highly morbid and dangerous," and this was "one of nature's methods of eliminating noxious matter from the body, in order that it may recover health."[17] The core belief of the miasma theory is the removal of poisonous substances from the living environment, which underlined the emphasis of ventilation and light. Miasma theory perhaps consolidated a long-standing search for methods of ventilation. In 1777, King Louis XV appointed a commission of the Académie Royale des Sciences to look into the problem of building hospitals, in connection to the rebuilding of Hôtel-Dieu which burned down in 1772, searching, over a decade, for the best and most hygienic plans for a 1,000-bed hospital. The hospital was seen to be a machine for ventilation, an architecture shaped by the movement of the air,[18] and perhaps not primarily understood as an architecture of surveillance in Michel Foucault's conception. More relevantly, miasma theory raised the importance of white and off-white surfaces as a way of making poisonous substances visible. Nightingale was highly critical of "the gloom of a dark ward,"[19] and recommends "impervious material" with "a white or tinted surface."[20] Bathrooms should certainly be covered with white tiles.[21] It is important to use "good color, and not a dull dirty one" for the surfaces, Nightingale suggests, and "a sufficiently good surface might be obtained by applying some of the better class of light-colored paints."[22] Nightingale's recommendation of white or off-white surfaces probably appeared to be strange at the time, when hospital interiors, let alone general architecture, were mostly covered with colors arising from aesthetic schemes. For instance, the 572-bed Poplar and Stepney Workhouse Infirmary (designed by A. & C. Harston in 1871) used mauve-gray colored brick walls with their lower portions painted buff, with chocolate line and skirting.[23]

The philosophical and moral discussions of whiteness, over the twentieth century, have almost entirely eclipsed its hospital origins; this understanding of the ubiquitous white walls of modern architecture must be supplemented by a recovery of their practical roots in the promotion of health. This recovery is important in relation to Asian cities because it could be a way to enfranchise intellectually the architecture of a city such as Hong Kong where the normative understanding is either grounded in a spectacle of the Other or in a set of statistics. In its lack of care for the philosophical and moral content of whiteness, Hong Kong forces our attention away from familiar academic debates, turning it back to the stark reality of whiteness or off-whiteness in its own trajectory.

SHINE

Hong Kong's interiors, particularly newly completed commercial and domestic interiors, are often covered with layers of shine, which, together with its off-white environment, produces effects of off-white shine; an army of polishers, dressed in nurse-like uniforms, continuously mop and polish these surfaces with antiseptic solutions. It seems important that these surfaces should shine constantly, at a high cost. The newly renovated Grand Century Plaza in Shatin (developed by Sun Hung Kai Properties) and the show flats and clubhouse facilities of Lake Silver (a residential project in Ma On Shan developed by Sino Group in 2009) located at the basement of Tsim Sha Tsui Centre are two of many recent examples of the domination of the aesthetic ideal of off-white shine. The Chinese traditional sensibility for shine seems to be always limited to isolated objects – porcelain, precious metals, jade, lacquered furniture – which sustain a sense of preciousness, cultivation, and refinement. The colors of shiny objects tend to be intense, which again highlights the characters of the objects. Although the imperial palaces and gardens used glazed yellow tiles to signify grandeur and hierarchy, their use was not wide-spread; the private gardens in southern China are generally free of shine in their use of building materials.

Unlike whiteness, which has powerful intellectual and moral connotations, shine has a rather lowly aesthetic and intellectual status for modernist propagators despite, or because of, its high capacity to delight the senses: the shiny marbles in Roman interiors and the metallic and reflective shine of the French court point to a general moral decay. It is perhaps not difficult to understand the distrust of shine because of its direct appeal to senses; the Platonic philosophical tradition has always propagated this distrust in aesthetic theories, such as those of Shaftesbury and Kant. It is this turning away

Figure 8.3 Grand Central Plaza, Shatin, Hong Kong.

from sense-based aesthetics that compelled Shaftesbury to dismiss sense-based knowledge production (empiricism) advocated by leading scientists in the seventeenth century.[24] Le Corbusier spoke disparagingly of the "most disturbing contrivance" of "trees glitter, rocks shine, the sky glows, jade, jasper, onyx, agate, lapis, crystal" in relation to the 1925 Exposition des Arts Décoratifs in Paris.[25]

Hong Kong's fascination with off-white shine, like its vast stretches of off-white surfaces, possesses a similar philosophical and moral indifference. If shine has little currency in philosophical and moral constructs, it is essential to the understanding of the germ theory, firmly established since the discovery of bacteria by Louis Pasteur in the mid nineteenth century (1822–1896). It changed fundamentally the way we live and transformed the ancient practice of antisepsis. The germ theory provided a scientific basis for the miasma theory which Nightingale believed, and gave rise to vaccines and antibiotics which dramatically reduced the infection and mortality rate in and out of hospitals. Pasteur's discovery is commonly acknowledged as the single most important medical event of all time; the period 1879–1900 is considered the 21 "golden years" of bacteriology, during which "major diseases were being discovered at the phenomenal rate of one a year."[26] It was in Hong Kong where Alexandre Yersin (1863–1943), a Swiss scientist who was sent by the French government and the Pasteur Institute, and Kitasato Shibasaburo (1853–1931), a Japanese scientist who studied under Robert Koch (1843–1910), simultaneously discovered the bacteria *Yersinia pestis* which had caused the 1894 bubonic plague in Hong Kong, which was found to be transmitted through the rat.[27]

Bacteriology confirmed what Nightingale and many others suspected: diseases pass from human to human through poisonous effluvia, more than the process of contact: Nightingale thought the use of the term "contagion" a misconception. In addition to ventilation and light, Nightingale was very specific about the nature of surfaces in her recommendations for hospital design. "The amount of organic matter given off by respiration and in other ways from the sick is such that the floors, walls, and ceilings of hospital wards – if not of impervious materials – become dangerous absorbents."[28] She objected to the use of "common plaster" because of its absorbent quality,[29] and recommended "impervious material capable of receiving a polish."[30] Italian non-absorbent cement is a good choice for the warm climate, and polished oak floor saturated with beeswax would be a good choice for the English climate; however, "the means of producing a really good impervious polished surface, with little labor, have yet to be discovered."[31] Today, Nightingale's heritage can perhaps be seen in the *Guideline for Disinfection and Sterilization in Healthcare Facilities* (continuously updated) published by the Center for Disease Control and Prevention; here, through a division of critical, semi-critical, and non-critical areas (the Spaulding scheme), domestic interiors are readily understood as non-critical areas which are subject to a rigorous regime of disinfection. In Hong Kong, guidelines for infection control are prepared jointly by the Infection Control Branch of the Center for Health Protection under the Department of Health and the Hospital Authority, divided over three categories of general public, institutions and businesses, and health professionals.[32] Under this classification of degrees of disinfection, washable walls and cleanable floors, free of fissures, open joints, and crevices, continue to be understood as the standard hygienic architecture.[33]

The variety of contemporary building materials is bewildering today; the choices of impervious materials – natural and artificial – fulfilling Nightingale's criteria are countless. Industrial standards are being established on antiseptic materials with an extraordinary speed.[34] Hong Kong is deeply influenced by these developments in building material science. Over much of the twentieth century, the surfaces of Hong Kong's architecture – from its Art Centre to general public amenities – have been dominated by the use of off-white ceramic tiles, which created affordable impervious surfaces capable of receiving regular washing and wiping. Increasingly, buildings in Hong Kong make use of more refined impervious materials such as polished stone, stainless steel, plastic, and glass, expanding their building coverage at a high speed. The fast-improving technologies of cladding have made these expansions desirable and affordable.

In the indifference toward the intellectual debate on the nature of materials, roughness and ruin is more readily associated with dilapidation, aged materials with the lack of hygiene. Hong Kong's urban renewal, which has resulted in the regrettable demolition of many old buildings, was partly grounded in the argument of old buildings being unhygienic and unsafe in the city; the development pressure and high land prices perhaps also deliberately cultivated the association of the old with the unhealthy. Roughness and age in building materials have served fundamentally important intellectual purposes in the academic discourse of architecture; the Greek and Roman ruins played critical roles in different constructions of the discipline of architecture throughout history. Like whiteness, roughness suggests potentiality.[35] Roughness and age possess a capacity to indicate time (aging process of materials) and space (sitedness of materials), which underpins a broad urban environmental framework that supports much of our intellectual and cultural activities. Hong Kong's off-white shine moves away from this traditional scheme of meaning in urban environment, and seeks other methods of spatial and temporal location. Perhaps paralleling the nature of industrial processes in the context of the self-referential Beaux-Arts architecture in the nineteenth century, Hong Kong is an unintentional avant-garde city; it signals, often in visually unpretentious ways, the emerging sensibilities and aesthetic potentials in future cities in Asia. Like washing the body, wiping buildings inside and outside is becoming essential and desirable in our continuously renewed relationship with bacteria and viruses; our aesthetic sensibilities may have to internalize these critical requirements.

The ubiquitous off-white shine, represented in one way by Hong Kong's urban reality, perhaps inspired the Chinese artist Zhan Wang in his installations *Urban Landscape* (from 2003) with shiny stainless-steel cooking utensils. Zhan Wang began his artistic career with a performance piece *Clean Ruins* (1994), in which he painted some of the ruinous surfaces of traditional courtyard houses in Beijing just hours before they were demolished to make way for a shiny building constructed with investment from Hong Kong. In his *Urban Landscape*, Zhan Wang's initial protest has turned into deeper reflection; the polished stainless steel represents one of the most enduring and

Figure 8.4 Zhan Wang, *Urban Landscape*, from 2003 (Image courtesy of artist and Pekin Fine Art).

effective antiseptic materials which transformed our urban landscape. Zhan Wang commented that his installations were driven by a sensibility that is "forced on him" in Asian cities, like a never-ending storm on the senses. Similar to his shiny stainless-steel versions of the ornamental rocks in traditional Chinese gardens, the cities with off-white shine in stainless steel is "a reinterpretation of our urban life through a change of materials, a reluctant acceptance of a new fact of life imposed on us by a new material."[36] Zhan Wang's metallic shine is a tremendous challenge to architects; "reluctant acceptance" has been a constant feature in the history of architecture, and this particular version we are facing today is no exception. However, architects, unlike artists, always have a delayed reaction.

THE CITY AS INFECTION BARRIERS

Among all the varied conceptions of the city, barriers remain a constant feature. The city as barriers is a paradox: an act of creating a community enclosing ceaseless struggles for isolation; this is manifested in urban realities resulting from enemy invasions, class struggles, trade wars, and now infection control. High density produces high infection rates; this was patently obvious during the outbreak of SARS (Severe Acute Respiratory Syndrome) in 2003 in Hong Kong, where almost 300 people died from 1,755 infections within a few months, recording one of the highest mortality rates in major infected areas in the world. Unlike city walls, gated communities, and trade regulations, infection barriers in cities are taking place in line with the principles of antibiotics, fighting bacteria and viruses from within the tissues of architecture. Beyond ventilation and light, it is the environment of off-white shine that best fulfills the requirement of antisepsis, and that provides the conditions for a new urbanism of infection barriers. Whiteness and shine have their roles in traditional aesthetic and moral formulations, but the necessity for bacteria and virus control in cities is reconstituting their roles, fundamentally regulated by a determination to keep bacteria and viruses at bay.

Unlike other barriers, infection barriers have to be constantly refreshed in order to be effective; normal disinfection procedures are only effective for a few hours.[37] To establish effective infection barriers, the city has to first reform the behavior of its inhabitants. In Hong Kong, the entire urban structure is now mobilized as a behavior-reform machine; posters, audio announcements, and television broadcasts on public transportation, as well as television broadcasts at private homes orchestrate hygiene campaigns. This is reinforced by regulating behaviors at schools and extra-curriculum classes through handwashing, mask-wearing, and temperature measuring. One of the most visible rituals of disinfection takes place at meal tables where eating utensils are ritually washed in tepid tea; there is no evidence to show that lukewarm tea can be used as an effective antiseptic solution, but the deeper purpose of this ritual, like the nature of many other rituals, is to constantly reinforce a commonly shared anxiety. Constant disinfection fills interior spaces with the smell of antiseptic solutions, and the homogeneous and impervious surfaces produce a distinctly long background reverberation, which contribute crucially to the urban experience in Hong Kong. In the Chinese cultural context, silence does not have religious significance associated with the monastic life and vibrancy is understood as "hot and noisy" (renao); human noise here is regarded as a life-affirming trait of living environment.

Perhaps the deepest impact of the city as infection barriers is the consequence of what may be described as "disposable architecture." The relative disconnection between the off-white shiny surfaces and philosophical and moral discourses enables a much faster cycle of reconstruction, much like a disposable plastic table cloth. Discarding items by-passes disinfection and sterilization, and is therefore more effective as an antiseptic procedure. In Hong Kong, renovation is relatively frequent and unsentimental; this is perhaps both a consequence of linking old buildings with a lack of hygiene and safety, and a result of construction economy in materials and in details that do not anticipate long-term viability. The fast changes in Hong Kong's architecture contrast strongly with traditional conceptions of permanence of cities and architecture. "Architecture aims at Eternity" – Christopher Wren began his treatise of architecture in the seventeenth century with this often repeated statement,[38] echoing and anticipating long lists of architectural treatises assuming the essential importance of the permanence of architecture. The "disposable architecture" in Hong Kong, as well as in many other cities in Asia and China, exhibits a reality of building cities which invites speculations on some of our most deep-rooted ideas on design, construction, materials, and economy of architecture.

One of the most intriguing signs of our time is that the foyer sinks at Villa Savoy and Rufer House have already been replaced by stations of antiseptic

Figure 8.5 Self-help disinfection station at the Information Desk, Grand Central Plaza, Shatin, Hong Kong.

hand-gel dispensers throughout the entrance lobbies in Hong Kong. These dispensers in place of wash basins are invitations for us to think about twenty-first-century cities, where antisepsis, among other important transformations, demands theoretical attention; these developments seem to be no longer rooted in classical or phenomenological sensibilities. If Adolf Loos imagined bravely a new world of daily washing and a new architecture that could emerge from this freshly minted necessity through technological development, we should be encouraged to reformulate and articulate a new architecture, placing it in critical discourses grounded in these new conditions, so that appropriate intellectual space and stimulus for exploration, much like Zhan Wang had done in relation to shine with his *Urban Landscape*, can be developed. The off-white shine in Asian architecture, instead of being a ground for dismissal, should serve as a theoretical and design opportunity.

NOTES

1 Adolf Loos, "Plumbers," *Spoken into the Void*, trans. Jane O. Newman and John H. Smith (Cambridge, MA: MIT Press, 1987), p. 49.
2 Ibid., p. 45.
3 Anthony Ley, *A History of Building Control in England and Wales, 1840–1990* (Coventry: RICS Books, 2000), pp. 20–32.
4 Ruth Rogaski, *Hygienic Modernity: Meaning of Health and Disease in Treaty-Port China* (Ewing, NJ: University of California Press, 2004), p. 141.
5 On the relationship between religion and dirt, see Mary Douglas, *Purity*

and Danger, An Analysis of Concepts of Pollution and Taboo (London: Routledge, 1966/2002).

6 Nadir Lahiji and D.S. Friedman, "At the Sink, Architecture in Abjection," *Plumbing, Sounding Modern Architecture* (New York: Princeton University Press, 1997), pp. 35–60.

7 For instance, as discussed by Mohsen Mostafavi and David Leatherbarrow in *On Weathering, the Life of Buildings in Time* (Cambridge, MA: MIT Press, 1993), and in *Surface Architecture* (Cambridge, MA: MIT Press, 2005).

8 Mark Wigley likens this aspect to Xenophon's description of husbandry as a woman, "the mother and nurse of all other arts" as well as Alberti's characterization of architectural as a virtuous woman, in "Untitled: the Housing of Gender," *Sexuality and Space*, ed. Beatrice Colomina (New York: Princeton Architectural Press, 1992), p. 361.

9 Ibid., p. 360.

10 Le Corbusier, "A Coat of Whitewash, the Law of Ripolin," *The Decorative Art of Today*, trans. James I. Dunnett (Cambridge, MA: MIT Press, 1987), p. 192.

11 Ibid.

12 Ibid.

13 Ibid.

14 Mark Wigley, "Introduction," *White Walls, Designer Dresses* (Cambridge, MA: MIT Press, 1995).

15 Florence Nightingale, *Notes on Hospitals* (London: Longman, 1863), p. iii.

16 Ibid., p. 4.

17 Ibid., p. 17.

18 John D. Thompson and Grace Goldin, *The Hospital: A Social and Architectural History* (New Haven and London: Yale University Press, 1975), pp. 125–126.

19 Nightingale, op. cit., p. 19.

20 Ibid., p. 68.

21 Ibid., p. 72.

22 Ibid., p. 69.

23 Jeremy Taylor, *Hospital and Asylum Architecture in England 1840–1914* (London and New York: Mansell, 1991), p. 18.

24 Anthony Ashley Cooper, the Third Earl of Shaftesbury, *Characteristicks of Men, Manners, Opinions, Times* (London, 1714).

25 Le Corbusier, op. cit., p. 4.

26 Roy Porter, *The Greatest Benefit to Mankind, A Medical History of Humanity from Antiquity to the Present* (London: HarperCollins, 1997), p. 442.

27 Ibid., pp. 443–444.

28 Nightingale, op. cit., p. 44.

29 Ibid., p. 45.

30 Ibid., p. 68.

31 Ibid., p. 70.

32 I am grateful to Professors Jean Hee Kim and Kristal Lee of the School of Public Health, the Chinese University of Hong Kong, for sharing their knowledge of public hygiene practices in Asian cultures and for guiding me through the extraordinary maze of infection-control guidelines in Hong Kong.

33 The American Institute of Architects Academy, *Guidelines for Design and Construction of Hospital and Health Care Facilities* (Washington, DC: The American Institute of Architects Press, 1998), p. 46.

34 For instance, the Japanese Industrial Standard JIS Z 2801:2000 measures the antibacterial activity in hydrophobic materials, which has influenced

the formation of a draft ISO standard, and a host of industrial standards of building materials in other countries. This includes those relating to antiseptic plastic and glass coatings specified by the Building Material Industry Standard of China currently being established.

35 David Leatherbarrow, *Architecture Orientated Otherwise* (New York: Princeton Architectural Press, 2009).

36 Zhan Wang, www.zhanwangart.com/news/work_cn/2007/11/07_11_6_ 3A9BC.shtml, accessed 24 July 2009. My translation.

37 Center for Disease Control and Prevention, *Guideline for Disinfection and Sterilization in Healthcare Facilities* (2008), pp. 29–30.

38 Christopher Wren, "Tract I," collected in *Parentalia* (London, 1750), p. 351.

9 BEYOND URBANISM
Mumbai and the cultivation of an eye

ANURADHA MATHUR AND
DILIP DA CUNHA

THE EYE OF URBANISM

Urbanism refers to the culture of cities, a way of life, an environment, an economy from points of view based in various disciplines or schools of thought. It has gathered a field in academia over the last few decades. But even as it has pulled together a field it has splintered into a growing number of urbanisms, a reference not to a multiplicity of cultures as much as to an assortment of advocacies. Each urbanism – new urbanism, landscape urbanism, ecological urbanism, emergent urbanism, transurbanism, tacit urbanism, etc. – carries a formational and transformational agenda built into its lens. With cities becoming settlements of choice by the majority of the world's population and increasingly fashioning their own relations with one another, urbanism and urbanisms are assuming center stage in academia and design practices.

However, well before the academic, professional, and popular imaginations were overrun by cities, urbanism had the world in its grip, promoting not just a choice settlement but an eye. This eye is unique in that it distinguishes things in geographic space, beginning with the singling out of the city itself. It separates before it relates, distinguishes before it unites or divides. It creates a world of articulated things, i.e., things that are not only drawn out visually from the messy stuff of a material world but can also be drawn on paper, in maps, sketches, or paintings. Ultimately this eye distinguishes the articulated from the amorphous; the city where it is most at home and the wildness which it reaches out to articulate. The colonizing work of this eye is described well by Rudyard Kipling in *Kim*. Being groomed to be a pioneering surveyor in hostile territory, to surreptitiously "Go across those hills and see what lies beyond," Kim is told by Colonel Creighton: "Thou must learn how to make pictures of roads and mountains and rivers – to carry these pictures in thy eye till suitable time comes to set them upon paper."[1] What Kim does in Kipling's work of fiction across the Himalayan ranges in the late 1800s for the Survey of India, the British Empire, and the discipline of geography, had been done across the Indian subcontinent through the eighteenth and nineteenth centuries by men educated to see with the eye of urbanism. Indeed the three tasks of this eye – picturing, carrying, and setting down on paper – were repeated in ordinary and extraordinary ways across the world by pioneers of the European Enlightenment whom Barbara Stafford calls scientific explorer-artist-writers (with people like Kim at their service). These pioneers, she writes, had a "profound conviction ... that something really is out there and that art and language were to be used to get beyond imitation – that is, beyond a hallowed art and language – in order to grapple with real things."[2] The "real things" – the roads, mountains, rivers, but also plants, animals, minerals, people, settlements, and other "visually extractable" entities – that they articulated would become the material ground for empirical science, professional disciplines, and progressive governance. Much attention has been paid to the use, value, and meaning of these "things" and to the schemes by which they have been ordered, understood, and, to some, exploited; but the extractions of these things set on paper remain the largely unquestioned vocabulary of place. Importantly, these extractions communicate in ways that allow others to picture places without being there.

Such is the power of the eye of urbanism. It had colonized much of the globe well before urbanization reached levels that are giving policy-makers in developing countries and academics across the world so much anxiety and opportunity today; and well before the city sprawled into surroundings that had been articulated to receive it and technologies made it possible for urbanites to be suburban and exurban. In fact, the eye of urbanism is so pervasive (and powerful) that to question it seems absurd, calling for a question rather than an answer in response: how else can it be?

Over the past decade, on the Lower Mississippi, New York, Philadelphia, Bangalore, and, most recently, Mumbai we have asked what it is for design to begin by questioning the eye of urbanism and the separations that it perpetuates such as between city and river, land and sea, formal and informal, infrastructure and landscape, and what it takes to posit not just a different view but another eye. It calls, we believe, for a design activism that works as much through public exhibition as it does through strategic projects. In Mumbai we come closer than we have at any time before to the ultimate propaganda tool of the eye of urbanism, the "Cities and Town Planning Exhibition" of the early 1900s. It was brought to India as an instrument of education and visualization by Sir Patrick Geddes, widely known as the father of modern city planning, to promote the City as a "real thing" and the land-uses of surveyors and geographers as "real things" that made cities. Some 90 years, many promises, and numerous disasters after it was shown in Mumbai, we suggest that it is time for a new exhibition, one that challenges the eye of urbanism and opens the possibility of an eye more accommodating of the fluid and ambiguous world of the estuary in which Mumbai is situated.

SETTING DOWN BOMBAY

Bombay was a pioneer of the eye of urbanism in India. In 1995 the name was officially changed to Mumbai which is argued to be its indigenous name. However, the image on the drawing board and in the imagination of most planners, designers, administrators, and the fraction of the public cultivated, like Kim, to see with the eye of urbanism, continues to be peculiarly Bombay.

Bombay was set down on paper not merely as an English settlement when Charles II acquired it from the Portuguese in 1665, but as an island separated from the wildness of, on the one hand, a little-known subcontinent and, on the other, an open sea traversed by fierce trading competitors. The early "situation of Bombay," writes Patrick Cadell, was "an island surrounded by powerful enemies, actual or potential, and with no territorial possessions outside its own limits."[3] The more immediate wildness at the time, though, was the sea itself or rather the flux of an estuary that brought together the sea, multiple fresh-water run-offs, and the southwest monsoon in complex and often unpredictable ways. This flux, which is the west coast of India, made significant room for wishful sightings of what constituted the "Island of Bombay in the East Indies" when it was granted to the English as part of the 1661 treaty between Kings Charles II and John IV "with all the rights, profits, territories and appurtenances whatsoever thereunto belonging." It further complicated a transfer already made difficult by reluctance, tragedy, suspicion, and misgivings. The Portuguese Viceroy based in Goa, Antonio de Mello de Castro, complained to his king that Sir Humphrey Cooke, to whom he had been ordered to hand over Bombay in 1665, had grabbed more than Bombay:

> The first act of Mr. Humphrey Cooke ... was to take possession of the island of Mahim in spite of my protests, the island being some distance from the island of Bombay, as your Majesty will see from the map I send herewith. He argues that at low tide one can walk from one end to the other, and if this is conceded your Majesty will be unable to defend the right of the other northern islands, as at low tide it is possible to go from Bombay to Salsette, from Salsette to Varagao.[4]

But Cooke appeared to experience another landscape:

> They would have Maim and Bombaim to bee two severall islands, but cannot well make out. I never tooke boate to pass our men when I tooke the possession of it, and at all times you may goe from one place to the other dryshod.[5]

In the century that followed, Bombay was made extractable without dispute. The grounds which Cooke crossed "dryshod" and de Mello de Castro believed was the sea were filled beyond doubt by basalt rock and soil of hills that were leveled. And a place that John Fryer, a visitor in the 1670s, described as "Spots of Ground, still disputable to which side to incline: For at Low Water most of them are fordable to the Main, or from one to the other; and at Spring-Tides again a great part of them overflowed"[6] was made what John Maclean in the 1870s would describe as "a precious stone set in the silver sea."[7] Such clarity served men like Creighton and Kim. It eased the task of picturing, carrying, and setting down Bombay with certainty and little doubt on the drawing board.

The eye of urbanism, however, did not stop at making an island in an estuary; it was deployed across Bombay, singling out not just visually extractable things but things which like Fryer's disputable ground carried the possibility of being made clear and distinct in the future – buildings, open spaces, streets, rivers, fields, groves, native towns, etc. Here, the *pucca* (cooked, "finished," firm, perennially inclined) was more easily drawn out than the *kuccha*

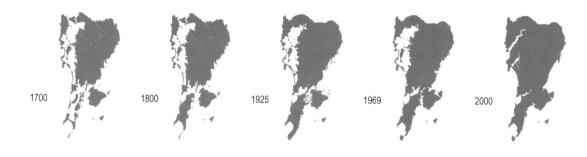

1700   1800   1925   1969   2000

Figure 9.1 Island of Bombay. The making of an "island" owes as much to an eye reinforced by measures of geographic space as to land reclamation schemes, which besides claiming land from the sea, also sought to remove any ambiguity in the meeting ground of land and sea.

(raw, in-process, soft, seasonally inclined); the garden, which derives its meaning from enclosure that is different from its surroundings, was more readily set down than the *maidan*, a non-descript dusty plain that not only accommodates a vast range of temporal activities but also leaks through appropriations; the market, with little doubt surrounding its objective of commerce, was more acceptable than the bazaar where transactions extended momentarily, invisibly, and beyond the realm of exchange; the definitive edge of land-reclamation schemes and rocky outcrops was more appreciated than the saline and muddy mangrove gradient where ground is constantly made and remade between land and sea; the river as a flow from source to destination between two lines was articulated with more ease than a surface of overflowing terraces, fields, and tanks that received a monsoon that fell everywhere and not just between lines; land which placed water and uncertainty beyond its edge was more readily appreciated than the fluid terrain of an estuary where a sea meets land across an ambiguous, temporal, and mysterious depth that reaches from monsoon clouds above through the labyrinthine world of tidal creeks and backwaters, to the web of aquifers beneath.

The separations made by the eye of urbanism and the clear and distinct things that it presumed possible were not necessarily considered or perhaps even seen by ordinary people. But drawn in maps, worked into administrative schemes and educational agendas, and made part of everyday conversation, they provided the language of governance that set the island on track to becoming the Island City. Here the *kuccha* held the possibility of being made *pucca*, the *maidan* promised a park, the bazaar a market, overflows could be channeled into drains and mangrove swamps were "badlands" to be replaced with a definite edge between land and sea. This is Bombay that was created as much by the visualizing demands of a cultivated eye as by the heroic efforts of land reclamation, harbor building, water-supply schemes, and other grand projects that have realized the determination of one of Bombay's early Governors, Gerald Aungier, in the late 1600s that Bombay is "a city which by God's assistance is intended to be built."

BOMBAY: A CITY IN HISTORY

Many instruments were and still are used to enforce the eye of urbanism in India. They include *maps*, which with a view from above are powerful articulations of separations such as between land and sea, building and landscape, thoroughfare and property, *government gazetteers* that inform administrators and the public on the "real things" of their place, and *textbooks* that formulate things and form the imagination. A lesser-known instrument is the *civic exhibition*. It came with Patrick Geddes who was a resident of Mumbai in the late 1910s and early 1920s and was for a time Professor of Sociology and Civics at the University of Bombay. It was part of his effort to take city improvement, which had become a primary concern at the time in India, beyond "betterment of the present" to "planning the future." Indeed he was responsible for making master planning of cities in India (and elsewhere) a critical task of local governance, particularly its demands for "diagnostic survey" and "conservative surgery."

Through the civic exhibition Geddes sought to instill in people an expectation, involvement, and way of seeing their place as a prelude to planned solutions implemented by government. To this end he traveled through a number of settlements across India with an exhibition of maps, plans, photographs, views, and other representations of what began in London in 1911 as the "Cities and Town Planning Exhibition."[8] It revealed the problems and potentials of the places that it traveled to by situating them in a history of the "City," a settlement that aspired to a universal civilization with roots, as he saw it, in Athens, Rome, and Jerusalem because the heritage of these cities "underlies all subsequent civilization, up to that of to-day, and necessarily also that of to-morrow."[9] From this root the visitor was taken through the medieval, renaissance, and industrial cities of Europe before culminating in the "garden city" that had taken root in Europe as the "city of the future," a city that grew in a planned manner, and was organized by "land-uses" which compartmentalized the terrain (and urban life) with clarity and certainty into residential, commercial, recreational, industrial, drainage, transportation, open space, or any deliberate "mix" of two or more of them. Geddes always intended, though it did not happen in Bombay, to devote a part of the exhibition to a local survey. These "smaller local surveys required the presence of the larger general section [of the exhibition], as it provided information on the general development of cities and their solutions."[10] The civic exhibition informed people about their own place in the context of the City-in-history.

Geddes's exhibition was not instrumental in bringing the eye of urbanism to India; but it displayed the projective nature of this eye, the possibility and promise of the City that its act of separation offered places. Bombay here was not necessarily a city; but it could be made one through planning.

MUMBAI: A PLACE IN AN ESTUARY

Some 60 years after independence from British rule, Mumbai, a name widely assumed to refer to the same place as Bombay, refuses to conform to the aspirations of the City held out by Geddes's exhibition. The *kuccha* infiltrates, grows and overwhelms as do the many uncertainties and ambiguities that administrators through the twentieth century have sought to remove through city plans and projects that promise the garden-city objectives of containment, land-use clarity, and orderly growth. Indeed the twenty-first century began with Mumbai singled out as a prime contributor to the "slumming of the planet."[11] But there is another emergent condition attracting as much attention as the *kuccha* today: the diffusion of the city facilitated as much by technologies as by diasporas and networks which operate in a haze of under-world and above-board, private and public realms, local and global worlds. Melvin Webber in the 1960s saw such "communities without propinquity" as making the "non-place urban realm."[12] Others in more recent times describe it as an "urban field, a collation of activities instead of a material structure," a "space of flows," and a "transnational attenuation of local space."[13] Here, Mumbai is a city too complex, dispersed and, perhaps, all-consuming to extract. "'The' city no longer exists," writes Rem Koolhaas, "What if we simply ... redefine our relationship with the city not as its makers but as its mere subjects, as its supporters? More than ever, the city is all we have."[14] Others like Saskia Sassen are still open to refining "cityness," a notion that allows "far greater variations in what constitutes urbanity" and "forms that ... are almost illegible to the foreigner."[15] Mumbai, it appears, is not any different from Fryer's "spots of ground" in the 1600s that allowed numerous wishful sightings of a Bombay of varying shapes until English administrators pictured, carried, and set down Bombay Island firmly on paper.[16]

Mumbai has a choice. It can continue on the path of the eye of urbanism which placed Bombay Island on a map and continues to believe in the act of separation, or it can accept its place in the fluid terrain of an estuary and forge another path not preoccupied with island and islandness, city and city-ness.

The fluid terrain of an estuary was brought momentarily into view with the events of July 26, 2005, which made headlines a month before Hurricane Katrina devastated New Orleans. Most people were too overwhelmed by tragedy to see it. They rather saw a "flood" devastating the "city," claiming hundreds of lives and damaging much property. They saw drains that did not perform, a ground that was saturated or too impervious, a sea that was too high, a rainfall of 944 mm in a day that probability analysis suggests occurs only once in a century. Efforts are underway to construct deeper, wider, and firmer drains (although for far lesser, more "probabilistic" amounts of rain), flood walls to keep out the sea, pumping stations to get rid of excess monsoon waters. But beyond the flood, the events of July 26, 2005 can also be seen as a momentary sighting of the aqueous terrain that John Fryer described in the 1600s, a sight that occurs each monsoon season, though not at the same magnitude. It calls into question the firm line of the island's edge but also by logical and analogical extension, the edges of so many enforced "land uses" that are gross simplifications of a surface that extends into an intricate tempo-ral and material depth. If Bombay took the route of the map (the view from above), the plan, and the master plan, Mumbai demands the section, the gra-dient, and a design approach that works not by probabilities, control or end-scenarios as master plans do but by possibilities, resilience, and initiations, i.e., seed-projects that evolve by a visual, political, and technological fluidity and agility that befits the temporality, uncertainty, and complexity of a terrain between land and sea.

This is a task not merely of design but design activism directed to taking charge of how and what place is seen and lived when we say Mumbai. This is the aspiration of SOAK, an exhibition that contests the inherited islandness of

Figure 9.2 Sections of Mumbai. Sections reduce the significance of boundaries and edges in the landscape, positing gradients, rhythms, and horizons which one approaches but never crosses.

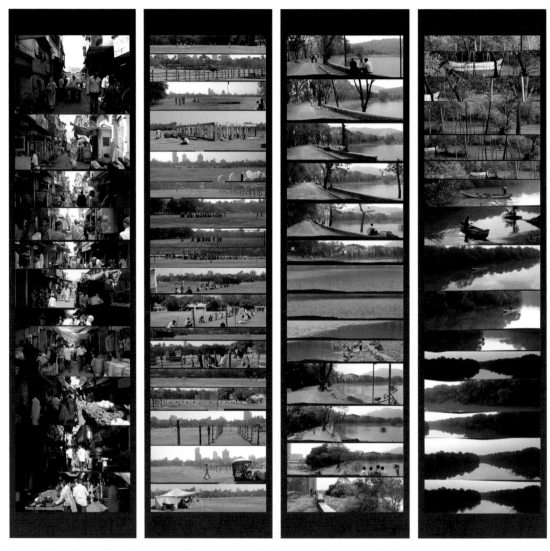

Figure 9.3 Landscapes of an Estuary. Just as the drawing out of an island with a line between land and sea was the forerunner of an eye that reached out to make islands of fields, buildings, roads, rivers, and other objects of a land surface, a gradient accommodates landscapes such as the bazaar, maidan, talao, and mangrove swamp that are flexible and elastic in time, demanding to be seen in movement, in depth and through the practices by which they are operated. Their openness accommodates uncertainty and multiple possibilities that are difficult to situate on a map.

Bombay that pervades the imagination. It seeks to cultivate a visualization of Mumbai and with it practices that accommodate gradients and rhythms rather than locate edges and boundaries; that elude visual clarity while exercising the tenacity and negotiating sensibility of the estuary; that bring together actors and agents in a terrain, not through property rights and land-uses, but through materials and adjacencies in time more than space; that acknowledge the sea not as a threat but as a challenge in a time when it is gaining a presence across the world. It presents a Mumbai that is not the entity that planners struggle to contain and social scientists work to comprehend, but rather a field of initiations. It makes the case that Mumbai in an estuary changes the script of the past as it does the future.

Figure 9.4 (continued from p. 146) SOAK: Mumbai in an Estuary. SOAK is a public exhibition that opened at the National Gallery of Modern Art in Mumbai at the start of the 2009 monsoon. It takes the events of July 26, 2005 – popularly called the 2005 Flood – as an opportunity to call attention to the limitations of a landscape created as much by a cultivated eye driven to draw lines of separation as by infrastructural efforts of land reclamation, harbour-building, and other grand projects for which Mumbai is known. It explores the role played by maps in dividing land from sea, Mumbai from the monsoon, and in relegating the many landscapes of the estuary to the "informal". It presents a new visualization of Mumbai's terrain, one that is open to its aqueous nature, encouraging interventions that work with the gradient of an estuary and accommodate uncertainty through resilience, not overcome it with prediction.

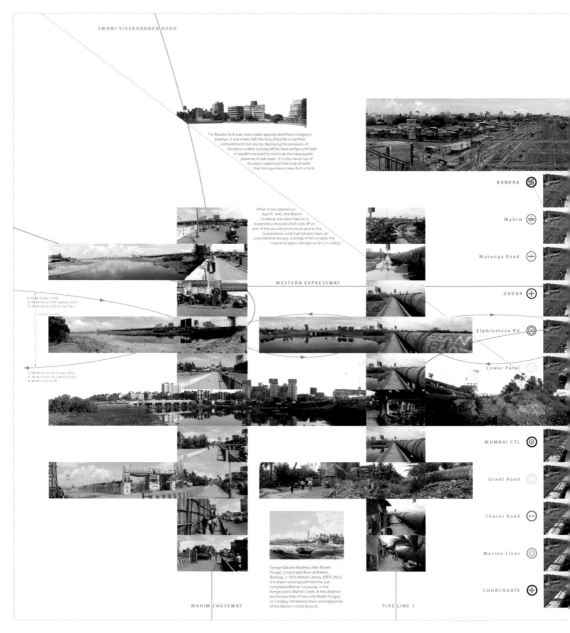

Figure 9.5

Figures 9.5–9.7 Mahim Crossing Project. SOAK presents 12 projects for an estuary. They demonstrate the possibilities of a new visualization. Each project comprises seeds that unfold in more than one way, extending opportunistically with agility and tenacity befitting an estuary *in* the monsoon. Each gathers moments, rhythms and adjacencies of a terrain and proposes multiple initiations that work through naming strategic and tactical operators, sectioning ground, and notating material and temporal practices that work on a gradient. These projects solve the problem of flood not by flood-control measures but by making a place that is absorbent and resilient.

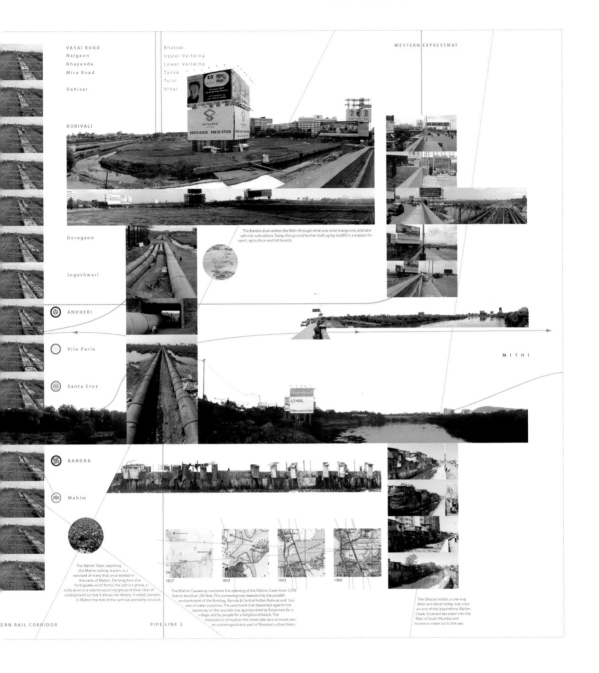

VASAI ROAD
Nalgaon
Bhayanda
Mira Road

Dahisar

BORIVALI

Bhatsai
Upper Vaitarna
Lower Vaitarna
Tansa
Tulsi
Vihar

WESTERN EXPRESSWAY

Goregaon

Jogeshwari

ANDHERI

Vile Parle

Santa Cruz

MITHI

BANDRA

Mahim

The Bandra drain enters the Mithi through what was once mangroves and later salt-rice cultivations. Today this ground further built up by landfill is a maidan for sport, agriculture and bill boards.

The Mahim Talao, adjoining the Mahim railway station, is a remnant of many that once existed in the oarts of Mahim. Deriving from the Portuguese word 'horta,' the oart is a grove, a cultivation or a natural occurring group of trees clear of undergrowth so that it allows the distant, if veiled, horizon. In Mahim the tree of the oart was primarily coconut.

1827   1855   1933   1960

The Mahim Causeway narrowed the opening of the Mahim Creek from 3,558 feet to less than 200 feet. The narrowing was repeated by the parallel embankment of the Bombay, Baroda & Central Indian Railway and two sets of water pipelines. The sand bank that deposited against the causeway on the sea side was appropriated by fishermen for a village and by people for a fairground/beach. The depositions of mud on the creek side have evolved into an undistinguishable part of Mumbai's urban fabric.

The Dharavi nullah, a one-way drain and sewer today, was once an arm of the labyrinthine Mahim Creek. It carried sea water into the 'flats' of South Mumbai and monsoon water out to the sea.

RN RAIL CORRIDOR   PIPE LINE 2

149

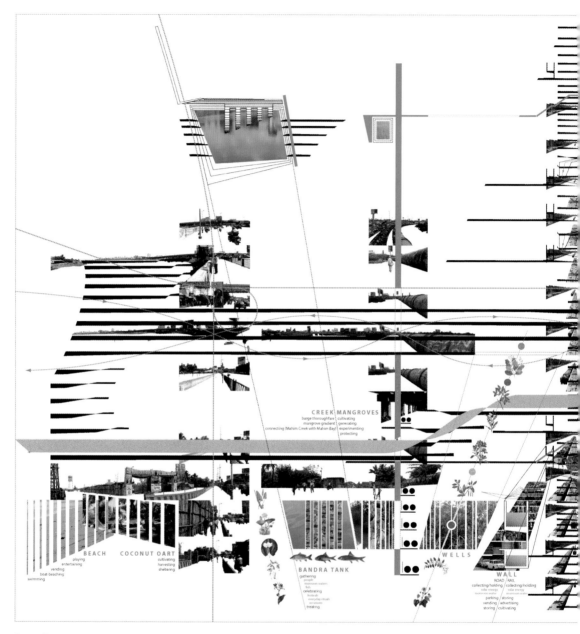

Figure 9.6

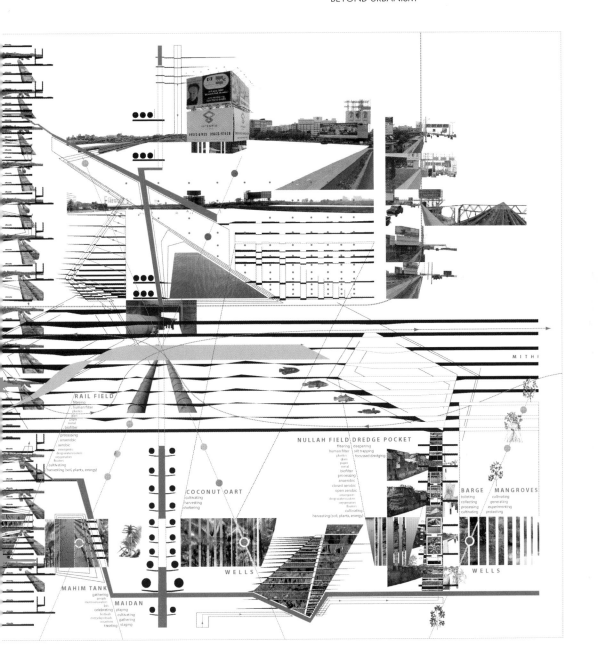

RAIL FIELD
filtering
human filter
plant
paper
metal
biofilter

processing
anaerobic
aerobic
emergents
deep water routers
oxygenation
floaters
cultivating
harvesting (soil, plants, energy)

MITHI

NULLAH FIELD DREDGE POCKET
filtering   deepening
human filter   silt trapping
plankton   focussed dredging
glass
paper
metal
biofilter
processing
anaerobic
closed aerobic
open aerobic
emergents
deep water routers
oxygenation
floaters
cultivating
harvesting (soil, plants, energy)

BARGE   MANGROVES
toileting   cultivating
collecting   generating
processing   experimenting
cultivating   protecting

COCONUT OART
cultivating
harvesting
sheltering

WELLS

WELLS

MAHIM TANK
gathering
people
monsoon water
fish
celebrating
festivals
everyday rituals
occasions
treating

MAIDAN
playing
cultivating
gathering
staging

151

Figure 9.7

NOTES

1 Rudyard Kipling, *Kim* (New York: Charles Scribner's Sons, 1902), 193.
2 Barbara Stafford, *Voyage into Substance: Art, Science, Nature and the Illustrated Travel Account, 1760–1840* (Cambridge, MA: MIT Press, 1984).
3 Sir Patrick Cadell, *History of the Bombay Army* (London: Longmans, Green and Co., 1938), 16.
4 F.C. Danvers, *Report to the Secretary of State for India in Council on the Portuguese Records relating to the East Indies* (London: India Office, 1892), 67–68.
5 William Foster, *The English Factories in India 1665–1667* (Oxford: Clarendon Press, 1925), 65.
6 John Fryer, *A New Account of East India and Persia Being Nine Years' Travels, 1672–1681*, vol. 1 (London: Hakluyt Society, 1909), 160.
7 J.M. Maclean, *Guide to Bombay, Historical, Statistical, and Descriptive* (Bombay: Bombay Gazette Steam Press, 1876), 304.
8 Jaqueline Tyrwitt (ed.), *Patrick Geddes in India* (London: Lund Humphries, 1947); Helen Meller, *Patrick Geddes: Social Evolutionist and City Planner* (London: Routledge, 1990).
9 Patrick Geddes and Frank C. Mears quoted in Volker M. Welter, *Biopolis* (Cambridge, MA: MIT Press, 2002), 100.
10 Volker M. Welter, *Biopolis* (Cambridge, MA: MIT Press, 2002), 125.
11 See, for example, Mike Davis, *Planet of Slums* (New York: Verso, 2006).
12 Melvin M. Webber, "Urban Place and the Non-place Urban Realm," *Explorations into Urban Structure*, eds. Melvin Webber et al. (Philadelphia: University of Pennsylvania Press, 1964).
13 Arjen Mulder, "TransUrbanism," *TransUrbanism*, ed. Arjen Mulder (Rotterdam: V2 Publishing, 2002); Manuel Castells, "Space of Flows, Space of Places: Materials for a Theory of Urbanism in the Information Age," *The Cybercities Reader*, ed. Stephen Graham (New York: Routledge, 2004); Homi Bhabha, *The Location of Culture* (London: Routledge, 1994).
14 Rem Koolhaas, "What Ever Happened to Urbanism?" *S,M,L,XL* (New York: Monacelli Press, 1995).
15 Saskia Sassen, "Seeing like a City," *The Endless City*, eds. Ricky Burdett and Deyan Sudjic (London: Phaidon Press, 2007), 276.
16 "Each of the surviving seventeenth-century maps," writes Gillian Tindall in *City of Gold: A Biography of Bombay* (London: Temple Smith, 1982), 25, "demarks the islands in a slightly different way, almost as if, like Prospero's Isle, they had been insubstantial, assuming different forms for different visitors."

10 RESURRECTING CITIES

Instant urban planning – real-time urbanization and planners' new role in emergency situations

IGNASI PÉREZ ARNAL, TRANSLATED BY
OSCAR YANEZ DEL MAZO

HOW CAN URBAN PLANNERS PLAY A MORE EFFECTIVE ROLE IN TACKLING REGIONAL PROBLEMS? BY PROVIDING SOLUTIONS

The role of the new generation of urban planners is to tackle the pathological outcomes of the heroic architecture of the past. Urban planners have histori- cally been agents of colonialism. Once didactic, they will now have to be reformists in the twenty-first century. This means being more sustainability- oriented, more cooperative and more responsible. In a planet full of chaos, the architect/urban planner/designer has to play the role of the peace-maker in the social and political framework in which they play a central role. Climate change, natural catastrophes, and continual disasters that are, for the most part, provoked by the actions of humankind, open new spaces between know- ledge and creative capacity, and between responsibility and social effective- ness. Emergency projects may well be the best platform for the realization of this new role. With the experience of recent years, we can consider Google Earth and some of its applications to be essential tools when rapid planning has to be projected, produced, and executed.

The future will generate a need for the creation of new professional direc- tions on every continent. This need will be amplified in light of differences between the Northern and Southern hemispheres. In many ways, it will support arguments for the continuing existence of "urban planning" in a time when civilized society agrees to leave urban processes to market forces and to urgent private needs. Resurrecting a city and its territories after its destruction by a catastrophe or accident has to be "the plan" of any urban planner. It is to be the proof that there remains any sense to urban planning.

After a catastrophe, we need to identify the affected area, its coordinates and the places that suffered most in order to imagine how the area might be developed through an urban project. We also need to look at all the environ- mental indicators so as to guarantee the sustainability of intervention.

TIME AND URGENT PRODUCTION: KEY FACTORS FOR A NEW "DIGITAL" URBAN PLANNING

Digitally designed settlements for tens of thousands of homeless people in Gulu (Uganda), Arequipa (Perú), Mostar (Bosnia-Herzegovina), Ambae (Vanuatu Islands), New Orleans (USA), and Trincomalee in Sri Lanka have been the first cases developed with responsive, sensitive, light, economical, and sustainable processes and materials. They constitute five sites in five continents that perfectly illustrate the new functionality of global software. Or software that works globally. Following these projects, works in five new

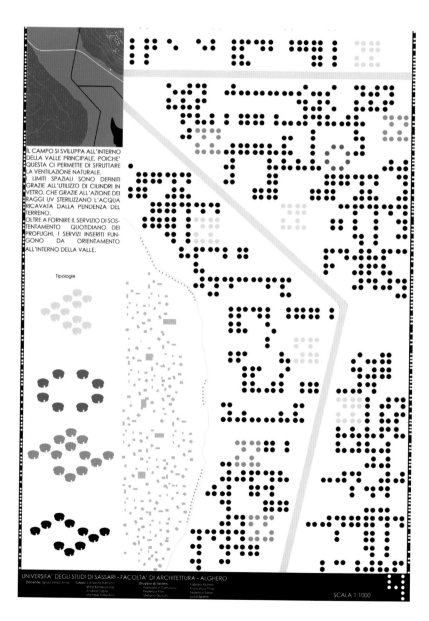

Figure 10.1 Detected patterns in small towns in Google Earth brought to give the solution of drought in Uganda into the main city, Gulu. By Google Earth, forced migration to gain access to water in Lake Victoria confirmed the proper planning realized (Carrucciu, F., Fois, F., Govoni, S., Muroni, F., Piras, F., Sasso, F., and Spano, L., Facoltà di Architettura di Alghero, Italy, 2007).

areas – Port-au-Prince in Haiti, Pakistan, Naples in Italy, Mar del Plata in Argentina, and RDC-Democratic Republic of Congo – were used to reconfirm the useful information this global software can provide and generate while introducing new parameters, like the Human Development Index, or specific climate data such as historical tendencies in wind and snow patterns.

It is interesting to consider what happens when there is no time to work with. This is a scenario that immediately appears in an emergency situation after a disaster or catastrophe occurs. It is in this precise moment that the tools of information have to work from a distance, in fact remotely from spaces that are completely removed from the actual site. Of course, these

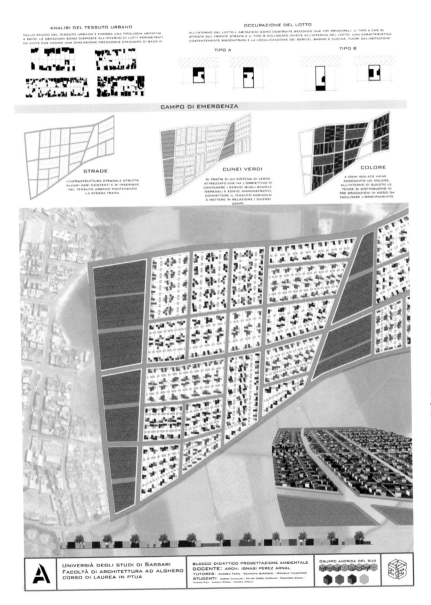

Figure 10.2 To limit the area affected by an earthquake is the first task of relief work after a seismic catastrophe. Arequipa (Perú) is one of the most active telluric areas in the world and year after year it suffers some event. The settlement was planned so that no one house could affect the next one in order to provide more security and long-life structures (Cavallini, C., Cossu, D., Ganau, F., Piga, M., Porcu, A., and Zirolia, A., Facoltà di Architettura di Alghero, Italy, 2007).

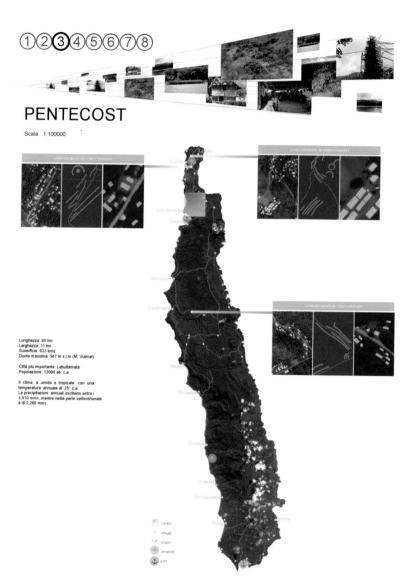

Figure 10.3 Combining Google Earth information with wind-increase analysis created an unexpected urban project. To prevent the wiping out of Ambae in Vanuatu (Pacific), the plan had to be made in Pentecost Island because any other solution would have brought death to the population while being transported to the nearest island because of wind and polluted air direction after the volcano explosion (Carboni, I., Cossu, B., M. Delazari, D. Meloni, F., Orrú, V., Piras, E., and Spanu, L., Facoltà di Architettura di Alghero, Italy, 2007).

technologies offer huge advantages in sites which are difficult to access, that lack resources or are cut off from transport as a result of the disaster itself.

These different case studies describe diverse needs where Google Earth, for example, satisfies the necessity to implement new tools.

GOOGLE EARTH AND URBAN PLANNING EDUCATION

Before entering into analysis of how solving the problems of post-catastrophic situations underlie such software programs, there emerge other difficult issues within our community. Namely the exponential increase of the use of Google throughout degree studies and the resulting frustration of educators not yet

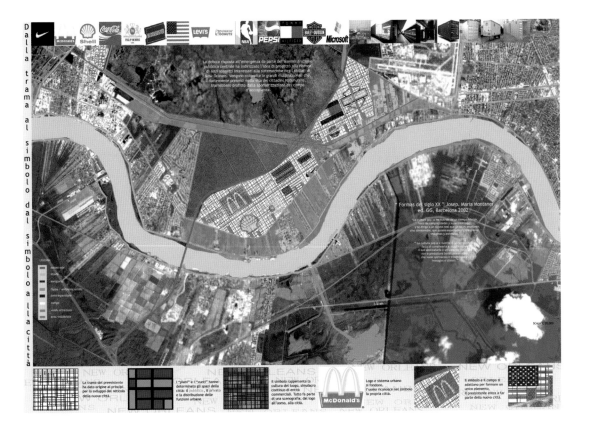

Figure 10.4 The approach to floods in New Orleans was solved with the cooperation of global brands. Global problems in advanced societies had to be made with global solutions ... (Cicolecchia, M., Destefanis, M., Frascaro, F., Mela, M., Pileri, F., Pileri, G., and Virdis, S.).

adapted to the inclusion of new technologies in education. It is true that academic rigor and fear for the academic spirit lie behind questions arising from the use of Google, such as the choice of terminology used in any given search. However, there are many educators who still do not accept web citations, or definitions that do not appear in printed dictionaries. *Wikipedia* is nevertheless superseding encyclopedias and dictionaries for the simple reason that these cannot be updated daily nor are they equipped with such ample groups of reviewers at any one time. In fact when I attempted to submit my final degree project in 1992 at the Barcelona School of Architecture, there appeared a ban on the submission of projects executed "by" the computer.

We have since moved on from such assessments. Even so, we are neither examining the scope of information technology, given its continual supply, nor allowing a moment to reflect on what it means. Without being nostalgic for attitudes like that of Oscar Niemeyer, whose texts were handwritten, we should consider the growing loss of "the hand" when using any design or layout software. If creative processes (literature, music, architecture, and of course urban planning) on the one hand incorporate new techniques and on the other reflect on what these techniques provide or no longer provide, we need to contrast what we have explored so far with the latter. Practice has always served to consolidate useful criteria. From now on, it must be used to integrate these criteria with urban works.

The use of Google Earth can also impart error. Our most recent work with the Department of Sustainability (Barcelona School of Architecture, International University of Catalunya) during the 2008–2009 academic year involved a sustainability project with the town of M'Hamid in Morocco. When entered as a search, M'Hamid appeared as one would expect, or as what Google Earth understood by that name. As it turned out, the inhabited area is referred to by this name but its correct name is actually M'Hamid El Ghizlane and it lies 2 km south of M'Hamid. The result was that part of the investigation team worked for months on a site that according to Google Earth was there but actually wasn't – something nobody could have anticipated nor confirmed.

THE NEW PRINCIPLES OF URBANISM (DIGITAL)

We might agree that, apart from the consolidation of the hypertextual infrastructure that is the Internet, we have contributed to the birth of the hypertext society. A society in need of security, citizenship, and rule of law will continue pushing for urban planning as an assurance of vigilance, not of the city but of its citizens. The kind of intense drama that brutally dissolved European society during the nineteenth and twentieth centuries is occurring on other continents, leaving them on the outer edge of globalization and in sinking famine, war, and the diseases of the twenty-first century. Will real-time tools be capable of offering solutions to these problems?

CITY TIES: ONCE ABOUT PEOPLE, NOW ABOUT RELATIONSHIPS

Cities are no longer made up of people who are united by firm ties, laws, and regulations. If previously "people spent their lives alongside their own people," as Francois Ascher explained in a lecture delivered at the Metapolis Festival in Barcelona in 1993, today people are neighbors because of their geographic location rather than out of kinship. Ties that are flimsy in their traditional urban form (of the city) become very potent in their social character as new cities emerge from disaster and these relationships become the backbone of those who suffered common events.

These events are no longer predictable and form an unforeseeable future. They cannot be planned for. If urban systems were once based on the possibility of reducing spatial uncertainties even within the realm of industrial production, we now use the city as a formal expression of a territory of the "new economy" – that system based on new information and communication technologies, activity based on Internet use and the exchange of knowledge, information, and processes. If the city was once the expression of its industrial production (ships with smoking chimneys, iron thoroughfares through which trains connect with the exterior, roads, etc.) and therefore its "material" production, they should now be an expression of the integration of information and communication technologies (IT) and therefore their digital (immaterial) production.

If cities were once planned by and for industrial production via paper-based design with strict regulations on its streets, public spaces, and utilities,

Table 10.1 The dynamics of the relationship between globalization and context within the third modern and meta-modern urban revolution dealing with long-term urban planning or urban planning post-catastrophe and emergency

	Stable	*Emergency*
Social ties	Inherited	Determined
Economic ties	Generated	Destroyed
General conditions	Beneficial and productive	Security-focused
Urban characteristics	Identifiable	Unknown
Emerging paradigms	Politics of the urban (banal)	Disrupted systems (skeptical and uncertain)
Project development	Long term	Reactive
Urban culture	Stable	Transient
Urban patterns	Nuclear-productive (centralized)	Hybrid-mesh (rhizomatic)
Planning bodies	Local (with resources)	International (without resources)

they should now be planned via the Internet as the dynamic of cognitive capitalism bases its projections on the variables of time, mobility, and the displacement of people, goods, and overall information. If the Internet functions as a supporting mechanism to this economy, shouldn't it do the same for developing cities?

DELIBERATING ON URBAN INFORMATION

Is it better or worse to access all urban information via Google? Will cities that have been planned with digital systems of global visualization be better or worse? If urban populations quickly grew from 220 million to 2.8 billion during the twentieth century, the design of the future will have to contend with unprecedented urban growth. This growth will be most notable in Africa and Asia where the population will have doubled between 2000 and 2030. That is to say that the urban growth of those regions, accumulated throughout the respective histories will double within one generation. Urbanization – the increase of the urban populace as a proportion of the total population – is inevitable but it can be turned into a positive. No country in the industrial age has successfully achieved economic growth in the absence of urbanization. Cities are a concentration of poverty but they also represent the best means of escaping it.

One aspect of modern civilization is that cities cause harmful effects on the environment. Nevertheless, the experts and those charged with formulating policy are ever more conscious of the value of the city's potential for long-term sustainability. Jose Miguel Iribas, a Spanish sociologist who specializes in rural and urban studies, offers a perfect explanation when he defines urban tourist centers as hotspots of negative environmental impact, but defends the city as a place for growth, even in regard to the environment. If cities are generating problems for the environment they also hold solutions. Will the potential benefits of global urbanization be able to adequately compensate for its drawbacks? Jaime Lerner, among others, thinks that the city is not the problem but rather the solution. It is something that a multitude of professionals who are familiar with global statistics hope to be the case. The data shows that in 2008 half of the world's population lived in cities and predicts that by 2030 that figure will rise to between 60 and 80 percent – a figure that leaves little margin for error when building cities. In 2008, the world reached an invisible yet unprecedented landmark – for the first time, 3.3 billion people lived in urban areas and it is anticipated that by 2030, the number will reach almost 5 billion. We could expand on what this would mean for global poverty but this is not the place to delve deeper into this issue.

COST OF THE GLOBALIZATION OF LARGE CITIES

The Third World Urban Forum, a program of the United Nations for Human Settlement, UN-Habitat, and a report entitled *The State of the World's Cities 2006/7* both raised worldwide interest in the deteriorating social and environmental effects of urban expansion. Globalization has also brought attention to the growth of cities and its human cost. Nevertheless, people in general have not yet grasped the enormity of the scale and implications of future urbanization.

So far, thinking has centered to a large degree on more immediate concerns, problems such as housing the poor and improving their living standards, job creation, the city's carbon footprint, improving government and managing better, more sophisticated urban systems. These questions are obviously important, but they are all eclipsed by the problems associated with the inexorable future growth of urban populations. In order for the urbanization of developing countries to contribute to solving social and environmental problems rather than aggravating them, with catastrophic results, it is necessary to anticipate these events and adopt a proactive approach.

Consequently, we should try to look beyond present problems, real and urgent as they are. They are a call to action. The report attempts to make sense of the implications of the imminent doubling of the developing world's urban population and to analyze what needs to be done in order to be better prepared for that enormous growth. It takes a detailed look at the demographics that underlie urban growth in developing regions and the political implications of this. It also makes a concrete analysis of the effects of the transition to urbanization on issues of sustainability and the reduction of poverty. It analyzes the different needs and conditions of underprivileged men and women in urban areas and the obstacles they face in the defense of their rights as well as in shaping their own potential as productive members of an urbanized world.

WILL GOOGLE BE CAPABLE OF OFFERING SUFFICIENT URBAN INFORMATION TO AVOID THE NECESSITY FOR LIVING IN MEGACITIES?

If megacities, with good reason, have been the object of attention because of what they may represent, this is precisely why we must consider in greater depth the conditions of less dense urban areas. Contrary to popular belief, it is probable that the majority of urban growth occurs in small-to-medium-scale cities where planning capabilities and implementation might be extremely poor. It is also true that some of the most populated continents like Africa and Asia lack the kind of planning strategies that we are accustomed to in Hispanic, Anglo-Saxon, or French culture. Nevertheless, the global decentralization of government departments is conceding the mounting responsibilities for these cities. Regulatory urban plans that define what cities should be no longer exist. Instead, those who inhabit cities have the final word and in many cases hold the reins. As the population of small cities grows, their already feeble capacity for administration and planning are left increasingly overcommitted. It will be imperative to find new ways to better equip them for planning future expansion, making sustainable use of resources and providing basic services. The message is clear: local and federal governments, in conjunction with broader society and with the support of international organizations, can adopt immediate measures to bring about enormous improvements to social, economic, environmental, and living conditions for the majority of the world's population.

Attempts to prevent migration are futile, counterproductive, and erroneous, not to mention an infringement on the rights of the individual. If policymakers think urban growth is too high, they have at their disposal effective options that are respectful of human rights. Advances in matters of social development like the promotion of equal rights or gender equality, universal access to education and sexual health, are important in their own right. But they will also empower women to avoid unwanted pregnancy and therefore reduce the principal cause of urban growth and the expansion of farming: an area of growth that limits and is limited by the planet's resources. It is easy to understand how natural resources are affected by the urbanization of the world's population. In the event of a catastrophe, the majority of the affected population reverts to the solution of moving to the big city in order to escape the situation. But this option limits the development and growth of the city itself. Therefore the solution lies in devising an immediate urban plan that provides resources and better exit points in impacted areas for those who are affected. Google Earth could be of enormous assistance if its photographic data over an affected territory could be updated on demand, for example.

Furthermore, cities need boundaries that expand beyond urban limits in order to reduce poverty and promote sustainability. This includes paying specific attention to the grassroots needs of the poor. For impoverished families, there is urgent need for sufficient land, incorporating basic access to water, sanitation, electricity, and public transport, upon which to build housing and therefore improve their lives. If we plan to respond to these requirements of space and infrastructure, bearing in mind the specific needs of impoverished women, the welfare of underprivileged families will be able to be greatly improved. This type of development, centered on people, illustrates and strengthens social fabric, as the experience of permacultural eco-villages around the world has shown.

In a similar vein, the protection of the environment and the management and regulation of eco-systems in anticipation of future urban expansion requires spatially determined structures that take into account basic human needs. A city's footprint extends far beyond its physical limits. Cities influence their greater environmental surroundings and are in turn ultimately affected by them. Proactive sustainability policy is no longer merely desirable but fundamental, taking into account climate change in many urban areas that lie at or close to sea level.

Third, population experts and institutions can and should play a pivotal role in support of community organizations, social mobility, government, and the international community in order to improve the environment and modes of urban expansion thus reinforcing the possibility of "capacity building" and future viability in this area. In these critical times, arranging international action in clarifying matters of public policy and providing information and analysis that support strategies geared toward the improvement of our urban future is of crucial importance. We can look to websites like www.unhcr.org that link to Google Earth as examples of ways of following international conflicts, the location of encampments, establishments, disasters themselves, etc.

GOOGLE EARTH FOR (NEXT) URBAN PLANNERS

This research has three points of origin. The first is the work developed by Massimo Faiferri, Samanta Bartocci, Michele Valentino, Erika Bonacucina, Andrea Tapia, Luca Melis, and myself, for an eight-month course (four two-month seminars) entitled "How to act as urban planners after a disaster." Held at the University of Sassari's Faculty of Architecture in the Italian city of Algheri, 48 students produced work that was so comprehensive that they were awarded a *cum laude* score of 30 – the highest score in the Italian system. Their work has consequently contributed to the faculty's national standing. In fact, a survey of architecture schools in Italy published by the national newspaper, *La Repubblica*, in June 2009 proclaimed the faculty as the best Italian School of Architecture, despite its location on Sardinia, an "isolated" island between Spain, France, and Italy.

The second origin of this study was a project that took place in 2007 concerning the development of urban planning in remote locations via Google Earth. Initiated by Agnes Tzouma, and assisted by Dennis Dollens, Jan Bayo, Jorge Lobos, Virginie Amiot, Mauri O'Brien, Stephane Villafane, and myself, it was entered into a UIA Competition organized by the Technical Chamber of Greece and the UIA-ARES Work Program. The international architectural competition was initiated to better understand natural disasters, and how renewable energy sources and bioclimatic architecture can be used in the design of "shells," to shelter people.

Lastly, XFrog (a growth software developed by German-based company, GreenWorks)[1] was also used in this project. Its use in conjunction with Google Earth made it possible for XFrog to "grow" designs within available space, to locate shelters and generate digital emergency planning as well as to re-grow and heal a city according to bio-mimetic criteria. The planning looked at the site as a permacultured new settlement – of self-sufficient living – that creates a plan that will colonize the destroyed urban fabric as a positive virus. The chosen location was Trincomalee (Sri Lanka) and it was therefore

(a)

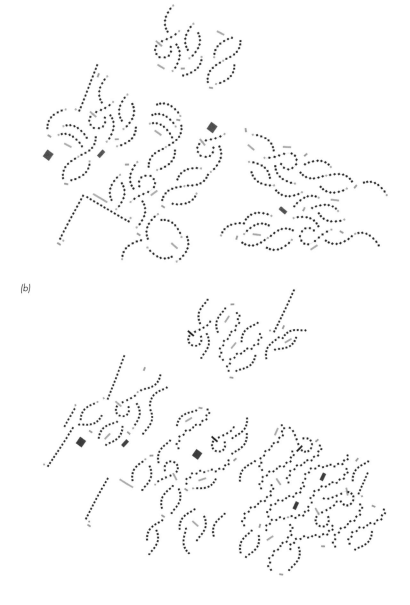

(b)

Figure 10.5a, 10.5b Two different phases of the new urban settlement in Trincomalee (Sri Lanka) showing the gradual influence of Google Earth information on transforming primary concepts into adjusted streets and number of tents-to-be-developed-as-houses (Agnes Tzouma, Dennis Dollens, Jan Bayo, Jorge Lobos, Stephane Villafane, and Ignasi Pérez Arnal, 2007).

crucial we know its atmospheric conditions, rain levels, climate variables, composition of ground, and its building systems.

DIGITALLY GROWN SETTLEMENT: FROM CLUSTER TO VIRUS INVASION

The "shells" provide semi-permanent housing for families of up to ten members; they are designed to be clustered in irregular patterns with particular

165

emphasis on the quality of urban design and the environment while also taking on characteristics of traditional Sri Lankan village groups. Units were grouped in clusters derived from natural forms grown in software in order to avoid the militaristic, bureaucratic planning of most emergency camps. Using XFrog coordinated with Google Earth, experimental clusters were extrapolated from digitally grown flowers and branching and then analyzed and transformed into configurations that maintain a spatial relationship to the biological precedent. These clusters, like the botanic forms that seeded them, have the potential to develop in many forms over various landscape typologies. When clusters reach a certain density, urban or social amenities are suggested, for example schools, clinics, communications pavilions, and are inserted into the plan as if they were flowers in a branching structure respecting the environment and creating non-gridded but easily understood urban and village circulation and service routes.

We have endeavored to create a landscape stressing community development utilizing green spaces, small plazas, and safe zones for small children, areas for family gardens, recycling stations, communication centers, community services, and even the possibility of family, home businesses such as cafes as well as bike paths and emergency routes. These environmentally friendly plans for the clustered villages, inspired by forms following natural plant algorithms, digitally grown as botanic simulation in software, creates an organic unity for shelter-villages to adapt to local terrain and climate.

ONE, TEN, HUNDREDS, THOUSANDS, HUNDREDS OF THOUSANDS

The process for evolving the structure and the village clusters emerged out of our discussions on desirable qualities such as durability and simplicity for the structure and its impact on the site – especially when considering that hundreds of units will be placed in a fragile landscape. And, while macro-site conditions are varying, some general properties are known for all settlement villages as inserts into existing site conditions – factors such as infill housing and cluster villages influenced our proposal to create two basic, square floor plans for the shelters while giving the site plans maximum flexibility for use as infill emergency housing or for larger camp developments. Here the shelter pavilions are customized for environmental conditions in Sri Lanka – for example, the seams of the pavilions are tied together giving the possibility of various configurations of openness or the complete removal of the front and two sides, whereas for a colder climate these front and side panels would be sealed for environmental protection and heat retention. So, with minor modifications and some difference in materials this proposal could easily and quickly be adjusted for use in desert or mountain environments.

Most emergency camps and displaced-population communities are spatially organized in impersonal, regimented, grid-formation shelter after shelter. It seems appropriate that design ideas and innovation could simultaneously attempt to make the camps more civic, environmentally sound, and visually interesting. Our proposal considers housing shelters in an environmental context that includes social, economic, and urban issues and seeks to address the needs of displaced people in a civilized manner. We attempted, with organizational clustering, to create public and private spaces that will encourage emergent social possibilities. We have organized the distribution of the shelters in a more environmentally friendly way with spatial qualities such as small plazas so that children may be safely overseen by the family or neighbors, and cooking areas are relatively localized. The plan enables the potential for paths, small vegetable gardens, and services more akin to those found in traditional villages or small cities and each cluster includes emergency routes and access for ambulances and fire equipment.

USEFUL CITY-PLANNERS: PROJECTS FOR A BETTER FUTURE OR BETTER PROJECTS FOR THE FUTURE

[W]e recognize that there is no one right path forward and that it is impossible to predict all future consequences of today's actions. And thus we must endure a condition of unpredictability, choose amongst a large variety of possibilities and pursue various options at the same time.

In this way Friedrich von Bories and Matthias Böttger[2] introduced their lecture at the 2008 Venice Biennale. Somehow, Google should be used not to create new urban planning or new cities but rather better urban planning and better cities. What use is an instrument, a tool, if not to make more and better things?

If Google Earth is a better and more intelligent network, it should be able to help us to unravel the complex process of global planning. It should be able to help us indentify hitherto unknown fluctuating cyclical patterns. It should help us observe the interactive, interconnected relationships that appear when we are able to create layers that we never thought could interact in locations that we need to develop.

NOTES

1 It was used during the competition and, in fact, Dennis Dollens held a conference titled "Emergence Urban Planning and Structural Systems," on August 22, 2007, 12:30 p.m., Redfish Conference Room, Santa Fe, NM (USA), where he pointed out the challenge that would suppose that programmers could use Google Earth to automatically coordinate XFrog designs with available space to locate shelters and create digital emergency planning.
2 Von Borries, Friedrich and Böttger, Matthias: *Updating Germany. How Do We Want to Live?* www.updatinggermany.de, Berlin, 2008, 11. Mostra Internazionale di Architettura. Partecipazioni nazionali. La Biennale di Venezia.

11 PRODUCTIVE RESIDUE
The casting of alternative public space

DAN PITERA

UNDERPINNINGS: DETROIT, MICHIGAN

In a capitalist system of development, growth is good and shrinkage is bad. The life of a city does not fit within this paradigm. Cities are ecological systems. Their populations grow and shrink. Their boundaries and land area grow and shrink. Currently, many models exist for cities that expand and very few exist for those cities losing inhabitants. Neither a plan for growing nor a plan for shrinking is sustainable on its own. Systems fluctuate. Social systems, economic systems, and political systems change. Cities must adapt. What is needed is not a pattern or plan for either growing or shrinking. Instead, what is more appropriate is a strategy for adapting to the inevitable and often unpredictable changes that cities undergo.

This chapter submits that shrinkage is not a pathological condition that requires reversal. In fact, it is not the city that is shrinking; it is the population. Land area remains the same. Infrastructure has not changed. Vacancy and abandonment become the differential. All efforts are directed into turning this around. However, shrinkage may reveal or uncover other methods of development rarely considered by urban-design strategies. This may point to an alternative urban public space that does not necessarily need to be filled in with buildings.

Detroit, Michigan, a collection of communities undergoing an apocalyptic[1] urban transformation due to a shrinking population will serve as the context for this chapter. Some suggest that Detroit is perhaps one of the few cities in this particular condition. However, studies have shown that Detroit is listed as thirty-second in a long list of 374 cities worldwide that have sustained a loss of population over a 50-year period. There are 59 cities in the United States alone.[2]

Several estimates suggest that there are 35–40 square miles of undesignated open space (i.e., vacant land and buildings) within the city limits of Detroit. This is similar to the land area of the City and County of San Francisco (46.69 square land miles – US Census Bureau). The City of Detroit at the beginning of the twenty-first century offers us a chance to begin again – to recast the typically negative perception(s) of the city and its future. Detroit has the opportunity to construct and construe another urban paradigm.

The scale of the city ... The scale of the issues ... The scale of the vacant space has Detroit standing in a state of paralysis. Some area residents think

Detroit is getting better. Others think it is getting worse. And some do not think about it at all: they have given up on the city's future. On the one hand, Detroit continues to lose population. On the other hand, there are many people who continue to live and work in Detroit and are passionate about the city. Detroit is in a unique position of crisis and opportunity. At the time this chapter is being written, Detroit has a 17 percent unemployment rate – the worst in the United States. Approximately one-third of its land area is abandoned. The City is potentially at a turning point in history based on its economic and physical reality. Old models have not worked. Perhaps a study of the slow and deliberate actions of the city residents can help provide an alternative viewpoint.

READING BETWEEN THE LINES

Many researchers, politicians, and community organizations have already speculated returning Detroit to its prior existence. They have attempted or proposed filling in the vacant gaps with buildings – to return to an appropriate urban density.

What does it mean to have an "appropriate urban density"?

The life of any city encounters dramatic shifts. The perceived problem in Detroit is seen as the problem of a shrinking population; however, it is the problem of "lines" – racial lines, social lines, economic lines. Detroit's shrinking population is a by-product of the lines that have been drawn by people, places and things. A mosaic of interactions makes a healthy city, as opposed to color-by-number and staying within the lines. These lines are drawn with distinct clarity, rejecting the blurriness inherent in a city. The limited space of a city engenders multiple uses and functional overlaps. The edges of things and of activities are blurry and indeterminate. To live in the city requires us to understand this blurriness. Essentially, it is *out of focus*. To live in a city, a person must color with many colors and outside of the lines.

Viewed in this way, urbanism may be defined as the simultaneous overlap of activities, programs, and things, where distinctions between each of them are indeterminate. For the sake of brevity, what if we exchange the word "urbanism" with the term "density"?

"Density" is the simultaneous overlap of activities, programs, and things, where distinctions between each of them are indeterminate.

This word exchange reveals a potential reading (or perhaps misreading) of density as more than the typical definition that refers to closeness of buildings and structures. Perhaps, it could be stated that density is directly related to intensity. Urban density suggests a higher intensity than a rural density. Thus, this work does not oppose a heightened density in Detroit, or other similar dis-urban cities; it opposes the limitation of density's definition to buildings and structures. An appropriate urban density may have large gaps and open spaces, and should be *out of focus*. It should include the density of landscape, the density of events, as well as the density of the built environment.

It is a fruitless effort to continue to fill in the vacant gaps with buildings alone. Buildings may be an inappropriate response. Perhaps these gaps are required moments in a paradigm of shrinking. These gaps offer a space of opportunity. As one of my thesis students stated: "They are the gifts of being able to forget the trauma." Detroit was a city of 1,850,000 people in 1950. It was also a city that housed these people in predominately single-family homes within a city limit totaling 138 square land miles – more than the land area of Boston, San Francisco, and Manhattan combined (US Census Bureau). Through time, neglect, and abandonment, many of these homes have become vacant or have been demolished. To rebuild or to fill in the gaps presupposes the regrowth of the city to its prior population and with a similar urban fabric. It does not question the social, racial, or economic patterns that generated this urban fabric. It could be argued that these vacant gaps are the residue of these prior social, racial, and economic structural systems. To rebuild the city to its prior form is to merely repeat history.

PRODUCTIVE RESIDUE[3]

Because the urban space of Detroit has lain fallow for so long, its traditional urbanism – its dense human production-oriented fabric – has weakened and the city's ecological system has adapted. Wetlands are developing. Ringed-neck pheasants have moved in. As a result, Detroit is a comprehensive landscape and urban hybrid. This hybrid Detroit is the residue of a shrinking population and continued disinvestment.

The residue left by vacant land and abandoned buildings offer possibilities of another Detroit. When one looks across the landscape in certain areas of Detroit, they do not see spaces between buildings; instead, they may see a building within open space. This open space has become the dominant space of Detroit, and can no longer be seen as the gap between things. The vacant gap has become the object and the object, the building, has become the gap. The reconsideration of this open space provides the territory for urban revitalization and change. Though ignored by traditional development strategies, these spaces are still appropriated and activated every day by Detroit residents. Through their actions they reveal an alternative public space, a public realm they have the power to alter and transform. Their spatial appropriation turns vacant land into productive landscapes, landscapes that produce products, create jobs, and engage the public. Their everyday activities, which include urban agriculture and art making, are part of an organic process that probes into strategies that activate this hidden public territory. They are transforming blighted land into neighborhood assets. Whether conscious or unconscious, they inherently seek to investigate the residue of "shrinking" and "decay" not as *pathological conditions that require reversal*, but for their potential as strategies and opportunities for urban development. This chapter does not wish to foster an attitude to clean-up or to erase the productive residue developed through this adaptation. It can coexist simultaneously and be a part of a revitalized urban fabric. The residue itself – the gap, the vacant parcel, the abandoned building – has become the space of social, cultural, and environmental actions, interactions, and reactions by Detroit residents. This existing condition of Detroit harbors clues – complex ecological systems, human activities, and creativity – that point to potential next steps. What may be seen as void of culture is actually culturally rich.

RESIDUAL INSERTIONS

The Heidelberg Project

The Heidelberg Project is a two-city-block art installation on Heidelberg Street on the near-east side of Detroit. It is a 23-year-old work in progress by artist Tyree Guyton. From the beginning without permits or permission, Mr. Guyton began to paint and sculpt every square inch of this two-block area. It began as an artist's desire to change the image of his community. It is situated in an area of Detroit that has been listed as one of the top three poorest zip codes in the United States by the US Census Bureau. The Heidelberg Project began as a work of art that engaged the community in an attempt to alter its decline. It has added a summer day camp for local youth, art programs in the

Figure 11.1 The Heidelberg Project, Eastside of Detroit.

local schools, and other economic development and community assets. Over the past five years it has evolved from a single artist's installation/vision into a creative artists' village – The Heidelberg Cultural Village. The Heidelberg Project is an art action that offers an example of an alternative method of developing in an area where tradition development is completely missing.

FireBreak: architecture and community agitation[4]

Through time, neglect, and abandonment, the physical space of speculative development, the urban single-family home has been revealed as a possible alternative urban public space that is different than the riverfront park or the central square. FireBreak is a series of guerrilla insertions by the Detroit Collaborative Design Center at the University of Detroit Mercy School of

Figure 11.2 The Heidelberg Project, Eastside of Detroit.

Architecture. It is a part of our process of searching and re-searching potential strategies to activate the urban residue and engage covert public territories. It focuses particularly on the burned urban single-family home. It investigates "shrinking" and "decay" not as *pathological conditions that require reversal, but on their potential as strategies for development*. Located in Detroit, Michigan, FireBreak builds upon works of other community residents like the Heidelberg Project who operate in this open space through their everyday rituals and artistic actions. With this in mind, FireBreak posits a possible alternative urban interference that appropriates or reclaims public space within the burned houses of Detroit. A private individual space has become a collective community place.

Presently, there are 8,000 burned houses in Detroit. What were once people's homes have been violently treated and left bare on the side of the road as urban artifacts. Without permits or permission, the Design Center, alongside community artists and residents, are interfering within this urban space. What motivates these mercenary or guerrilla actions is the intense desire to appropriate and transform urban blight into a public asset. Fire-Break is centered on the position that everyone – the next-door neighbor or the person down the street – can shape her or his world. These catalytic interventions and interferences have thrown the urban context and one's power over it into the public discourse through both event and word.

This project was developed out of a community meeting in which we presented a master plan for an area on the east side of Detroit. One of the participants asked the simple but difficult question:

> We are very happy with this master plan, but what can I do tomorrow? What can I do to the burned house that is next to my home? There are several more down the street. How can I change my neighborhood tomorrow?

We suggested that we as a community could spend a weekend and transform the house through an artistic installation. Two weekends later we covered all the openings of a burned abandoned house with fabric that was the color of fallout-shelter yellow. Inside the house we hosted a local community band and had a large community picnic. Since this first action we have completed ten houses in collaboration with community residents, organizations, artists, and the Detroit Collaborative Design Center. The City of Detroit has, outside of our knowledge, demolished each of these houses. We do not see our installations as precious. Instead they are mercenary acts that attempt to alter neighborhood perceptions. In other words, each neighborhood has been trying for years to have these houses removed. Following these installations, they were demolished within weeks.

Frequently we are asked why do we, as architects, concern ourselves with this type of project? Why is this the work of an architect? We simply respond: We should concern ourselves with the built environment, not merely with building buildings. We should seek creative ways to engage these spaces – the burned house and the abandoned building – in ways that look beyond simple demolition.

SELECTED HOUSING TYPES: URBAN EPHEMERA

HayHouse – 2001

Figure 11.3 FireBreak–
HayHouse, northeast corner,
Detroit Collaborative Design
Center.

Figure 11.4 FireBreak–
HayHouse, west wall, Detroit
Collaborative Design Center.

175

The east side within the city limits of Detroit has become noted for its attempt to fill in the vacant land with agricultural crops. For example; alfalfa has been planted due to its ability to partially detoxify the contaminated soil. Detroit residents have transformed old "crack houses" into "hay houses" (bundles of hay are stored inside of these houses). Before the HayHouse event the Design Center and neighborhood participants made 3,000 miniature bundles of hay. Some 3,000 nails were evenly spaced on all exterior faces of the house. The event attracted 100 surrounding residents ritualistically placing the hay on the house – Urban Field.

HouseWrap – 2004

The entire exterior of a burned house on the west side of Detroit was wrapped in 8,070 lineal feet of clear plastic – Urban Body Bag. The event of wrapping

Figure 11.5 FireBreak–HouseWrap, east wall detail, Detroit Collaborative Design Center.

Figure 11.6 FireBreak–HouseWrap, northeast corner, Detroit Collaborative Design Center.

the house was collaboration between the Design Center and the Woodbridge Neighborhood Development Corporation. It marked the dedication of new affordable housing on the site by the WNDC.

HouseBreath – 2005

Figure 11.7 FireBreak–HouseBreath, west wall detail, Detroit Collaborative Design Center.

Figure 11.8 FireBreak–
HouseBreath, west wall, Detroit
Collaborative Design Center.

Vertical strips of fabric were connected solely to the top and bottom of all exterior walls – Urban Re-Veiling. The autumn wind passed through the cracks in the house and caused the fabric to flutter.

PublishingHouse – 2008

"What I have learned, I learned from you." "I don't need you to die for me. Live for me." "Are you fighting for me or against me?" Several quotes by southwest Detroit young people were enlarged to 16-foot-long vertical banners. They were mounted and hung on a burned house situated directly across the street from a local high school – Urban Echo.

Figure 11.9 FireBreak–PublishingHouse, north wall, Detroit Collaborative Design Center.

Figure 11.10 FireBreak–PublishingHouse, south wall, Detroit Collaborative Design Center.

PlayHouse[5]

The burned houses in Detroit are blight on both the physical and the psychological landscape. Some are renovated but due to costs most are demolished. There is no "middle ground." As stated earlier, the FireBreak houses were intentionally temporal acts. PlayHouse: An Exterior Urban Community Theater offers a long-term installation that is neither full renovation nor complete demolition. The overall intent is to design and fabricate a community theater with residents, artists, and young people that will become an artistic and cultural centerpiece in an area of Detroit that has been listed as one of the top three poorest zip codes in the United States by the US Census Bureau.

The design will completely remove a two-story sidewall of a burned house so that the interior will be visible to its exterior side yard, which currently exists as a half a block of vacant and abandoned properties. Three of the adjacent properties will be designed to be exterior seating facing the interior of the house, making it a two-story stage. A new exterior "skin," completely composed of rotating and sliding panels, will open to reveal all or only a portion of the stage. We do not see this project as a single event. It is the first step in formulating a strategy through art and architecture to re-inhabit these houses with community spaces in alternative ways.

IMPLICATIONS

Can we view Detroit without nostalgia? Without this lens, it is possible to see that the city offers the opportunity to rethink the paradigm(s) of other cities. We must view Detroit with a sense of amnesia. There are 374 cities worldwide that have continued to lose populations over the last 50 years. At the same time, every city harbors areas characterized by disinvestment and neglect, whether due to race, class, etc. A reconsidered study of these types of spaces and cities without the intent to eliminate them would foster other

Figure 11.11 FireBreak–PlayHouse, partially open, Detroit Collaborative Design Center.

approaches and strategies of urbanism, landscape, or architecture. Potentially these strategies would center on productively engaging the residue of abandonment as opposed to trying to erase it. The FireBreak projects presented here operate at the scale of the intervention while considering the implications of multiple interventions at the scales of the neighborhood and the city. FireBreak is one possible urban interference that appropriates or reclaims public space within the burned houses of Detroit. They are not seen as the only possible intervention or solution. They do not attempt to celebrate Detroit as an apocalyptic post-industrial fetish. Rather, they illustrate the power of design as a community organizing tool that can alter and shape a person's surroundings. They are about synthesizing and repositioning altered viewpoints, points of view, pointed views, or (perhaps?) anointed views.

NOTES

1 The use of the term "apocalyptic" refers to a richer meaning than the common definition of a "tragic destructive end." It also refers to a point of uncovering or revealing.
2 As part of a study produced by the German Federal Cultural Foundation titled "Shrinking Cities," Detroit was listed at 32 with reference to the percentage of urban citizens lost since its peak population of 1,850,000 in 1950. Saint Louis (12), Youngstown (25), Pittsburgh (27), and Buffalo (30) have all lost a larger percentage of people when compared to their peak population, though they have lost less people than Detroit. I was "curator" of the Detroit section of this international research effort.
3 Residue is defined here as the intersection between verb and noun. It is not necessarily an end-product, but the by-product of an action. It is a resultant, but often the "other" – an unintended resultant.
4 Disclaimer: The issues surrounding Detroit or other cities and the strategies required to alter them are far more complex than a single action, a single idea, a single organization, or a single person. It must be a collaborative act – many people and many actions. Thus the project that follows, FireBreak, is not an attempt to find a single solution or to solve the surface problems. It is only the first cut in this process.
5 In progress, estimated time of completion summer 2010.

12 BUBBLE CITIES
Islands, airports, and nomads

GRETCHEN WILKINS

As abandoned cars fill residential parking structures and airport lots in Dubai it becomes harder and harder to argue this region's immunity to fluctuations in the global economy. Speculations about the sustainability of Dubai's massive urbanization began almost as soon as the first towers rose, but given its phenomenal internal wealth and relative autonomy, the boom was not obviously attributable to an economic bubble. In oil-rich Abu Dhabi this may still be the case, but since Dubai has based its economy on global finance and tourism it is inherently linked to international patterns of spending and travel, all of which have slowed. Media about Dubai's delirious and seemingly unstoppable development has been replaced with speculations about how this extraordinary urban project will take shape in the wake of the 2008 Global Financial Crisis.

Dubai's emergence was so well publicized because the urbanism it was creating was so unprecedented; a beach-y resort hub of super-tall towers in the once vast and remote Middle Eastern desert was only the beginning of the emirate's exceptional ambitions. But despite the unique and anomalous conditions surrounding Dubai's architectural emergence and expansion, many of the development patterns are in fact well documented elsewhere. It is as if the cut-and-paste technique so often used to describe Dubai's architecture also applied to its economic, demographic, and infrastructural landscapes, as we can find traces of other "bubble cities" in Dubai's recent history. Detroit and Tokyo, for example, both emerged on the back of an economic boom, from the automobile industry and real-estate speculation respectively, and both are still negotiating the aftermath of boom-turned-bust. Once seemingly invincible, Tokyo and Detroit now share the title of "shrinking cities"[1] as populations decline, migrate, or age, as vacancy rates increase, and as the primary economic industry contracts or converts into something else altogether. These patterns of retrenching are as equally well documented as Dubai's rapid expansion, and as Dubai re-evaluates its trajectory post-GFC, these patterns reveal several moments of convergence between very disparate cities.

DETROIT>DUBAI: NOMADS

The similarities between Dubai and Detroit are already mutually recognized, having established themselves as Sister Cities in 2003. They share a history of trading, are both key transportation hubs for their regions, and to some degree share culture, Detroit having one of the largest Arab populations outside of the Middle East. This population migrated like many others to enable Detroit's automobile industry in the first decades of the twentieth century, when hundreds of thousands of people arrived from around the world to take advantage of the financial opportunities only Detroit could then promise. Henry Ford's announcement of the five-dollar workday in 1914 more than doubled the average salary for autoworkers at the time, enticing workers to migrate overseas and endure the harsh conditions of factory work. From 1910 to 1950 Detroit's population surged from 285,000 people to over 1.8 million, 500 percent growth, and with 30 percent of those people coming from foreign countries.[2] Due to a confluence of many factors occurring mid-century, this steady growth abruptly reversed in 1950 and Detroit lost 50 percent of the population in the next 50 years.

The patterns of growth and population change in Detroit virtually mirror that of Dubai, even if occurring many years earlier. In the 1960s, when Detroit's population continued to migrate (this time away from the city, in the cars they could now afford because of the money they were being paid by the auto industry), Dubai discovered oil, a moment which would do for Dubai what Ford's five-dollar workday did for Detroit. In the next 40 years the population of Dubai grew from 60,000 to 1.5 million where it stands today, an astounding growth rate of over 2,500 percent, even if not yet having reached Detroit's 1950 peak. Workers came, like they did to Detroit, for the promise of professional opportunity and financial compensation unlike

Figure 12.1 Chart of population history, Detroit and Dubai.

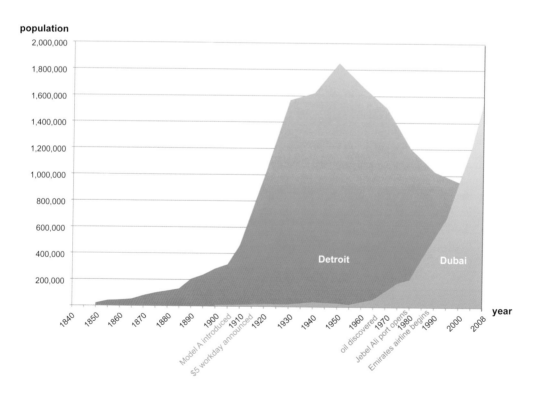

wherever they were from, and this was also the incentive to endure unfamiliar or, in the case of construction workers, extremely harsh living and working conditions.

Unlike Detroit, however, these migratory populations in Dubai tend not to remain in the country when the opportunities recede, but repatriate or migrate elsewhere. This difference is at least partially due to differences in the economic structure of the industries upon which the cities were built. Where Fordism created both the product and the market for the product simultaneously, expanding the middle class and the industry in a perpetual cycle, the imported workers in Dubai are not integrated into the larger economic system beyond the tasks they are paid to do. This is true for both manual laborers and white-collar workers alike; there is no place in the local system for expatriates, economically or socially, so when the job is complete everyone leaves. As Rem Koolhaas reported in 2007, the expats that comprise 80 percent of Dubai's population come either to enable the construction boom or to use it, but "with little emotional investment both plan to leave eventually."[3]

In this context it would seem that both Detroit and Dubai emerged quickly through a process of mass immigration for financial opportunity and continue to experience an urbanism defined by migration and contemporary nomadism. As Jerry Herron said about Detroit earlier in this volume, "The people who came here never intended to stay."[4] In short, both cities are perpetually "on the way to becoming something else,"[5] an uncommon and perhaps uncomfortable mode of urbanism, but also one which offers a wholly new model to the far more dominant paradigm of urban permanence and stability. Detroit and Tokyo, and so far also Dubai, have all presumed permanence in the midst of (not so obvious) economic volatility, but an alternative position, especially for these cities, might be to embrace perpetual change, as Roger Sherman suggests in an essay about Los Angeles:

> Perhaps, rather than assuming stability and explaining change, one needs to assume change and explain stability. Elastic planning strategies are needed to facilitate surfing the highly unstable and unpredictable evolution of the contemporary city without, at the same time, merely accommodating this evolution. It is precisely this question – how to provide sufficient looseness with regard to future scenarios – that constitutes the principal paradox of urban development today. Overcoming this paradox hinges on learning the ability to operate at the cusp between control and disorganization.[6]

TOKYO>DUBAI: BUBBLE INNOVATIONS

An economic bubble often enables the most supportive and innovative periods in a city's architectural history. Architecture rarely receives the same level of public media, financial backing, and cultural significance than during an economic boom. Detroit experienced this architectural upsurge in the early twentieth century, when 95 percent of all downtown Detroit high-rises were completed in a four-year span, between 1925 and 1929.[7] An economic bubble acts as a sort of architectural shock-treatment out of which new talent, new types of building, and in some cases wholly new cities emerge. Dubai and Tokyo certainly share this particular history, as the explosion of building projects during the bubble years allowed younger architects to gain commissions previously reserved for an established few, and where experimental approaches were not just supported but were strongly in demand by clients, city administrators, and the general public alike.

Interestingly though, bubble architecture in both Dubai and Tokyo served to elevate the role of the engineer as equally or more important than the architect, as the combination of immensely scaled projects and push for iconic innovation demanded structural innovation across architectural and urban scales. Botand Bognar's description of bubble-era architecture in Japan rings true in contemporary Dubai when he says,

> [It] did not shy away from applying cutting-edge technologies. On the contrary, the bubble years seem to have been a time when architects and engineers were poised to test how far they could push the limits of their abilities in harnessing the potential of technology. This held true in terms of both "hardware" (structural or constructional) but, even more so, "software" (electronic or computer) technologies, although the two in most cases complemented each other, as at Kansai airport or Sendai Mediatheque.[8]

In Dubai as well, new structural and technological techniques go hand in hand with architectural design, the combination of which enabled the "superlative urbanism" it strives for.

And like Tokyo, Dubai also became a proving ground for smaller or less established practices from all over the world, offering a seemingly endless number of commissions at scales unimaginable in the United States, Australia, or Europe; in Dubai a "small project" could mean anything less than ten buildings. Ultimately, however, Koolhaas suggests that Dubai may actually establish the domain of the junior engineers over the junior architects, as smaller, younger firms push beyond the limits set by their elder colleagues,

> Just as the diminishing distance between the Starchitect and his or her stand-in discredits the former's claims of idiosyncratic uniqueness, there appears a parallel in engineering. While the established geniuses of intuition+computing can make things happen at large cost – actual and metaphorical – and very visible effort, heights that they told us could only be reached with fantastic structural ingenuity – super-tubes, carbon fiber matrices, bundles and sheaves, are routinely surpassed – in Dubai, Hong King and Bangkok – by their less prominent colleagues.[9]

The results of this form of architectural and urban practice in Dubai have proved largely unpredictable when actual results are assessed, leading more often to mediocre projects than to the lofty ambitions suggested in the renderings. Bognar's description of bubble-architecture in Tokyo is again relevant in this description of Dubai, as he said,

Three themes seem to characterize well the developments of the new, and now overwhelmingly commercial and public architecture: experimentation, innovation and spectacle. With practically unlimited commissions and budgets, and working in largely unrestricted conditions, architects enjoyed the freedom of shaping their buildings any way their personal talent or fancy could afford. Seeking only cheap novelty and merely a marketable image, the majority of the vast design output of this time was unquestionably trivial, garish and inferior in quality – if one could speak about quality at all in these cases.[10]

In this environment the rapid pace of development is at odds with the measured pace of architectural design and construction, requiring expedient resolution over meticulous and premeditated design. This isn't inherently an equation for poor quality, but it does promote a particular brand of "bubble" architecture, more likely a result of economic pressures than design or cultural agendas.

In its strive toward superlative urbanism Dubai has been retesting some previous experiments conducted elsewhere, such as artificial islands and indoor environments that emerged during Tokyo's bubble years. One of the first indoor slopes appeared in this context, the LaLaport Skidome SSAWS (stands for Spring Summer Autumn Winter Ski), constructed in 1993 and closed ten years later – 15 years before reaching the projected financial break-even point. It was demolished and replaced by an IKEA, a clear shift from

Figure 12.2 Tokyo LaLaport Skidome, SSAWS (2003).

Figure 12.3 Ski Dubai (2008).

high to low financial risk given IKEA's status as the world's largest furniture company and often a harbinger of suburban expansion. SSAWS redux is Ski Dubai, a slightly smaller version opened in 2005. It is physically attached to the Mall of the Emirates on Sheik Zayed Road, the 12-lane highway and central nervous system linking the distributed "cities" of Dubai to each other and to Abu Dhabi 100 km to the west. Given the incredible costs associated with maintaining an Arctic environment in the desert, this project is just as financially risky as the Tokyo dome, but attaching the slope to the mall allows the risky business to be absorbed into the safe one, SSAWS into IKEA. However, this also makes it more difficult to separate should the facility suffer the same fate as in Tokyo, especially as the wall connecting the two buildings is a giant window between the slope and the food court, turning the mall into an expanded "ski lodge" where both skiers and shoppers congregate, eat, and watch.

The significance of engineering in bubble-era urbanism isn't just limited to buildings and interior climates, but extends to the creation of entirely new urban territories through land-reclamation projects. In Tokyo the extreme inflation in land prices made the production of even more land a very lucrative endeavor and resulted in a series of major reclamation projects in the Tokyo Bay. At that time one square foot of land in the posh Ginza district was selling

for upwards of $24,000, making the prospect of creating new property in the bay potentially cheaper than buying existing land in the mainland city.[11] Teleport Town is one such example, an island in the Tokyo Bay originally designed as a model for a self-sustaining city of 100,000 people. The island was built but the economy crashed before the larger ambitions could be realized, leaving a vague and largely empty landscape dotted with mega-structures, all of which are linked by an elevated monorail. The buildings are currently in use but only just, perpetually waiting for new development plans to be implemented. It is unlike any other space in Tokyo in its vast openness and thinly distributed program, a landscape that begins to resemble the current organization of Dubai – a flat piece of ground composed of equal parts infrastructure and mega-structure, awaiting the middle-ground to fill in between.

The land-reclamation projects in Dubai are speculative financial engines as they were in Tokyo, but not for want of additional land. Rather, multiplying the coastline of Dubai's waterfront also multiplies tourism, the primary industry upon which Dubai's financial projections are based given its very limited oil resources. In this context the coast is treated in an elastic, linear way to create as much valuable waterfront as possible, as opposed to consolidating the new land into a singular island block like Tokyo's Teleport Town. The coastline in Dubai is a malleable contour bent into palm-shaped housing

Figure 12.4 Ski Dubai food court (2008).

189

Figure 12.5 Teleport Town, Tokyo, Fuji headquarters building (2007).

Figure 12.6 Beach in Abu Dhabi (2008).

developments and other symbolic shapes, each of which also serves the secondary (or maybe primary?) function as a global icon, constructed as they are at a scale that is only legible in their entirety through aerial photography. To know what Dubai looks like is to view its coastline through Google Earth, as the rest of the city is largely indistinguishable at this scale and has no imageable identity. Unlike aerial images the experience of being on the Palm Jumeirah is strangely urban; the roads are canyons carving between large, closely spaced housing estates, and the only point at which the water is visible is from private properties.

190

Figure 12.7 Beach in Dubai (2008).

DETROIT>DUBAI: HUBS

As cities that are both "on their way to becoming something else," with a per-petually transient population, Dubai and Detroit share a quality of spatial precariousness. It is as if the city is not where you expect it to be, or that the common urban indicators seem to exist in name only, the Detroit "down-town," or the Dubai "beach." This may be a result of the condition of incom-pleteness they share, one currently emerging from the ground and the other retreating back to it, one voraciously reclaiming land and the other being slowly reclaimed by it. Or it may be because they are both primarily function-ing as transit hubs, Dubai being "halfway to everywhere"[12] and Detroit still a primary link to the Asian automobile industries. Indeed the airports of Detroit and Dubai are currently the most "complete" and recognizable aspect of these cities. Detroit Metro Airport is surprisingly busy and polished given the city's overwhelmingly dominant identity as a crumbling ruin, moving over 35 million people through it every year, more than Dubai in 2008.[13] Indeed Detroit's entire airport is new, completed in two stages with the most recent terminal opening in 2008 and another master plan already approved to accommodate up to 60 million passengers by 2027,[14] the same target Dubai airport is projecting. Rather than centrally located within the city grid, perhaps this space is the emerging "downtown" Detroit?

POST-BUBBLE PRACTICES

The rapid expansion during a bubble era is often followed by a far slower pace of contraction, as the clear direction and collective momentum give way to uncertain projections and reassessment of individual projects. In Tokyo, as potentially in Dubai, the economic crash happened so abruptly that many

Figure 12.8 Dubai.

projects were affected mid-stream, creating a landscape of partially complete developments whose cultural identity shifted from one of prosperity to one of vulnerability almost overnight. As Thomas Daniell describes in his book *After The Crash: Architecture in Post Bubble Japan*,

> Major construction projects are very difficult to launch, yet once in motion their armatures of vested interests make them equally difficult to stop – witless, unwanted golems that continued lurching toward completion throughout the worst years of the post-bubble recession.[15]

As these "unwanted golems" continue to lurch forward in Dubai post-GFC, it is perhaps easier to see how they might be completed given the wealth of Abu

Dhabi and the collective interest in sustaining the momentum of development in the United Arab Emirates more broadly. However, this will undoubtedly impact the nature of future architectural practice in this region.

In Tokyo, the pendulum of practice swung from big and audacious during the bubble to small and clever afterward, from a practice of insertions to one of forensic detections. As Daniell describes, "Though major projects did continue, the pace of new construction drastically slowed. Architectural experimentation for its own sake became more difficult to justify. Adaptive reuse became a pressing necessity rather than a romantic choice." And further,

> big public projects never completely disappeared, but politicians and citizens alike began to demand far more accountability in price and purpose ... The recession also provided a welcome period of respite from the earlier delirious excesses, a time to rethink the architect's mandate and, quite literally, take stock of the existing city.[16]

Practices like Tokyo's Atelier Bow-Wow emerged during this period, focusing primarily on the existing conditions of the city and documenting the "intelligent and witty inventories of the detritus left in the wake of decades of rampant industrialization and urbanization."[17] They produced this work in two books, *Made in Tokyo Guide Book* (2001) and *Pet Architecture Guide Book Volume 2* (2002), both very influential in the analysis of other cities and in the nature of work that emerged from it.

This pattern of close-reading and documentation post bubble was similar in Detroit, when the architectural perspective of the city shifted from one of dismissal and hopelessness to something that raised new and critical questions and that warranted a second look. *Stalking Detroit* (2002) was one of the first books to "take stock" of Detroit in this way, suggesting as a wholly other form of urbanism than could be found anywhere else in the United States, somewhere that offered a new perception and potential for practice in the city. But Detroit's decline wasn't a sharp collapse like that of Tokyo, rather it was a 50-year period of slow transformation. In this context we might see other examples of shifts in practice by looking back further, such as the century-old Detroit architecture firm Smithgroup (originally Smith Hinchman Grylls, SHG), who acquired a landscape architecture firm in 1971 and a historic preservation firm in 1998 – diversifying into fields that were perhaps becoming more relevant to contemporary practice than were large public buildings or government contracts – the bulk of their practice in the first half of the twentieth century.

The quickness with which Dubai transformed from desert colony to international tourism and financial hub is nothing short of astounding. It stands to reason that a similar transformation could happen in the next phase of its development, whether this occurs along architectural, economic, or political lines. Perhaps Dubai will shift into a "forensic" practice or perhaps it will be bailed out by Abu Dhabi, the latter a project that extends beyond economics and into the political and familial (or politico-familial) structure of the country. But the major difference between Dubai's post-bubble context and that of Tokyo and Detroit that cannot be underestimated is a technological one; public use of the Internet didn't even exist in the context of Detroit and

Tokyo's expansion and contraction. Dubai on the other hand would have been impossible without it, given the international network of practices that helped shape it and range of web-based tools that allowed broad participation. These tools have triggered a wholly new form of urbanism in Dubai and elsewhere, one which links Dubai concurrently to other economic and architectural networks. In this sense we will all participate in the next phase of urbanism in Dubai, whether remotely, vicariously, or directly.

NOTES

1 Shrinking cities was a research project directed by Philipp Oswalt of Berlin from 2002 to 2008, documenting depopulating regions around the world. See www.shrinkingcities.com.
2 Detroit census history.
3 Koolhaas, Rem, "Import Expat," in *Al Mahakh*, vol. 12, eds. Ole Bouman, Mitra Khoubour, and Rem Koolhaas (Netherlands: Stichting Archis, 2007), p. 292.
4 Herron, Jerry, Chapter 5 in this volume.
5 Ibid.
6 Sherman, Roger, "If,Then," *Log*, vol. 5, ed. Cynthia Davidson, guest eds. R.E. Somol and Sarah Whiting (New York: Anyone Corporation, 2005), p. 51.
7 Jerry Herron, "Chronolgy: Detroit since 1700," from *Shrinking Cities: Detroit*, Working Papers Part 1, March 2004 (ed. Philip Oswalt).
8 Bognar, Botand, *Beyond the Bubble: The New Japanese Architecture* (London: Phaidon, 2008), p. 17.
9 Koolhaas, Rem, "The Gulf," presented at the Venice Biennale's Tenth International Architecture Exhibit, published by Lars Muller Publishers, Switzerland, 2007.
10 Bognar, op. cit., p. 25.
11 Ibid., p. 10. This refers to the cost of land in the Ginza district, but estimates vary, some as high as $93,000 per square foot.
12 Koolhaas, op. cit., p. 138.
13 According to the Airports Council International, www.airports.org/cda/aci_common/display/main/aci_content07_c.jsp?zn=aci&cp=1-5-54-55-71 53_666_2__.
14 Detroit Metro Airport press release: www.metroairport.com/about/history.asp.
15 Daniell, Thomas, *After the Crash: Architecture in Post-Bubble Japan* (New York: Princeton Architectural Press, 2008), p. 13.
16 Ibid., pp. 13–14.
17 Ibid., p. 14.

BIBLIOGRAPHY

Airports Council International, Published on the Internet. Available: www.
  airports.org/cda/aci_common/display/main/aci_content07_c.jsp?zn=aci&cp
  =1-5-54-55-7153_666_2__.
Allen, S., "From Object to Field," in *AD Profile 127 (Architecture after
  Geometry)*. *Architectural Design*, 24–31, 1997.
American Institute of Architects Academy, *Guidelines for Design and Con-
  struction of Hospital and Health Care Facilities* (Washington, DC: The
  American Institute of Architects Press, 1998).
Bacon, Edmund N., *Design of Cities* (New York: Penguin Books, 1976).
Bandera, Maria Cristina and Miracco, Renato, eds., *Morandi 1890–1964*
  (Milan: Skira Editore, 2008).
"Best Places to Live," *Money*, Published on the Internet. Available: http://
  money.cnn.com/magazines/moneymag/bplive/2007/index.html.
Bobbitt, Philip, *The Shield of Achilles: War, Peace and the Course of History*
  (New York: Knopf, 2002).
Bognar, Botand, *Beyond the Bubble: The New Japanese Architecture*
  (London: Phaidon, 2008).
Bouman, Ole, Khoubour, Mitra, and Koolhaas, Rem, eds., *Al Mahakh*, vol.
  12 (Netherlands: Stichting Archis, 2007).
Brogan, H., *Alexis de Tocqueville: A Life* (New Haven: Yale University Press,
  2006).
Center for Disease Control and Prevention, *Guideline for Disinfection and
  Sterilization in Healthcare Facilities* (2008).
Close Up at a Distance, Published on the Internet. Available: www.l00k.
  org/?s=closeupatadistance.
Cooper, Anthony Ashley, the Third Earl of Shaftesbury, *Characteristicks of
  Men, Manners, Opinions, Times* (London, 1714).
Corner, J., ed., *Recovering Landscape: Essays in Contemporary Landscape
  Architecture* (New York: Princeton Architectural Press, 1999).
da Cunha, D. and Mathur, A., *SOAK: Mumbai in an Estuary* (New Delhi:
  Rupa and Co., 2009).
Daniell, Thomas, *After the Crash: Architecture in Post-Bubble Japan* (New
  York: Princeton Architectural Press, 2008).
Daskalakis, Georgia, Waldheim, Charles, and Young, Jason, eds., *Stalking
  Detroit* (Barcelona: ACTAR, 2001).
Debord, G., "Théorie de la Dérive," *Les lèvres nues*, no. 9, November
  1956.
Debord, G., Statement 6, *The Society of the Spectacle*, Published on the Inter-
  net. Available: www.bopsecrets.org/SI/debord/1.htm.

de Botton, Alain, *The Art of Travel* (London: Vintage International, 2004).

DeLong, J.B., "Creative Destruction's Reconstruction: Joseph Schumpeter Revisited," *The Chronicle of Higher Education*, December 7, 2007, B9.

de Sola-Morales Rubio, Ignasi, "Terrain Vague," in Davidson, Cynthia C., ed., *AnyPlace* (Cambridge, MA: MIT Press, 1995).

Detroit Metro Airport, Published on the Internet. Available: www.metroairport.com/about/history.asp.

Doctorow, E.L., *Ragtime* (New York: Random House, 1974).

Douglas, Mary, *Purity and Danger, An Analysis of Concepts of Pollution and Taboo* (London: Routledge, 1966/2002).

Dunnigan, Brian, ed., *Frontier Metropolis: Picturing Early Detroit 1701–1838* (Detroit: Wayne State University Press, 2001).

Ferry, W.H., *The Buildings of Detroit* (Detroit: Wayne State University Press, 1968).

Florida, R., *Who's Your City: How the Creative Economy Is Making Where to Live the Most Important Decision of Your Life* (New York: Basic Books, 2008).

Ford Motor Company, *Helpful Hints and Advice to Employes [sic] to Help Them Grasp the Opportunities Which Are Presented to Them by the Ford Profit-Sharing Plan* (Detroit: Ford Motor Company, 1915).

Fuller, R. Buckminster, "Proposal to the International Union of Architects," in Krausse, Joachim and Lichtenstein, Claude, eds., *Your Private Sky: R. Buckminster Fuller: Discourse* (Baden: Lars Müller Publishers, 2001).

Heard-Bey, F., *From Trucial States to United Arab Emirates* (Dubai: Motivate, 2004).

Herron, Jerry, *AfterCulture: Detroit and the Humiliation of History* (Detroit: Wayne State University Press, 1993).

Herron, Jerry, "Chronology: Detroit since 1700," in Ostwalt, Philip, ed., *Shrinking Cities: Detroit, Working Papers Part 1*, March 2004. Published on the Internet. Available: www.shrinkingcities.com.

Hoffman, Dan, "Erasing Detroit," in Daskalakis, George, Waldheim, Charles, and Young, Jason, eds., *Stalking Detroit* (Barcelona: ACTAR, 2001).

Holli, M., *Detroit* (New York: St. Martin's, 1976).

Hwang, I., ed., *Verb Natures* (Barcelona: Actar, 2006).

Jacobs, J., *The Economy of Cities* (New York: Random House, 1969).

Jacobs, J., *The Death and Life of Great American Cities* (New York: Modern Library, 1993).

Jintao, Hu and the Chinese Communist Party, *Draft Abstract for the Eleventh Five Year Plan for China – "Building a New Socialist Countryside"* (Beijing: CRP, 2006).

Koolhaas, Rem, "The Generic City," in Koolhaas, Rem and Mau, Bruce, eds., *S,M,L,XL* (New York: Monacelli, 1995).

Koolhaas, Rem, "The Gulf," presented at the Venice Biennale's Tenth International Architecture Exhibit (Switzerland: Lars Muller Publishers, 2007).

Kramer, M., "Optimism and Turmoil," *Crain's Detroit Business: Living and Investing in the D*, 24, no. 32a (2008).

Krauss, Rosalind E., *The Optical Unconscious* (Cambridge, MA: MIT Press, 1993).

Lacey, R., *Ford: The Men and the Machine* (Boston: Little Brown, 1986).

Lahiji, Nadir and Friedman, D.S., "At the Sink, Architecture in Abjection," *Plumbing, Sounding Modern Architecture* (New York: Princeton University Press, 1997).

Leatherbarrow, David, *Architecture Orientated Otherwise* (New York: Princeton Architectural Press, 2009).

Le Corbusier, "A Coat of Whitewash, the Law of Ripolin," *The Decorative Art of Today*, trans. James I. Dunnett (Cambridge, MA: MIT Press, 1987).

Lerup, Lars, *After the City* (Cambridge, MA: MIT Press, 2000).

Ley, Anthony, *A History of Building Control in England and Wales, 1840–1990* (Coventry: RICS Books, 2000).

Loos, Adolf, "Plumbers," *Spoken into the Void*, trans. Jane O. Newman and John H. Smith (Cambridge, MA: MIT Press, 1987).

Mack, Michael, ed., *Reconstructing Space: Architecture in Recent German Photography* (London: AA Publications, 1999).

McShine, Kynaston, ed., *Joseph Cornell* (New York: Museum of Modern Art/ Prestel, 1990).

Mangurian, R. and Ray, M., *Caochangdi Beijing Inside Out* (Beijing: Time-zone8, 2009).

Maynard, M., "After Many Stumbles, the Fall of an American Giant," *New York Times*, June 1, 2009, sec. A, pp. 1, 12.

Mendelsohn, Erich, *Amerika: Livre D'Images d'un Architecte* (Paris: Les Editions du Demi-Cercle, 1992).

Mostafavi, Mohsen and Leatherbarrow, David, *On Weathering, the Life of Buildings in Time* (Cambridge, MA: MIT Press, 1993).

Mostafavi, Mohsen and Leatherbarrow, David, *Surface Architecture* (Cambridge, MA: MIT Press, 2005).

Mumford, L., "What is a City?" quoted from *The City Reader*, Richard T. LeGates and Frederic Stout, eds. (London: Routledge, 1997).

Neuwirth, R., *Shadow Cities* (New York: Routledge, 2006).

Nightingale, Florence, *Notes on Hospitals* (London: Longman, 1863).

Oswalt, Philipp, "Shrinking Cities." Published on the Internet. Available: www.shrinkingcities.com.

Payne, H., "Cross Country: Murder City," *Wall Street Journal*, December 8, 2007: A10.

Perkins, J., *Confessions of an Economic Hitman* (Melbourne: Australia, 2006).

Pierson, G., *Tocqueville in America* (Baltimore: Johns Hopkins University Press, 1996).

Porter, Roy, *The Greatest Benefit to Mankind, A Medical History of Humanity from Antiquity to the Present* (London: HarperCollins, 1997).

Rogaski, Ruth, *Hygienic Modernity: Meaning of Health and Disease in Treaty-Port China* (Ewing, NJ: University of California Press, 2004).

Rybczynski, W., *City Life: Urban Expectations in a New World* (New York: Scribner, 1995).

Schumpeter, J., from *Capitalism, Socialism and Democracy*, quoted in Thomas K. McCraw, *Prophet of Destruction: Joseph Schumpeter and Creative Destruction* (Cambridge, MA: Harvard University Press, 2007).

Sherman, Roger, "If,Then," *Log*, vol. 5, ed. Cynthia Davidson, guest eds. R.E. Somol and Sarah Whiting (New York: Anyone Corporation, 2005).

Smithson, Alison, ed., "Team X Primer 1953–1962," *Architectural Design*, no. 12, December 1962.

Smithson, Alison and Smithson, Peter, Grille 1953, section House + x = street, quoted in Jesko Fezer, "Die Idee der Strasse ist vergessen worden" [The idea of the street has been forgotten], *Starship Magazine*, no. 5, 2002.

Smithson, Robert, "A Thing Is a Hole in a Thing It Is Not," in Flam, Jack, ed., *Robert Smithson, The Collected Writings* (Berkeley, University of California Press, 1996).

Solnit, R., "Detroit Arcadia: Exploring the post-American landscape," *Harper's Magazine*, July 2007: 66.

Studio Sputnik, *snooze: Immersing Architecture in Mass Culture* (Rotterdam: NAI, 2003).

Taylor, Jeremy, *Hospital and Asylum Architecture in England 1840–1914* (London and New York: Mansell, 1991).

Thompson, John D. and Goldin, Grace, *The Hospital: A Social and Architectural History* (New Haven and London: Yale University Press, 1975).

Tocqueville, A., *Democracy in America*, ed. and trans. Harvey C. Mansfield and Delba Winthrop (Chicago: University of Chicago Press, 2002).

United Nations, *World Urbanization Prospects, The 2005 Revision* (New York: United Nations, 2006).

Venturi, R., Scott Brown, Denise, and Izenour, Steven, *Learning from Las Vegas: the Forgotten Symbols of Architectural Form*, rev. edn. (Cambridge, MA: MIT Press, 1977).

Von Borries, Friedrich and Böttger, Matthias, "Updating Germany. How Do We Want to Live?" Published on the Internet. Available: www.updating-germany.de.

Waldheim, C., ed., *The Landscape Urbanism Reader* (New York: Princeton Architectural Press, 2006).

Wang, Zhan, Published on the Internet. Available: www.zhanwangart.com/news/work_cn/2007/11/07_11_6_3A9BC.shtml.

"What Ford Plans for New Tractor," *New York Times*, September 21, 1915, sec. X.

Whitman W., *Leaves of Grass* (New York, 1860).

Wigley, Mark, "Untitled: the Housing of Gender," in Colomina, Beatrice, ed., *Sexuality and Space* (New York: Princeton Architectural Press, 1992).

Wigley, Mark, "Introduction," *White Walls, Designer Dresses* (Cambridge, MA: MIT Press, 1995).

Wilson, E., "Detroit Motors," *The Edmund Wilson Reader*, ed. Lewis M. Dabney (New York: Da Capo Press, 1997).

Winthrop, J., "A Model of Christian Charity," in Baym, Nina, ed., *The Norton Anthology of American Literature*, vol. 1, 5th edn. (New York: W.W. Norton, 1998).

"Without Immigrants, Metro Areas Would Shrink," *U.S. News*, April 5, 2007. Published on the Internet. Available: www.msnbc.msn.com/id/17954186.

Wren, Christopher, "Tract I," collected in *Parentalia* (London, 1750).

INDEX